Population Change
and
Social Policy

OTHER BOOKS BY NATHAN KEYFITZ

Applied Mathematical Demography.
New York: John Wiley & Sons, 1977.

Mathematical Demography: Selected Papers. *(With David P. Smith)*
Heidelberg: Springer and Co., 1977.

Introduction to the Mathematics of Population: With revisions.
Reading, Mass.: Addison-Wesley and Co., 1978.

NATHAN KEYFITZ

Population Change and Social Policy

Abt Books
Cambridge, Massachusetts

Library of Congress Cataloging in Publication Data

Keyfitz, Nathan, 1913–
 Population Change and Social Policy

 Bibliography: p
 Includes index.
 1. Population   2. Demography   3. Social Policy
 I. Title
 HB871.K47   1982   304.6   82-6866

© Abt Associates Inc., 1982

All rights reserved. No part of this publication may be reproduced or transmitted in any form or by any means, electronic or mechanical, including photocopy, recording, or any information storage or retrieval system, without specific permission in writing from the publisher: Abt Books, 55 Wheeler Street, Cambridge, MA 02138.

Printed in the United States of America

ISBN: 0-89011-568-0

For Beatrice

CONTENTS

Part One	POPULATION THEORY AND ANALYSIS		
	Chapter 1	Population Theory and Doctrine: A Historical Survey	3
	Chapter 2	The Evolution of Malthus's Thought	26
	Chapter 3	Causes and Consequences of Population Change	34
	Chapter 4	Values and the Ceiling on Population	49
	Chapter 5	Upward Mobility in a Stationary Population	65
Part Two	DATA AND ITS LIMITATIONS		
	Chapter 6	The Use of Censuses for Allocation	79
	Chapter 7	How Do We Know the Facts of Demography?	91
	Chapter 8	Population Appearances and Demographic Reality	111
Part Three	ECONOMIC AND SOCIAL DEVELOPMENT		
	Chapter 9	Resources and the World Middle Class	125
	Chapter 10	Development and the Elimination of Poverty	146
Part Four	FORECASTING POPULATIONS		
	Chapter 11	The Mechanics of Forecasting	165
	Chapter 12	Forecasts as an Aid to Analysis	175
	Chapter 13	The Limits of Population Forecasting	184
Part Five	POPULATION CHANGE AND POLICY		
	Chapter 14	Social Security and Solidarity	201
	Chapter 15	How Birth Control Affects Population	216
	Chapter 16	Equity Between the Sexes: The Pension Problem	233
	Chapter 17	What Difference If Cancer Were Eradicated?	237
	BIBLIOGRAPHY		245
	INDEX		255

LIST OF TABLES

Upward Mobility in a Stationary Population

Table 1:	Age of Passing Various Gateways	69
Table 2:	Effect of Mortality	70
Table 3:	Values of derivative 0.01 dx/dr	72
Table 4:	Values of derivatives 0.01 dx/dr for $k = 1$, $k = 0.6$, and $k = 0.2$	73
Table 5:	Rapid Decrease or Increase	74

How Do We Know the Facts of Demography?

Table 1:	Proportion Aged 65 and Over and Rate of Natural Increase, 18 Latin American Countries	94
Table 2:	Features of the Stable Age Distribution and Rates of Increase Obtained by Combinations of Female Birth and Death Rates from Five Countries	99

Development and the Elimination of Poverty

Table 1:	World Population and Its Division into Poor and Middle Class	151

The Mechanics of Forecasting

Table 1:	Age Distribution of American Girls and Women Under 45 Years of Age, 1960	167
Table 2:	1960 Population of American Girls and Women under 45, Projected to 1975 at 1965 Death Rates	168
Table 3:	Millions of Girls and Women under 45 Years of Age in the United States if Birth and Death Rates Remain at the 1965 Level	170
Table 4:	Increase of Girls and Women in the United States from 2050 to 2065, 1965 Birth and Death Rates	170
Table 5:	Main Component of Female Population in the United States, 1960	171
Table 6:	Departures of Projected Population in Table 3 from Geometric Progression in Millions	171
Table 7:	Numbers of Girls and Women Under 45 Years of Age in the United States if Birth Rates are at Replacement Level from 1975 Onward	173

The Limits Of Population Forecasting

Table 1:	Root-Mean-Square Departure of Forecast from Subsequent Realization	188
Table 2:	Four Measures of Error Shown for United Nations Forecasts Made in Three Jumping-Off Periods	190
Table 3:	Root-Mean-Square Error of United Nations Forecasts for Three Jumping-Off Years	192
Table 4:	Root-Mean-Square Error in Percentage Points of 1955–1975 Forecast	195

Social Security and Solidarity

Table 1:	Estimate of Persons 15–64 and 65 and Over, U.S. 1980–2060	204
Table 2:	Ratio of Population 65 and Over to that 20 to 64 at Last Birthday for Various Rates of Increase	206

How Birth Control Affects Population

Table 1:	Calculation of Births Averted by Contraception	225

LIST OF FIGURES

Population Theory and Doctrine: A Historical Survey

Figure 1:	Production as a Function of Population, and Location of the Welfare Optimum of Population	14
Figure 2:	Optimum Population and the Surplus	15
Figure 3:	Cost and Utility Curves for a Child of a Given Birth Order	23

Upward Mobility in a Stationary Population

Figure 1:	Contrast of Increasing Population and Stationary Population	68

The Use of Censuses for Allocation

Figure 1:	Fraction of Population Counted at Various Levels of Expenditure on the Census: Suggested Relation	81

How Do We Know the Facts of Demography?

Figure 1:	Average Annual Increase of Per Capita GNP and of Population for Countries with over 20 Million Population	92
Figure 2:	Relation of Proportion of the Population over Age 65 to the Rate of Population Increase: 18 Latin American Countries	95

Population Appearances and Demographic Reality

Figure 1:	Age Distributions Resulting from Fixed Survivorship in a Stationary and a Stable Increasing Population	119
Figure 2:	Typical Relation of Stable to Stationary Age Distribution	120

Resources and the World Middle Class

Figure 1:	"Population Explosion" Curve	129
Figure 2:	Rate of Increase of Population	132
Figure 3:	Widening Gap between Per Capita Incomes in the Developed and in the Less Developed Countries	134
Figure 4:	Increase in U.S. Energy Consumption	136

Figure 5:	Future Impact on World Resources of the Growth of the Middle Class	139
Figure 6:	Consumption and Production of Energy in the Developed Countries	141
Figure 7:	Reduction in U.S. Share of Energy Consumption, Durable Goods, and Other Indicators of Wealth	144

Preface

Population objectives vary with time and circumstance. The rulers of Rome were right in wanting all the warriors that they could induce women to bear. The Renaissance princes were right in wanting more people, for they could put them in workshops and turn them into gold. In the modern debate, the objective is not as simple as conquering barbarian lands or enriching the treasury of the ruler; it is a wider notion, nothing less than the well-being of all members of the community. This book concerns some of the dilemmas of modern population analysis and policy, and the way that data can contribute to their resolution.

Population and demography are among the most empirical of the social sciences, and yet many of their most important questions are not empirically answerable. Is the population aging, with the difficulties for old age pensions that entails, because of improved survivorship or because of lower births? The answer, not easily derivable from either common sense or empirical observation, is lower births. Stable theory helps to attain such knowledge.

Similarly, for the effect of population growth on promotion, stable theory can tell us how much earlier promotion will come in a fast-growing office or factory compared with one that is growing more slowly. Population growth makes more difference than high mortality, which also helps promotion (for the survivors) but not as effectively.

The pro-growth conclusion from this encounters another argument of quite a different kind: the limited ability of resources and the environment to support well-being. Sooner or later we will have to forego rapid promotion based on population increase. The judicious balancing of these two opposed forces should be determinable by facts, but the facts are not readily accessible. The facts include what the condition of our soil will be under intensive cultivation over the next hundred years or more, as well as productivity rates, the fraction of the labor force unemployed and similar matters. Underlying every assertion on present policy are implicit estimates of such future quantities.

The spread into poor countries of middle-class consumption patterns is clearly an inducement to modern production. But the high consumption of the middle class draws heavily on resources; its meat requirements, for example, take up much land. The consequences of these two opposed forces for the emergence of the three quarters of the world population that does not have the means to support automobiles and air conditioners have yet to be investigated.

Thus the future, including the long-range future, is crucial to policy-making. We need further serious study of forecasting. Forecasting is made difficult by the way everything is connected to everything else in the real world. To know what population will be 50 years from now, one would have to know the conditions of war and peace, prosperity and depression, the environment. These independent variables affect population, though our knowledge of just how is incomplete. That puts us at two removes from effective forecasting of population—ignorance of the values of the independent variables on which the future population depends, and ignorance of the equations describing how these variables affect population.

Given all the difficulties, we should at least know how accurate past forecasts have been. That is a start on knowing how much we can rely on current forecasts of what is still the future, and for choosing among methodologies to find out how to do better. In the history of demography, the need to forecast and the large errors of forecasts led researchers deeper into the nature of population change, a positive result even where the forecast itself was a failure.

Paradoxes abound within the field of population studies. An effective treatment for cancer would seem to reduce deaths by one person each time it is applied. But, in fact, such cures would raise death rates from heart disease and other causes. The eradication of cancer makes much less difference than is thought by those who forget that heart disease is waiting to carry off those saved from cancer.

A similar difference between individual results and collective effects on population is to be found in fertility. Each abortion of a pregnancy that would result in a live birth does indeed prevent one birth from coming into existence. But 1000 abortions in a population cannot possibly prevent 1000 births. Statements on individual effects need not carry over to population effects.

Maintenance of the aged is not possible without the assistance of their children, but since the 1930s we have preferred that the assistance be collective, principally in the form of old-age pensions, rather than individual within the family. The preference suggests that the institution of the family has weakened, or at least changed, so that it can no longer sustain the burden of the old, just as in the 19th century it ceased to educate the young, and schools took its place. But collective maintenance of the old with cash is necessarily more expensive than having aged parents live with their children; moreover, costs rise further with the aging of the population. The demographic pressure on the social security system has had a small effect up to now; it will start to become important a generation from now, when the baby boom reaches retirement age. The tension between the needs of the old and resistance to higher taxes will be with us through the first third of the 21st century. It is all very well to say that the old cannot be supported within the family because the old-time solidarity is gone, and so they must be taken over by the state; the question is whether the state will show the needed solidarity that the family lacks.

Such considerations weigh on a wide range of policies. Whether we should be concerned about the low birth rate, about the high immigration rate, about age distribution in relation to social security—each involves a host of conflicting questions. This book contains essays that begin to explore them, based on my work of the past twenty years. I have tried to make the solution of policy problems appear no more difficult than it actually is, but I have also tried to stay clear of facile answers.

Acknowledgements

Many colleagues have read and commented on my writings or otherwise helped me. These include, among others: William Alonso, Brian Arthur, Barbara Bailar, Michel Balinski, Daniel Bell, Ansley J. Coale, Paul Demeny, Nathan Glazer, Morris H. Hansen, Robert Hauser, Philip M. Hauser, Irving Louis Horowitz, Beatrice Keyfitz, Leslie Kish, William Kruskal, Ronald D. Lee, Juan Carlos Lerda, Gary Littman, Robert Lundy, Margaret Martin, James N. Morgan, Fred Mosteller, William W. Murdoch, Robert J. Myers, William Petersen, Robert Potter, Samuel H. Preston, Roger R. Revelle, Andrei Rogers, Richard Savage, Donald Shepard, Jacob Siegal, David P. Smith, Michael Stoto, Leon Tabah, Conrad Taeuber, Judith Tanur, James Trussell, James Vaupel, William O'N. Waugh, Harrison C. White, Hal Winsborough, Peyton Young, Richard Zeckhauser. The book's errors are not their fault.

Material support by the Ford Foundation, the Harvard Center for Population Studies, the International Institute for Applied Systems Analysis, and the National Science Foundation is gratefully acknowledged.

Most of the pieces here contained have been published before in one form or another; all have been extensively revised for this book. Thanks are due to the copyright owners for permission to use their materials. Following is the list:

Chapter 1: Population Theory and Doctrine: A Historical Survey, in *Readings in Population*, edited by William Petersen, pp. 41–69. Macmillan Co., New York, 1972.

Chapter 2: Malthus as Demographer, in *Malthus: Past and Present*. Selection of papers presented at the Malthus Conference of IUSSP, edited by J. Dupaquier and A. Fauve-Chamoux. Academic Press, London, 1983.

Chapter 3: Causes and Consequences of Population Growth, in Amos H. Hawley, editor, *Societal Growth: Processes and Implications*, pp. 76–95. The Free Press, New York, 1979.

Chapter 4: Population Growth: Causes and Conseqences, in *Environment*, edited by W.W. Murdoch, pp. 40–63. Sinauer Associates, Sunderland, Mass., 1975.

Chapter 5: Individual Mobility in a Stationary Population, *Population Studies*, Vol. 27, No. 2, 1971, pp. 335–352.

Chapter 6: Information and Allocation: Two Uses of the 1980 Census, *The American Statistician,* Vol. 33, No. 2, 1979, pp. 45–50.
Chapter 7: How Do We Know the Facts of Demography? *Population and Development Review,* Vol. 1, No. 2, 1975, pp. 267–288.
Chapter 8: Population Appearances and Demographic Reality, *Population and Development Review,* Vol. 6, No. 1, 1980, pp. 47–64.
Chapter 9: World Resources and the World Middle Class, *Scientific American,* Vol. 235, No. 1, July 1976, pp. 28–35.
Chapter 10: Development and the Elimination of Poverty. *Economic Development and Cultural Change,* Vol. 30, No. 3, 1983, pp. 649–670.
Chapter 11: How Crowded Will We Become? in *Statistics: A Guide to the Unknown,* edited by Judith M. Tanur, et al., pp. 297–309. Holden-Day, San Francisco, 1978.
Chapter 12: Models, *Demography,* Vol. 8, No. 4, 1971, pp. 571–580.
Chapter 13: The Limits of Population Forecasting, *Population and Development Review,* Vol. 7, No. 4, 1981, pp. 579–593.
Chapter 14: How Secure is Social Security? Working Paper WR-81-101, July 1981. International Institute for Applied Systems Analysis, Laxenburg, Austria.
Chapter 15: How Birth Control Affects Births, *Social Biology,* Vol. 18, No. 2, 1971, pp. 109–121.
Chapter 16: Equity Between the Sexes: The Pension Problem, *Journal of Policy Analysis and Management,* Vol. 1, No. 1, 1981.
Chapter 17: What Difference Would It Make if Cancer Were Eradicated? An Examination of the Taeuber Paradox, *Demography,* Vol. 14, No. 4, 1977, pp. 411–418.

Population Change and Social Policy

Part One
Population Theory and Analysis

CHAPTER 1

Population Theory and Doctrine: A Historical Survey

The number of people in the city, the nation, or the world—what determines that number and how in turn it affects power and welfare—has been a persistent theme of social science. Philosophers, theologians, counselors to princes, and legislators have espoused population doctrines and promoted policies based on them, or else promoted policies and created doctrines to buttress them.

We can learn from all of them, ancient and modern, even where the views of a particular society are hardly appropriate for us. Most premodern thought was pronatalist. The Romans wanted men to fill the legions that would extend the boundaries of the empire. The mercantilists wanted workers on the land or in manufactures, who would produce goods to sell abroad and so add to the riches of the prince. Imperial and mercantilist thought was directed toward turning people into power or into gold. High death rates made populations seem fragile, in danger of dying out if not fostered and encouraged from above.

In the late eighteenth century the center began to shift from the emperor or prince to the people. Sincerely or not, the arguments in population debate came to revolve around the prosperity or misery of the masses. The optimum population for high average income is a smaller number than the optimum for the wealth and power of the ruler. When people ceased to be regarded as the property or instrument of the ruler, restrictions on growth could be seriously argued. The following paragraphs sketch the historical course of discussion. They are especially indebted to Vialatoux (1959), the United Nations (1953, Chap. 3) and Sauvy (1956).

ANTIQUITY

Greek thought on population developed in city-states with constitutional rule by the minority who were citizens. According to Plato (*Laws*, Book V, para. 637), a population must be sufficient to defend itself against its neighbors, and the optimum thus depends partly on the strength of these neighbors; but no city should exceed its capacity to provide materially for its citizens. Effective rule and civil order depend on the citizens knowing one another, which sets another limit to size. In his discussion he used the arbitrary figure of 5,040 landholders, a number sufficient for the various specialties the state requires. This total is divisible by fifty-nine numbers, and so would facilitate the allocation of tasks and the division of property. When more or fewer children were needed to attain the ideal, the change in fertility could be realized by appropriate honors or negative sanctions; fostering immigration or dispatching citizens to the colonies were also acceptable policies for influencing the total. Aristotle was especially concerned that the city not be too large; he advocated abortion, rejecting infanticide except as a eugenic measure (*Politics,* Book I, para. 1; Book VII, para. 4; see Barker 1959: 407–8; United Nations 1953).

In India not long after Plato—around 300 B.C.—Kautilya wrote *Arthasastra* (Book VII, chaps. 1, 11; Book VIII, chap. 3; Book XIII, chap. 4; cf. Spengler 1963), which discussed population as a source of political, economic, and military strength, the necessary complement of land and mines. Though a given territory can hold too many or too few people, the latter is the greater evil. Kautilya restricted asceticism to the aged, favored the remarriage of widows, opposed taxes so high as to provoke emigration.

With their tightly administered land empire and ceaseless wars on their borders, the Romans needed men even more than did China or India. Being superior to their neighbors in the arts of warfare, they could send any excess men across their frontiers to conquer the lands that would sustain them. Women were useful for producing warriors. Roman writers condemned celibacy and advocated monogamous marriage as the type that would produce the most offspring. Vice leads not only to individual ruin but to collective depopulation (Cicero, *De republica,* Book IV, para. 5).

The literary emphasis on virtue and on Rome's need for men did not prevent small families, especially in the upper and middle classes, or an increasing dependence on hired barbarians.

CHRISTIAN THOUGHT

Christian thought developed in the declining Roman Empire, but encouraging population growth to meet the secular needs of the empire formed very little part of it (Noonan 1965). To the church fathers virginity was the ideal; only for those too weak to abstain from temptation of the flesh was marriage recommended. Augustine reacted against the pessimistic heresies of Gnosticism and Manicheism, which condemned marriage and procreation as producing material human bodies in which the Light would be imprisoned. He sought a justification for marrige, and found it above all in procreation. His doctrine of the marital goods—offspring, fidelity, symbolic stability—dominated Christian thought for a thousand years, during which marriage remained the second-best state. "I am aware," Augustine wrote, "of some that murmur, 'What if all men should abstain from sexual relations, whence will the human race subsist?' ... I answer, so much more speedily would the City of God be fulfilled and the end of the world hastened."

The contrast to the prior Hebrew teaching is striking. The early Christian theologian did not refer to the injunction of Genesis to increase and multiply, nor did he speak of spreading Christianity by having children. The less austere Thomas Aquinas reintroduced the Aristotelian concept of nature; just as it is the nature of the eye to see, so it is the nature of the genitalia to procreate—the very word tells that. It is right and pleasurable to do what is according to nature.

In 1930, the encyclical *Casti Connubii* synthesized a variety of themes from many historical epochs. It condemned contraception on the grounds of the need to propagate the human race and to bear children for the Church of Christ, as well as on Augustine's three goods of marriage. It recalled Aristotle and Aquinas in arguing that "no reason can make congruent with nature what is intrinsically against nature." It used nineteenth-century theology to condemn the sin of Onan (Noonan 1965: 508). Following the lead of the Lambeth Conference, which in 1930 opened the door to contraception in the Anglican church, most other Protestant groups have found little difficulty in reversing their previous stand against birth control. But Catholic doctrine up to this writing has yielded only the theologically confusing concession of the rhythm method, sanctioned by Pius XII in 1950 after much debate within the church, which seemingly shifted from the intention of contraception to the method. Insistence at the highest level that contraception is wrong has proved incomprehensible to many priests and laymen.

The Cycle of Population and Empire

Ibn Khaldun, who lived before the eighteenth century invented the idea of progress, saw history as the rise, prospering, and fall of states and civilizations (Mahdi 1957: Part 4). When a tribe becomes numerous under an aggressive chief, it enters on a career of conquest, builds or captures a capital city, and adapts its tribal religion in order to strengthen loyalty to the chief. The tribal chief's successors make themselves absolute rulers of an expanding state, build palaces and temples, and sponsor the arts and the sciences. Rule comes to depend less on the respect for a senior kinsman and more on a tightly organized bureaucracy and army. The city expands with the expansion of the hinterland supplying its food.

Later generations of rulers, attracted to luxury, lose their martial virtues. The original population declines; foreign mercenaries are hired for the army, and foreign officials for the administration. These can be paid only by high taxes, levied on both the artisans and the surrounding peasantry. The absorption of the rulers in luxury, the decline of the native population, and the spread of intrigue in the bureaucracy and army lead to the loss of the provinces on whose food and other raw materials the state depends. Having broken the original bonds of kinship and perverted religion to the service of the state, the rulers are helpless when the artificial military and civil structure dissolves. In the last phase the provinces have fallen away, commerce is undercut by taxes and insecurity, and the birth rate declines further. If it is not conquered by a newly rising population, the state burns out like a lamp wick when the oil is exhausted.

Machiavelli, also a counselor to princes and a political realist, lived about a century after Ibn Khaldun, and like him saw population growth as initiating new cycles of history. He gave as an example the demographic expansion of the barbarians beyond the Rhine and the Danube. A community that became numerous would divide into three parts, each containing the same proportions of nobles and people, rich and poor, and draw lots to see which third would move out of their native country, generally toward the south. The migrating masses destroyed the Roman Empire. Population was indeed a matter for the ruler to be concerned about: "I think those princes capable of ruling," said Machiavelli, "who are capable, either by the numbers of their men or by the greatness of their wealth, to raise a complete army and bid battle to any enemy that shall invade them" (*History of Florence*, quoted by Malthus 1960b: 195).

In Europe of the sixteenth to eighteenth centuries, states competed ceaselessly for military, political, and economic power. Absolute rulers had an interest in maximizing their territories' populations, from which both armies and manual workers could be recruited. The monarch's wealth was seen as a function of the total value produced by his kingdom less whatever was paid in wages. Since the wage per worker would always diminish as the number of workers increased, people were an unqualified asset to their masters. A king could no more have too many subjects than a modern farmer can have too many cattle. Any limit is set by food in the one case and pasture in the other. "One should never fear there being too many subjects or too many citizens," wrote Jean Bodin, "seeing that there is no wealth nor strength but in men" (*La République,* Book V, chap. 2). The goods they produced could be exported for gold or silver, and so people were money. For Frederick the Great it was a certain axiom that "the number of the people makes the wealth of states" (Stangeland 1904: 131). For Süssmilch (1788, 1: 17ff), a chaplain in Frederick's army, the interests of the sovereign coincided with the divine order, and both would be furthered by more Germans (Mackenroth 1953: 301–2). With minor exceptions, other French, Italian, and Spanish mercantilists favored population growth unanimously. Botero (1956) offered advice on how larger populations might be attained: agricultural and especially industrial production should be encouraged; the export of raw materials should be forbidden and that of manufactured goods fostered. The English writers were more qualified in their populationism; Petty accepted the thesis that men create wealth but also feared the poverty and social turmoil consequent on too great numbers.

POLITICAL ARITHMETICK AND THE PHYSIOCRATS

The numerical study of population starting in the seventeenth century, rather than earlier speculations, marked the beginning of demography. When John Graunt (1662) worked up bills of mortality, he observed many constant features of deaths and births. Estimating that the ratio of deaths to births was fourteen to thirteen in London, as against fifty-two to sixty-three in the countryside, he calculated the immigration from the countryside needed to maintain and increase London's population. The statistics were poor, but Graunt made what reasoned adjustments he could and did not hesitate to draw conclusions. The concept of a cohort that is diminished by death as it goes through successive ages was clear to him, though his estimates of its diminution were too high. (The life table implied in his calculations has an expectation of life at birth of about 17.5 years, as against the 27.5 years of Halley's [1693] table for Breslau. The European urban average of the time was probably between these two figures.) He calculated age distributions from the life table, although he did not quite understand the notion of a stable (for a steadily increasing or decreasing population) as against a stationary age distribution, apparently first stated precisely by Euler in 1760. He made some corrections for misstatement in the bills' totals by cause of death, and noted that aside from the plague, the distribution by cause did not change greatly from year to year. The records of baptisms, which he also analyzed, showed a slight but constant excess of males over females at birth, and he considered that this excess held in the population as a whole. Childbearing women "one with another, have scarce more than one childe in two years," a birth interval close to that computed by present-day scholars from data on seventeenth-century Europe.

It is not clear, however, whether the credit for initiating demography goes to Graunt or to his more imaginative younger contemporary, Sir William Petty. Even the original authorship of the *Observations on the Bills of Mortality* has been attributed to Petty. At least, "Petty may have stimulated Graunt's initial interest in this sort of enquiry; he later carried through somewhat similar, but more superficial, observations on the Dublin bills of mortality; and he edited a posthumous edition of Graunt's *Observations,* published by the Royal Society" (Lorimer 1959: 126; Glass 1963).

Petty's new science of Political Arithmetick (1691), based on empirical work by Graunt among others, raised exciting perspectives in the Royal Society of London. Toward the end of the seventeenth century, Gregory King assembled enough data to produce a realistic estimate of England's population—5.5 million. Such work as that of Graunt, Petty, Halley, and King, who made good use of the crude data at hand, when combined with later theorizing on population convinced legislators of the need for censuses and vital statistics.

By the eighteenth century the mercantilists' emphasis on numbers was tempered by the recognition of poverty. Cantillon, standing between the mercantilists and the physiocrats, saw that an overcrowded state could acquire some relief by exporting manufactured goods and importing food—a frequent mercantilist theme (Hoselitz 1960: 26–42; Spengler 1942). Cantillon's masterpiece, *Essai sur la nature du commerce en général* (1952: 1), made land or nature the source of all wealth. Population is created by the means of subsistence, which depend not only on nature and such institutions as property rights in land but also on the decisions that princes and landowners make. If those who control the land want horses for hunting and war, the human population will be smaller than if they prefer domestic retainers. That French landowners preferred Dutch cloth reduced France's population and increased Holland's. The prince's way of living sets the style for smaller landholders. Cantillon does not moralize, but by implication he tells the rulers by what personal sacrifices they could increase population. Horses were the means of transport favored in Europe; that in China bearers carry travelers on litter-chairs explains why compared with Europe the human population is larger, the horse population smaller.

THE ENLIGHTENMENT AND MALTHUS

Some mercantilists feared a growth of population beyond the subsistence already in sight, but most expressed confidence that any number of new subjects could produce their own subsistence. The latter view was incorporated in the very different framework of the eighteenth century's new theory of progress and human perfectibility. Among others, Condorcet, Godwin, and Daniel Malthus held that the numbers of men determine available resources, rather than vice versa. In the era that they saw dawning, such past coercive institutions as property, the family, and the punishment of criminals would disappear, their objectives to be realized through the individual consciences of perfected men. No growth of population in an adequately organized society could conflict with progress, in Godwin's view, for the new City of Man (like Augustine's City of God) would harmonize all social classes and the whole of society with its material base. "There is in human society a principle whereby population is constantly maintained at the level of the means of subsistence," for "the goods of the world are a common fund from which all men can satisfy their needs" (Godwin 1793: 466, 520; Hutchinson 1967).

These views, which he heard first from his father, stimulated Thomas Robert Malthus (1960b) to seek a more realistic analysis of how population relates to resources. By his famous "principle of population," the number of people, if unchecked, grows in geometric progression, while the resources on which they depend at best increase arithmetically. Moreover, the capacity of men to multiply, and through their multiplying to make themselves miserable, would be accentuated by the very changes in institutions designed to attain an earthly paradise. Malthus's persistence in opposing this thesis to the optimism of the *philosophes* established him as the central figure of population doctrine. For his immediate predecessors—Hume, Wallace, Adam Smith, and Quesnay—population growth was primarily a sequel to an increase in produce; demand for labor (as for shoes) produces the supply in a self-regulating system (Coontz 1957; Smith 1921, 1: 82–83). Malthus opposed to Smith's natural harmony the conflict between population and its means of subsistence.

To ascertain the power of population one had to look at a territory where good land was plentiful. America showed a doubling in less than twenty-five years. In countries settled longer the pace was much slower, and most of Malthus's writing and research concerned the nature of the checks by which the rate of growth is held down. He found that in Europe late marriages made for small families. This moral restraint, incorporated in custom and in individual responsibility, he termed a *preventive* check. Also included under preventive checks were vices such as homosexuality, adultery, birth control, and abortion, and these Malthus certainly did not recommend (Petersen 1969: 149). When preventive checks were inadequate, such *positive* checks as wars and epidemics would supplement them. The ultimate positive check was famine; that did not often come into operation, but had always to be taken into account as a potential danger.

Malthus remains one of the most controversial figures in social thought. Regarded as a reactionary by those who dreamed of an earthly paradise, he in fact helped develop the economic theories that propelled the revolutionary social changes of the nineteenth century. The traditionally pious accused him of blasphemy for urging men to take responsibility for the size of their familes; had not the Creator himself enjoined all to be fruitful and multiply? Had not Luther declared that any man hesitating to start a family because he lacked property or a job showed a want of faith? One of the most vigorous attacks came from Proudhon, who held that early marriage is the surest guarantee of good morals. To defer love in the name of moral restraint would restrict marriage to superannuated spinsters and aging satyrs. Like other socialists, Proudhon argued that the imprudence of the working classes was not the cause of their misery but a consequence; with the institution of a society based on justice people would not want more children than could be provided for (Vialatoux 1959, 2: 375–98).

In the English language "Malthusian" or "neo-Malthusian" came to designate a proponent of contraception. This is despite the fact that Malthus explicitly disavowed birth control. In an appendix to the *Essay's* fifth edition he wrote: "Indeed I should always particularly reprobate any artificial and unnatural modes of checking population, both on account of their immorality and their tendency to remove a necessary stimulus to industry. If it were possible for each married couple to limit by a wish the number of their children, there is certainly reason to fear that the indolence of the human race would be very greatly increased." In recent years a similar opposition to contraception was expressed by Gandhi: "If Indians made the necessary effort, they could grow all the food they need;

but without the stimulus of population pressure and economic need they will not make the effort" (Clark 1964: 283).

Contraception goes back to the beginning of human history, with references to it in the Kahun Papyrus, the Bible, the writings of Charaka (an Indian physician of the first century B.C.), Herodotus, al-Razi (900 A.D.) and other Islamic scholars (McCleary 1953: 83; Himes 1936). Nearly all known human cultures have had sufficient knowledge of the facts of human reproduction to be able to use at least coitus interruptus, and most have had other devices as well. Among moderns it appeared in the writings of Moheau, Condorcet, and especially Francis Place (1822), who was followed by Richard Carlile, Charles Bradlaugh, and Annie Besant. These did not share the puritanical view that hunger and sex were the stick and carrot without which men would be slothful, and they found in contraception the full answer to the problem Malthus had posed. "Contraception . . . is both old and new; old in the sense that the *desire* dates back half a million years and some *practice* nearly as long; . . . new in the sense that democratized knowledge is an ultramodern phenomenon . . . that we have been able, more effectively than our ancestors . . . to winnow out the reliable, the harmless" (Himes 1936: 422).

In one of his last statements on the matter, a "summary view" published in 1830, Malthus (1960a: 13) went one step toward applying his principle to nonhuman populations. The principle of population was a direct forebear of the theory of evolution. "I happened to read for amusement Malthus on *Population*," Darwin (1961: 58) noted in his autobiography, "and being well prepared to appreciate the struggle for existence which everywhere goes on from long continued observation of the habits of animals and plants, it at once struck me that under these circumstances favorable variations would tend to be preserved, and unfavorable ones to be destroyed. The result of this would be the formation of new species. Here then I had at last got a theory by which to work." Wallace, who developed a theory of evolution independently of Darwin, also acknowledged a debt to Malthus. The directions in which Malthus's thought changed from the slim book of 1798 to the elaborate empirical studies of subsequent editions is the subject of Chapter 2.

THE BIOLOGICAL PERSPECTIVE

The tendency of species to outreproduce their means of support exerts a constant pressure toward differentiation. Each species seeks to adapt to a niche in which it will have some degree of shelter from competition. Some species become complementary to others and enter into symbiotic relations with them. "We can dimly see why the competition should be most severe between allied forms, which fill nearly the same place in the economy of nature" (Darwin 1962: 88). In Spencer (1867, 2: 406–10, 479–508) this leads to an escape from the original Malthusian predicament by way of biology: organisms become more complex in the process of adaptation, and complexity reduces the animal's drive to reproduce. Human individuation is a continuation of animal evolution: the nervous system becomes more active, with a consequent further reduction in reproductive activity. The theory has been used to explain why bacteria are more prolific than mice, why men are among the least prolific of the higher animals, why the Victorian upper classes had fewer children than the lower classes. In every case the group comprising more differentiated, more elaborately adapted individuals has a lower reproduction combined with greater adaptability. In Spencer's optimistic view, the evolutionary process that population growth initiated would persist until both fertility and mortality had reached a low-level harmony.

More immediately suggestive for our subject is the recent observation of ecologists and ethologists that fertility in many species of birds and animals depends on density. We all know that beyond a certain point mortality is density-dependent through the ultimate check of starvation. But starvation is not very often seen in nature and, even combined with predators, disease, harsh weather, and other disasters, does not seem to exercise the continuous control that would explain the relative constancy of numbers in most species of higher animals. The constancy has been explained by a territorial mechanism of reproductive control, to accord with long-term food supplies. Among some species of birds, at the beginning of the breeding season each male lays claim to an area of suitable size and keeps out other males; all of the available ground is thus parceled out as individual territories. The often furious competition for an adequate piece of ground takes the place of direct competition for food. This territoriality is a special case: some species compete merely for membership in a hunting group, and only so many are accepted. Those without territory, or left out of the hunting group, have no opportunity to reproduce. The pecking-order among birds has the same function: those low on the scale are a reserve that can fill in for casualties among the established members or be dropped, as circumstances require. (Wynne-Edwards 1962)

By such territorial and similar mechanisms population is maintained comfortably below the ceiling imposed by resources. The analogy to Malthus's preventive check comes as close as is conceivable for species lacking human foresight. Man has indeed the possibility of foresight, yet he offends more than most species in overgrazing, overfishing, and generally overexploiting his habitat.

POPULATION AND THE GIFTS OF NATURE

The classical school of economics developed from Malthus the law of diminishing returns: more work applied to given land produces less than proportional returns, and indeed increments of any one factor of production eventually generate lessening amounts of income. The doctrine was given mature expression in Mill (1876, Book I, chap. 13, 2): "The niggardliness of nature, not the injustice of society, is the cause of the penalty attached to overpopulation. An unjust distribution of wealth does not even aggravate the evil, but, at most, causes it to be somewhat earlier felt. It is vain to say that all mouths which the increase of mankind calls into existence bring with them hands. The new mouths require as much food as the old ones, and the hands do not produce as much." The operation of the law may be long postponed if there is vacant land to which people may move and, subsequently, if technical improvements are developed, but over the longer run its course is seen as inexorable. The law is applied to an increase in the land under cultivation through the presumed fact that rational men would start to till the most fertile and accessible portions first, so that any new lands added to the nation's agriculture would be less and less productive. As population grows in any country closed to trade, poorer lands will necessarily be brought into use, and any excess over the return to labor on marginal land will be taken as rent by landowners in the natural operation of the market. Population growth beyond a certain point would provide landlords with an increasing proportion of the national product. The model supposes an agricultural community of fixed land and techniques with a growing population.

But quite different conditions apply in industry, where the factors of production are extensible and the division of labor advantageous. True, industry depends on the availability of raw materials, but the limits of these are more distant than the coming shortage of agricultural land. If in some sectors of the economy returns increase with added effort while they diminish in others, then there will be a certain size of population at which overall production per head will be a maximum (Cannan 1895). It is useful to consider production a function of population whenever the economy is relatively static while population grows—the situation of many countries today. In Figure 1 the three curves represent, respectively, total, A; marginal, B; and average production, C. The maximum point on B is at the inflection point along A, where the slope of total production ceases to increase and begins to decrease, the maximum on C at the point of A tangent to a line drawn from the origin. The curve B can be shown to cut C at its maximum point; where the marginal product equals the average, the latter is at its peak. This is demonstrated by considering the output of the

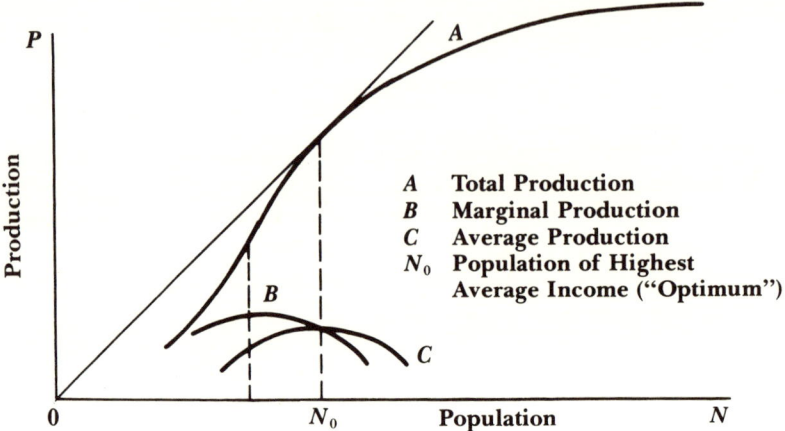

Figure 1: Production as a Function of Population, and Location of the Welfare Optimum of Population

last man; if it is greater than the average, the average will be raised by the presence of this last man. The reverse is true if the last man's output is lower than the average. Only if the last man's output is equal to the average will the average be at its peak and the population optimum from a welfare viewpoint. Call this optimum population N_0.

Consider now the curve of marginal production B along with line D, representing the minimum that will keep individuals alive, assumed to be equal for all sizes of population (Figure 2). The area below B and above D can be called a surplus, which is at a maximum for the population where B and D cross, or N_1. A technically primitive and static state that wants to maximize its armed strength or any other entity not dependent on immediate consumption will aim at population N_1 in its countryside. The surplus will be drained off and used to support an urban court, artisans, and armed forces, including the police and tax collectors who remove the surplus. The mechanism for this removal will vary and may include resident or absentee landholders taking rents. In modern times, a well-entrenched, development-minded government determined on heavy investment for industrial growth will appropriate the surplus for that purpose; it will be inclined to favor a population N_1, larger than the optimum N_0. But any diminution in the authority of government, reflected in a rise of the level D regarded as subsistence, lowers N_1 and moves it closer to N_0.

A state seeking the maximum population will aim at N_2—placed so that areas between curves B and D are equal in the intervals N_aN_1 and N_1N_2. Under mild assumptions the welfare optimum N_0 is smaller than the power optimum N_1, which in turn is smaller than the maximum

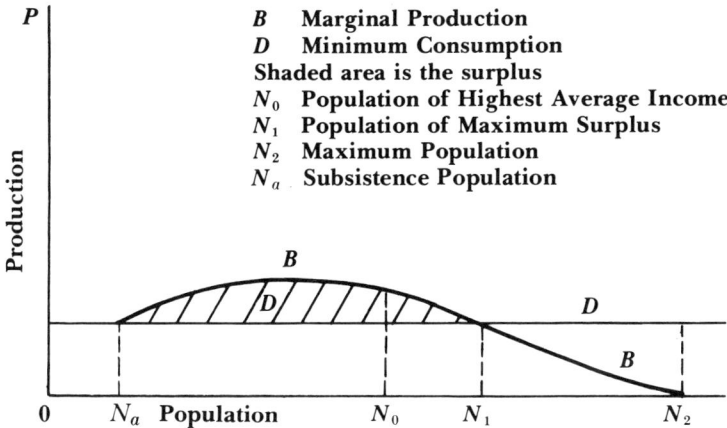

Figure 2: Optimum Population and the Surplus

population N_2 (Sauvy 1956, 1: 60). Fixed costs raise the optimum population, while lowering average income.

Nineteenth-century English economists tried to adapt these arguments, which apply to a closed economy, to one heavily based on foreign trade. Some thought that Britain could increase per capita production indefinitely; any excess population could emigrate to distant lands, there to grow food that would be exchanged for British manufactured goods. But since that time freely available lands have been appropriated by population growth elsewhere, and agricultural countries want to develop their own industry.

In the 1920s England and some other advanced countries seemed to have passed their optimum and arrived at the point of rapidly diminishing returns (Keynes 1920; Wright 1923; Overbeek 1970: 141–63). The best coal deposits were being exhausted, cotton was attacked by the boll weevil, and for these and other commodities prices could only rise in response to increasing scarcity, with a resultant fall in the standard of living. The question of resource adequacy raised in the nineteenth century by Jevons has been intermittently asked in the twentieth century. Population control is an important part of the answer.

The optimum depends on the criterion used and will be very different if it is national power or real income per capita. Even with the best of statistics on the present and past, the optimum is not readily calculable; it can be determined only if we know what income would accord with various levels of population. This lack of empirical applicability contrasts with the sharply defined theory. Any curve relating population and production may "for large spaces have a very level course" (Myrdal 1940:

142). Even if one proved that, for instance, a given country has double its optimum population and has also the power to reduce it by emigration, a sharp reduction might be a disaster; for the disadvantages of the change—particularly since most emigrants would be young adults, whose rearing their native country had paid for up to the age when they began to produce—could more than offset any advantages of arriving at the optimum level.

THE ENVIRONMENT

Contemporary ecologists are interested in optimum population, but they sharply reject the gradually diminishing returns and easy adaptations of classical economics. Their writings constitute a radical attack on the modern system of production and consumption (Ehrlich and Ehrlich 1970). At best, the kinds of damage not now entered in private or national accounting schemes must be deducted from our calculation of national product and income. At worst, the word *production* itself is seen as an ironic misnomer for such a process as depleting supplies of irreplaceable crude oil (that ought to be saved for lubrication), consuming it in an inefficient way of moving people from place to place, and creating unbreathable air that may well raise mortality rates. If the population of Malthus's time was pushing against a food ceiling, that of today seems to be pushing against a ceiling of space, air, water, and mineral resources (Wright 1923; Brown 1954).

The problem for us is whether such complaints really have a bearing on population. Parking space is short not because there are too many people in the country, or even too many automobiles, but because people want to live in large cities, or because they all want to go to the same place at the same time. The air is polluted either because automobiles are badly designed, or because some other solution to the transport problem should replace them. The present system of production would quickly direct itself along lines that preserve the environment and enable it to take care of far more people if manufacturers were charged for the damage their products cause. They receive income for their goods and should pay for their bads, as Kenneth Boulding says. He proposes (1966: 9) to rescue nation-income accounting by distinguishing "that part of the Gross National Product which is derived from exhaustible and that which is derived from reproducible resources, as well as that part of consumption which represents effluvia and that which represents input into the productive system again."

SOCIALIST WRITERS ON POPULATION

Marx was generally well disposed toward the classical economists, of whose school he was a wayward member. But he repeatedly attacked not only Malthus's doctrines but also his motives and personality:

> Malthus ... asserts that population constantly exerts pressure on the means of subsistence.... If there are too many people, then in one way or another they must be eliminated.... Now the consequence of this theory is that since it is precisely the poor who constitute this surplus population, nothing ought to be done for them, except to make it as easy as possible for them to starve to death.... The giving of alms would be a crime, since it would encourage the growth of surplus population (Meek 1953: 59).

Malthus had propagated a "vile and infamous doctrine, this repulsive blasphemy against man and nature." No general law of population could be valid for all societies; each had its own law. The irreducible opposition between population and welfare, far from being universal, was in Marx's view the special predicament of capitalism, with its impoverishment of the proletariat. The reproduction of the working class made new workers cheap and so permitted the bourgeoisie to extract surplus value from their work. But to ask the proletariat to be more responsible was futile, for the very degradation inherent in capitalism ruled out an appeal to their higher natures. The transformation of capitalist to socialist institutions would eliminate the Malthusian dilemma. As on other points, Marx started with the classical premises and reached a conclusion very different from the classical harmony.

The history of capitalist society, as he viewed it, is divided between a period of original accumulation and one of maturity and imperialism. In the period of original accumulation all the conclusions of Adam Smith and Ricardo are valid, with only a change of terms and some simplification. Marx divided capital into constant, C (for example, buildings and machinery), and variable, V (comprising consumer goods such as food bought with workers' wages). Constant capital is so called because it is merely reproduced without a quantitative change in the product; all surplus is imputed to labor. The capitalist tries to use all the labor he can employ, for thus he makes the largest profit. If it costs six hours per day to produce labor—the amount of time the average worker requires to feed, clothe, and house himself and his family at a subsistence level—and if the goods he produces sell for the equivalent of twelve hours' time, then the capitalist's surplus value is six hours multiplied by the number of workers he employs. The rapid increase of population in early capitalism was due to the demand for labor, just as Adam Smith had said.

For the second or "imperialist" period, however, Marx diverged sharply from the classical economists. The wage rate is V/P, variable capital divided by population, as before. But now as technical progress and competition force capitalists to substitute machines for men, the "reserve army" of the unemployed grows continually. Workers respond by lowering their birth rate as less labor is demanded, and Marx pictured a struggle around the ratio V/P, with the capitalists trying to shift the resources they control from V to C, and the workers seeking to counter this effort by reducing P. Unfortunately for the system as a whole, the birth rate cannot fall fast enough to prevent capitalism from producing the surplus workers that are its gravediggers.

That labor-saving methods of production make an increasing fraction of the population redundant has been a popular fear before and since Marx. Today the identification of surplus population with unemployment is found in underdeveloped countries, while the countries with the largest stock of capital have more often encountered a labor shortage.

The world at large sees Malthus and Marx as "the two great antagonists, battling eternally" (Sauvy 1963: 13). But the very vehemence of Marx's attack stemmed from the lack of a substantive rebuttal, as his *Critique of the Gotha Program* admitted: "If [Malthus's] theory of population is correct, then I can *not* abolish this [iron law of wages] even if I abolish wage-labor a hundred times, because this law is not only paramount over the system of wage-labor but also over every social system" (Marx and Engels 1959: 124). Marx and Malthus agreed that the condition of the proletariat was miserable and that its misery should be alleviated (Petersen 1964: 72–89). Malthus's solution relies on individual responsibility, Marx's on a collective condition called socialism; but both were better at posing the problem than at solving it.

Marx and Malthus agreed profoundly on the material base of social existence. At Marx's graveside Engels summed up his collaborator's contribution: "Marx discovered the law of evolution in human history: the simple fact, previously hidden under ideological growths, that human beings must first of all eat, drink, shelter, and clothe themselves, before they can turn their attention to politics, science, art, and religion" (ibid.). Malthus (1960a) made the same point with equal clarity in his own summing up, published four years before his death: "Elevated as man is above all other animals by his intellectual faculties, it is not to be supposed that the physical laws to which he is subjected should be essentially different from those which are observed to prevail in other parts of animated nature." Says Mehring (1962: 149) of the Marxist view:

> This theory, the contention that the capitalist mode of production impoverishes the masses wherever it prevails, was put forward long before the *Communist Manifesto* was published, even before either Marx or Engels put pen to paper.... first of all by bourgeois

economists. The *Essay on Population* written by Malthus was an attempt to refine this "theory of increasing misery" and turn it into an eternal natural law.

That the workingman can avoid increasing misery, both collectively and individually, by restricting his family, that mothers should in effect become a trade union and declare a childbearing strike, was a theme of leftist social reform in the writings of John Stuart Mill, Bernstein, and others. But Marxists insisted that advanced capitalism could always undercut the workingman with more efficient equipment; in the race between voluntary reduction of the work force and substitution of labor-saving devices, the latter would necessarily win. Relief must be sought in revolution rather than in contraception.

Marx bequeathed his opposition to Malthus to succeeding Marxist thinkers. Lenin in particular stressed that evolving technique would undercut the law of diminishing returns. Much of Stalin's argument has the tone of the mercantilists: the growth of population facilitates economic advance. Recent Soviet writings on population include a study of Europe's population increase during the past century (United Nations 1953, Chap. 3). The increasing growth under industrial capitalism was followed by a slower rate during the "imperialist" stage; and since private property in land or other means of production in itself diminishes fertility, Western birth rates will continue to fall. Although Soviet society was supposedly immune to these pressures, its birth rate over the past two decades has followed very closely that of the United States. Hungary's birth rate fell to fourteen per thousand, well below that of the capitalist countries of Western Europe. Evidently, fertility differs less between socialist and capitalist than between industrial and traditional societies.

DENSITY AND THE DIVISION OF LABOR

Durkheim (1902) marked society's change from a small undifferentiated clan or tribe to the complexity of his day, noting that interdependence increases with the greater specialization of groups and individuals. The complex society, he concluded, comes with population growth. As a tribe increases in volume and density, individuals and groups compete more and more intensely; only by specialization can they find shelter from competition. "In the same city the different professions can coexist without having to harm each other, for they pursue different objectives. The soldier seeks military glory, the priest moral authority, the statesman power, the industrialist wealth . . . ; each can thus reach his goal without preventing the others from reaching theirs" (ibid.: 249–50). For Durkheim population growth, through the "moral density" that arises from it, is responsible for the advance from a simple segmented society to a complex organic one.

Among peasant populations, one that is small and stationary is more likely to stay with slash-and-burn agriculture, which under many circumstances of low density produces more with less labor. Higher density forces a shorter fallow and ultimately annual crops, even though these mean more work. A "gradual adaptation to harder and more regular work is likely to raise the efficiency of labor in both agricultural and nonagricultural activities; the increasing density of population opens up opportunities for a more intricate division of labor" (Geertz 1971: Chap 2; Boserup 1965: 75).

POPULATION AND DEVELOPMENT

If a poor country somehow does manage to cut its birth rate, this improves its development prospects, in the theory worked out by Coale and Hoover (1958) and others. From alternative projections for India and other countries Coale (1969) concluded:

> Any low-income country that succeeds in initiating an immediate reduction in fertility would in the short run enjoy a reduction in the burden of child dependency that would permit a higher level of investment and more immediately productive uses of investment.
>
> After 25 or 30 years the advantage of reduced dependency would be enhanced by a markedly slower growth of the labor force, making it possible to achieve a faster growth in capital per worker from any given investment, and making it easier to approach the goal of productive employment for all who need it. . . . In sum, a reduction in fertility would make the process of modernization more rapid and more certain.

Between two countries with different birth rates, the one with a higher rate will initially be at a disadvantage by its lack of industrial capital rather than of food. For the underdeveloped countries, the choice is whether to use resources in order to produce more capital rather than more labor, so that each unit of labor will be better equipped in the next generation. This concentration on capital accumulation has dominated professional thinking on population and development (Ohlin 1967).

And yet it is far from universally accepted. Latin Americans argue that their empty spaces can hold many millions, and that the internal migrants to those spaces can construct their own agricultural and other capital. According to Nurske (1953), a dense rural population positively helps the development of a country with a sufficiently strong and singleminded government. Everyone in the countryside may appear to be working, at least for part of the year, yet some of the rural population constitutes disguised unemployment in the pertinent sense that it could be removed, even with no substituted technical improvements, without a loss in production. Such persons could engage in the construction of buildings, roads, and urban industrial projects that do not require much capital. Since they all somehow obtained a minimal diet before, the shift would entail merely transporting their food to the city. But it is not clear that fewer agriculturists can produce the crop merely by reorganizing the task and without major technical improvements (Schultz 1964). If there were genuine surplus of labor, moreover, it would not be easy to hold per-capita consumption fixed in a half-starving countryside; and if those remaining on the land simply eat better, the expected surplus from the land disappears with the out-migrants. This was the famous "scissors" problem in the Soviet Union of the 1920s; it has never been solved, for the punitive measures used to mitigate it generated new troubles.

Global development may be prevented by too many people, not through the difficulty of accumulating capital but by the absolute shortage of raw materials. After showing what large quantities of metals and fuels are now required to keep the advanced economies in operation, and noting the rate of increase in world population, Harrison Brown (1954: 226) considers it unlikely that the agrarian underdeveloped regions of the world will be able to attain their goal of industrialization. "The picture would change considerably if Western machine civilization were to collapse, thus giving the present agrarian cultures room into which they could expand. But the collapse of Western culture would have to come well in advance of the time when high-grade ore and fuel deposits disappear." The raw materials in the earth's crust set a limit on the volume of development, on the number of people—or more exactly the number of person-years—that can exist in the developed condition, as that condition is understood today in the United States. How the volume of development will be apportioned among peoples, and over time, could well be the major question of national and international politics in the next generation.

For the advanced countries population has often been seen as an aid to growth. Writing in the 1930s, Keynes and Hansen saw an increasing population as a guarantee of markets. Housing demand, for example, varies with the rate of growth of a population. Investors know that even a product that does not quite fit consumers' tastes still finds buyers in an expanding economy. But in recent decades it has been noted that an expanding economy could be arranged more easily by an increase of purchasing power than of population.

The basic prerequisite to expanding the economy is a high level of investment, and the chief argument against rapid population growth has been that it diminishes savings and hence investment. But expenditures on children do not necessarily reduce savings, for at least in advanced countries expenditures on children may be a substitute not for savings but for more consumer goods or more leisure (Kuznets 1960: 332). Looking into the past, Hicks (1939) asked whether the whole industrial revolution of the last two centuries has been nothing but a vast secular boom, largely induced by the unparalleled rise in population (Bladen 1956: 115). Myrdal (1940:161–66) held that the cessation of population increase "will have a restrictive effect upon young people's opportunities for advancement," and Coale (1968) also opposed any immediate policy to bring about a zero population growth in the United States.

These theories relating population and the economy in a macro-economic model say nothing about how individual parents are motivated. The route from micro-models that describe individual behavior to an explanation of aggregates was traveled at least as far back as Adam Smith. In his view, the demand for labor increases population by permitting individuals to marry earlier and to raise a larger proportion of the children born to them (Coontz 1957: chap. 4). But different mechanisms have been proposed in recent years to account for the quite different phenomena now observed.

The Economic Theory of Fertility

In a micro-economic framework the decline of the birth rate with economic development can be analyzed in relation to the utilities and costs of children to their parents (Leibenstein 1963). With increasing income the cost of a child of a given order rises, let us say in proportion to the family income. The consumption utility—that is, the pleasure of having the child in the house—is difficult to assess and can be estimated as fixed independently of income. The utility of the child as a source of security certainly declines: parents with more income can provide for their own security, or a wealthier state provides it for them; and if increased income is accompanied by weakening of family discipline, parents are less likely to be able to exercise claims on their children even if they are in need. The child is less valuable as a producer as income increases, because schooling is extended and the household ceases to be the unit of production (Figure 3). If these four elements (one of cost and three of utility) are exhaustive and correctly portrayed, then the individual family is likely to have fewer children as per-capita income increases and as development proceeds. At

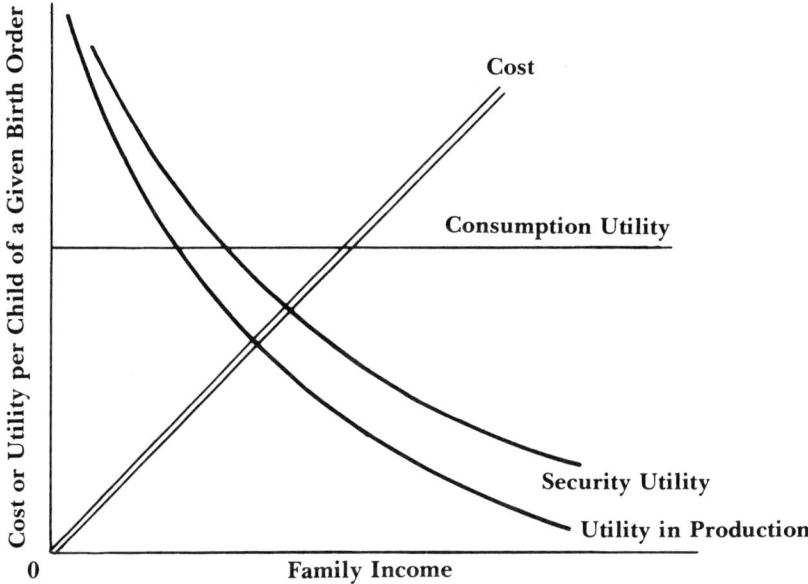

Figure 3: Cost and Utility Curves for a Child of a Given Birth Order (after Leibenstein 1963: 162)

any given stage, moreover, richer families would be inclined to have fewer children than poorer ones.

One can start with the opposite view, that the price per child does not go up with the parents' income. The rich could spend as little on their children as the poor, but *choose* to dress them better, send them to better schools, and so on; in effect, they purchase higher-quality children (Becker 1960). By this view the cost curve in Figure 3 for a given quality of child becomes horizontal. Thus, Becker comes to the opposite conclusion from Leibenstein: people have more children as they become richer, just as the well-to-do have not only better cars than the poor but more per household. In any large population the relation is hidden by the fact that the rich practice contraception more effectively; and among contracepting couples, according to data that Becker cites, income is related directly to family size, as his theory demands. Duesenberry (1960), Leibenstein (1963), and Okun (1960) reject Becker's distinction between price and cost, on the grounds that each family is constrained to house, clothe, and feed its children in accordance with the norms of its income group. If custom requires richer families to spend more on each of their children, one cannot conclude from their larger income that they will also want more children. If one controls for the differential knowledge of contraception, not by comparing the family sizes of birth control users but by using surveys of ideal family size, the correlation with income is negative. From such data, the poor *want* more children than the better off (Blake 1967).

These are micro-explanations in that they reason from individual behavior to certain aggregate phenomena of the community or country taken as a unit. Economics (like physics) tries to explain the mass in terms of the atoms, but such explanations cannot be successfully detached from the cultural and social context.

SOCIAL CAPILLARITY AND FAMILY STRUCTURE

The decline of the birth rate in industrial countries has followed a decline of the death rate. The populations involved have undergone a more or less uniform transition: first a slow and accelerating fall in mortality, followed at some interval by a corresponding fall in fertility. The pace varies from country to country; the later the fall in the death rate, the more rapid it is. In one country, France, the fall of births very nearly coincided with the fall of deaths; elsewhere there has been a considerable lag. Whatever its local variation, the phenomenon has been so widespread, and commented on by so many writers, that it has acquired a name: the demographic transition (Notestein 1945; Taeuber 1960; and others).

Both the fall in deaths and the slower fall in births may be a concomitant of modernization (Notestein 1945), or the decline of fertility may be a response to the earlier decline of mortality (Davis 1963). In either case, the literature is incomplete concerning the causal mechanisms operating. In particular, there is no answer to the big question: will the fall in mortality that by now has taken place in the underdeveloped countries by itself produce a fall in fertility, or will it do so only in the presence of development? Must poor countries wait for development before their birth rates can fall? If high fertility prevents capital accumulation and so development, then they will have to wait a long time.

A French social scientist, Arsène Dumont (1890), tied declining fertility to the structure of society and to the individual's desire to rise in the world. Trained as an anthropologist, Dumont was a passionate nationalist who saw in France's depopulation a harbinger of her downfall, and devoted his life to analyzing the familial conduct of his countrymen. (He never married, and at the age of fifty-three took his own life!) "All men," he wrote, "tend to raise themselves from the lower functions of society to higher ones.... Guided by an unerring and inescapable instinct, each social molecule strains with all the energy at its command.... to rise unceasingly toward a luminous ideal which charms and attracts it" (ibid.:106). This ascent is not by income alone, but in every field of manual work, of intellect, and of art (Sutter 1953). In the competition for higher places, the man with few or no children has as certain an advantage over the father of many as the liquid in a narrow tube has over that in a wide one. This is the law of social capillarity.

Social mobility gradually intensified over a century or more in Europe and America. It was functional for economic development, but signs of change are appearing:

> One does not have to be a prophet to foresee that our present passion for demographic and economic growth will some day be superseded by a concern for population quality and ecological balance. When this inevitable adaptation is effected—inevitable, that is, barring the catastrophe that will forestall all adaptation—perhaps it will seem more natural to espouse a hierarchy of values in which our assessment of men will not depend so heavily on their ability to "get ahead" (Duncan 1969:365).

THE USE OF PAST DOCTRINES

This account has sketched population ideas and doctrines that appear in writings over 2,500 years. Some of the ideas are thoroughly obsolete, some keep recurring and are to be heard on the street or read in newspapers today. The advantage of knowing the antecedents of what people are now saying is that one then knows the context in which they fit and the criticism that they aroused. When we hear someone say that more people will add to national power, we remember the Romans and appreciate how the then-current techniques, especially the organization of men, enabled the Romans to conquer the lands of their neighbors. When someone says that masses of people can be set to making goods for export, we think back to the mercantilists and the treasuries of their princes. To locate the argument in its setting may not dispose of it, but it is an aid to clear thinking.

CHAPTER 2

The Evolution of Malthus's Thought

Malthus made ingenious use of numerical data, struggled to reconcile the animal nature of man with his powers of thought and foresight, and showed a sense of the dilemmas among which policy choices must be made. Yet some would reduce Malthus to four words: population is food-controlled. That formula has been a convenient target for both praise and attack during the nearly two centuries since Malthus began to write.

No such formulation can possibly be original; this essentially biological one was clearly anticipated by both Adam Smith and Cantillon before him. "When food increases," wrote the latter, "men will multiply like rats in a barn." Malthus listed among his predecessors classical Greek writers, Montesquieu, and Benjamin Franklin (Preface to the 1803 edition, p. 148 in the Modern Library Edition). But the biology of population became steadily less important to Malthus as he extended his observation through his own travels, reports of the travels of others, and national statistical systems that were evolving from primitive beginnings during the thirty years over which his thought was evolving.

In fact, cases in which population is directly food-controlled do not dominate the experience of mankind. For each instance in which nature has applied the ultimate sanction of famine, say in China or India, or in the Sahel in some recent years, one can cite many instances where populations have lived comfortably for centuries at densities well below the maximum that their territory could sustain. The more subtle and important part of Malthus is not to be found in any simple secondhand condensation.

Malthus was practical, and he saw people as neither godlike nor irredeemably wicked. Godwin's scheme of a society based on benevolence was clearly unworkable, humans being what they are. Even as an ultimate ideal, said Malthus, it is so distant that it cannot give any guidance in practical affairs, and if we direct our efforts toward it, we will suffer repeated failures and "impede that degree of improvement in society that is really attainable" (*First Essay*, p. 100). And in a footnote a page later, he explains that "he is a much greater benefactor of mankind, who points out how an inferior good may be attained, than he who merely expatiates on the deformity of the present state of society, and the beauty of a different state, without pointing out a practical method, that might be immediately applied, of accelerating our advances from one to the other" (p. 101). He was throughout a Whig incrementalist: he promoted universal schooling, extension of suffrage, free medical care for the poor, state assistance to emigrants, more equal distribution of land and of income.

More Appropriate to Animals Than to Humans?

Malthus wrote not one book but at least two, the later editions being entirely different from the first. Malthus explains in the 1803 edition that he would have called it a different book, but he wanted to avoid reference to the first edition (Dupaquier 1980, p. 281). This sounds as though he was repudiating the 1798 work, except for the few parts that he incorporated in subsequent editions.

Seemingly uncompromising, the first book (Malthus 1798, chap. 1) starts from the two postulates that "food is necessary to the existence of man," and that "the passion between the sexes is necessary and will remain nearly in its present state" (p. 4 of the version edited by Kenneth Boulding), and proceeds to the conclusion that "the power of population is indefinitely greater than the power of the earth to produce subsistence for man" (p. 5). Human nature and human capacities have little to do with the matter: "The race of man cannot, by any efforts of reason, escape from [this great restrictive law]" (p. 5).

Yet a few pages later, even in the first essay, a qualification is put on this apparent assimilation of people to plants and animals. The preventive check (of late marriage and abstinence) "appears to operate in some degree through all the ranks of society in England" (p. 22). Class distinctions come naturally to Malthus: better-off people are above the animals in their ability to restrain childbearing, while "the positive check to population, by which I mean the check that represses an increase which is already begun, is confined chiefly, though not perhaps solely, to the lowest orders of society" (p. 25). Malthus was neither the first nor the last to see the lower classes as closer to the animal than the upper; but he had every hope, as the later editions clearly say, that education would eliminate such class differences.

Malthus asks us to look at man as he is: "inert, sluggish, and averse from labor, unless compelled by necessity" (p. 127). "Evil seems to be necessary to create exertion, and exertion seems evidently necessary to create mind" (p. 126). "Leisure is, without doubt, highly valuable to man, but taking man as he is, the probability seems to be that in the greater number of instances it will produce evil rather than good." Humans are not static, but can develop their talents, so hardship is genuinely creative: "The exertions that men find necessary to support themselves or their families frequently awaken faculties that might otherwise have lain forever dormant."

His dour view of the world has never been well received in continental Europe, and today it is everywhere out of fashion. It is accepted least of all in the matter of sexual relations, where Malthus expressed himself vigorously against the device of contraception: "If it were possible for each married couple to limit by a wish the number of their children, there is certainly reason to fear that the indolence of the human race would be much increased" (Appendix to the fifth edition). For him it was the pressure of population that gave individual and social life its tension and significance. To relieve that pressure (as the contraceptive device recommended by Condorcet would do) would destroy the essence of human life and destiny. It is a strange injury that posterity has inflicted on Malthus when it calls contraception "Malthusian" or "neo-Malthusian."

His ideas were congruent with the needs of the Industrial Revolution. Malthus anticipates Weber's Protestant Ethic of a century later in that they both call on the individual for endless labor and painful abstinence; there was much capital construction to be undertaken and very little in the way of consumer goods to pass around as rewards. With a different justification, contemporary China has also taken a puritanical view of life, that seems to fit with the needs of early industrialization.

DEMOGRAPHIC CONDITIONS OF THE LATE EIGHTEENTH CENTURY

One much debated question of the late eighteenth century concerned the size and rate of population increase. Some, like Montesquieu, argued that the actual numbers had decreased from ancient times due to poor government, but they adduced no data, and one suspects that their principal evidence was their conviction that the government of the time was bad. Malthus scorned such circularity and persistently sought numerical evidence in an age when precious little effort went into data collection. His use of data seems to have stimulated the more systematic gathering of it, and certainly his writing encouraged the initiation of the English censuses from 1801 and of vital statistics from 1837. As better data became available, Malthus made use of them, and successive editions of the *Essay* were more solidly empirical.

The number of people in England and Wales rose from A.D. 1066 (when it was estimated at 1.1 million) to the 1841 census (which counted 15.9 million). Malthus was aware of the pitfalls in earlier estimates and made some contributions of his own to improving estimates for 1780 and later. He analyzed the downtrend in England's death rate and again was exemplary in his critical approach to data. He was aware of the high death rate in the cities but, unlike Price and other scholars of the time, did not see urbanization as equivalent to depopulation. All this is brought out clearly by Petersen (1979). Malthus was one of the first to see how difficult to answer is such an easily asked question as: Why did the death rate fall in the late eighteenth century? A less conscientious proponent of the principle of population would simply have answered: greater food supplies.

MALTHUS AS FORECASTER

It is common to read that Malthus's forecast failed, since population has indeed increased since his time and, in the industrialized part of the world the increase has certainly not brought misery. This vulgar treatment of the principle of population as a concrete prediction disregards what Malthus never failed to keep in mind—that people-sustaining capacity depends on technology. Indeed, he wrote at length on the way that populations grew and became more prosperous in North America as European technology replaced that of the Indians.

Malthus did explicitly predict the future on differential fertility, as we now call it, and on the demographic transition, by which the whole community would move to low birth rates. He anticipated that people would come to control their childbearing as they rose in the social scale, and he urged that those at the bottom of society be encouraged to rise. Rationality in planning marriage and children, like any other type of planning, depended on faith in the future; as the lower classes saw a higher standard of living ahead, they would also adopt the small family pattern.

Such forecasts were based on cases found in his travels in which people did accommodate their fertility to resources. The summary of his views provided in the *Encyclopedia Britannica* article (1824, p. 44) quotes Süssmilch's figures on the way that marriages fell as mortality declined in various parts of Germany and Poland. He quotes figures that show how a supposed depopulation of parts of Switzerland—births that seemed insufficient to maintain the population and, if true, an instance where his principles did not apply—was really a response to falling death rates, so that fewer births were needed to keep up the population (p. 45). This is exactly what we too regard as progress and describe as the demographic transition.

Would a rise in wages be turned into children? Vulgar Malthusians have thought it would, but that is not the view of Malthus himself: "In the vast majority of instances, before a rise in wages can be counteracted by the increased number of laborers it may be supposed to be the means of bringing into the market, time is afforded for the formation of . . . new and improved tastes and habits. . . . After the laborers have once acquired these tastes, population will advance in a slower ratio, as compared with capital, than formerly" (from the *Principles,* quoted in Petersen 1979, p. 235). This is a clear advance on the simpler view of the *Essay* of 1798. In modern terms Malthus is here close to suggesting a positive feedback, a kind of beneficent circle, by which the rise in wages results in fewer children, and hence more capital per worker in the next generation that in its turn will obtain yet higher wages.

Moral Restraint

Malthus saw that Europe had indeed held its population under enough restraint during the preceding centuries that its famines had been few. The Chinese peasant was no less skilled and industrious than the European peasant, yet China was subject to recurrent famines. Europe owed its fewer famines to its less dense population, and that population was held below the carrying capacity of the soil through late marriage.

But with the spread of industry, migration to cities, and the weakening of traditional rural associations, this restraint was in danger of breaking down in Malthus's time. In accord with his realistic and antiutopian outlook, he advocated reverting to tradition. "He was recommending the intensification of a demographic characteristic peculiar, in his day, to Western Europe," says Coale (1979, p. 8). "In Western Europe at a given moment fewer than 50 percent of women of childbearing age were married; in Eastern Europe the fraction was 65 to 90 percent." Malthus recommended a means of control that he knew was feasible because it had worked in the past.

EDUCATION

Education of the masses is important because it will make people capable of the restraint in childbearing so important to Malthus—the preventive check will be stimulated. And if there is one demographic generalization that has stood from his time to ours, it is that the more educated have fewer children.

But he also thought of education in a broader sense, as along with liberty contributing directly to welfare; not the welfare of princes and rulers, but of individual people. He was a true child of the Enlightenment, in sharp contrast to many contemporary holdovers from mercantilism.

For few of us does the adjective "Malthusian" connote the education of the masses, yet that is how Elie Halevy (1928, cited by Petersen 1979, p. 234) used it: "As concerns the education of the poor in particular, the radical theory of popular instruction is Malthusian in origin." It was not only that educated people would be more capable of exercising the moral restraint that later editions of the *Essay* saw as the solution to the population problem, and not so much that education would make them better workers—Malthus was not even sure that the workman needed geometry and other academic subjects in his occupation—but that "an instructed and well-informed people would be less likely to be led away by inflammatory writings." Whether or not such confidence was justified, Malthus opposed the majority of his contemporaries who feared that education would only make people rebellious.

ECONOMICS AND POLITICS

Malthus's liberal orientation shows up clearly in his taking the side of the Irish. "The underlying reason [for the poverty in Ireland] was [its] degradation. The peasant, seeing no escape from his lowly condition, spent his life proliferating" (Petersen, 1979, p. 109). It is remarkable that a minister of the established church could say, "Let the Irish Catholics have all that they have demanded; for they have asked nothing but what strict justice and good policy should concede to them."

Malthus's demography and his economics were related to one another in a classic paper by Keynes (1937) that concerned the two devils of Malthus. For Malthus the world was not an easy place. His work comes down to two principles that for short might be called population and demand. When population grows, there will be no lack of effective demand. But, as Keynes says, "When devil P. of Population is chained up, we are free of one menace; but we are more exposed to the other devil U. of Unemployed Resources than we were before."

His opposition to the Poor Laws has enabled utopians to portray Malthus as a heartless reactionary. But let us recall what Malthus was objecting to in the Poor Laws. "Payments of the Speenhamland type, in which wage subsidies and family allowances were confused, meant that the relief received by the pauper-worker was based in part on the number of his children. Employers could therefore pay lower wages to those with larger families, and thus . . . preferred to hire fathers. . . . 'Men who receive but a small pittance know that they have only to marry, and that pittance will be augmented in proportion to the number of their children'" (Petersen, 1979, p. 120). The law was intended to provide payments to poor workers, but the real beneficiaries were employers, who had cheap labor immediately and more and cheaper labor later on.

The humane question then as now is how to aid children already born without providing the incentive to bear more children who will also be poor. "If . . . Malthus thus stressed one side of a painful dilemma, he at least saw that it was a dilemma, and not to be resolved with sentimentality" (p. 126).

Equality

By the eighteenth century bourgeois property was taking its place alongside the hereditary landed property of the nobility. Malthus oscillated a little, but on the whole he favored the breaking up of large estates, as the French Revolution was doing across the Channel. He wanted "a greater part of society . . . in the happy state of possessing property" (*First Essay*, p. 120), and spoke of the "permanent advantage that would always result from a nearer equalization of property." This, he felt, would promote responsibility and liberty as well as conservation.

In short, Malthus's thought took account of some dilemmas of policy that face us today as much as they did then. How to discourage excessive childbearing without making life more difficult for children already born is only the first of a series of difficult questions. How can we solve immediate problems of unemployment by emigration without hurting others (for instance the American Indians) and without encouraging parents to have more children to replace those departing? How can we provide poor relief in a way that does not merely add to the profits of employers?

The introduction of much data in the later editions could not but make the argument more subtle and more complicated. As Walter Bagehot says, "In its first form the *Essay on Population* was conclusive as an argument, only it was based on untrue facts; in its second form it was based on true facts, but it was inconclusive as an argument" (quoted by Himmelfarb, in Malthus 1960a, p. xxxiii).

One way to summarize the evolution of Malthus's thought is to compare the start of the first edition with the ending of the last. The first starts by referring to the progress of science, along with the change of institutions typified by the French Revolution, and how these are thought to be decisive for the fate of mankind (p. 1). In the next few pages he shows that the fate and happiness of mankind depend on quite other considerations embodied in the principle of population: our numbers will increase so that neither science nor laws can do much for our individual comfort. In the last sentence of the last edition he says, "We may confidently indulge the hope that, to no unimportant extent, [the virtue and happiness of mankind] will be influenced by [physical discovery's] progress and will partake of its success" (p. 594).

The world faces a population problem today, and that inevitably makes us look back to Malthus. But there is a deeper reason why Malthus has an appeal in the late twentieth century: his thinking was the opposite of facile; the difficulties and contradictions of life are his constant preoccupation. Not only population, but every aspect of existence presented dilemmas to him. That is why he lives again today, after the complacent Victorian period had seemingly buried him forever.

CHAPTER 3

Causes and Consequences of Population Change

Causes are elusive entities. Relations, correlations, comparisons, measures of change we can establish by just working hard. And these are needed, because though they are not equivalent to causal knowledge they provide evidence, incomplete evidence, on causes. It has been shown many times that more educated couples have fewer children; it nonetheless remains a mystery whether providing people with education and no other changes will cause them to have fewer children. If it does, we want to know what kind of education will have that effect; will merely educating people to the means of contraception be sufficient? Are accompanying changes in other variables like income and urbanization needed for the effect to show itself? The raw negative correlation between family size and education is a negative kind of knowledge: if that correlation did not exist, we would be less hopeful of finding causation in this direction.

That causes are elusive does not mean that they are scarce. They are very prominent in the literature of social science and even more so in journalistic writing. In fact, it is their abundance that makes trouble in the form of coexistence of arguments that both policy X and policy not-X will solve overpopulation (or inflation or anything else). The mutual contradictions among causal arguments are the main theme of this discussion.

Causes and consequences, whatever their status in the real world, are clearly properties of models. Any model, whether verbal or mathematical, is like a set of interconnected levers and wheels and valves, such that when one of them is pressed or turned or opened something happens elsewhere in the system. And when the world is modeled in different ways, different levers appear to cause change in a given variable. The levers are policies, and my theme will be the indeterminacy of policy in the face of a multiplicity of models and uncertainty as to which model applies.

Once we fix people's attention on a particular model so that it fills their consciousness, it seems obvious in the light of that model what causes what, and from that follows what ought to be done to change the variable in which change is sought. To say that someone is persuasive—whether he is a social scientist or a political leader—is to say that he somehow has the ability to fix our attention on a picture of how things work and to exclude other competing pictures from our thoughts. Models, whatever purer purpose they serve, are also powerful means of persuasion. To make the most use of this feature, it is customary to present the model first, and let it exercise its almost hypnotic effect, so that the policy conclusion will be readily accepted. Opponents who can resist the hypnotic effect suspect that the policy conclusion came first in the mind of the model maker, and the model followed after as a device of rhetoric.

All this and worse has been said of Malthus, on the one hand, and the demographic transition, on the other. What happens to the birth rate when income rises? The Malthusian says it goes up, and he can prove it from a carefully worked-out model. The proponent of the demographic transition says it goes down, and he is equally convincing. We need not review the arguments here, except to say how wholesome it is to juxtapose one commonly believed model with another, and to see how in practice the decision between them is made. The real world, through the empirical data that it throws up or that can be coaxed out of it, to some degree constrains the choice of model, but to some degree leaves the choice indeterminate. If facts do not decide between models, then the decision among them is relegated to fashion, to a prevailing ideology, or to the interest of the powerful.

Students have approached population in at least three different ways—from the viewpoint of engineering, economics, and sociology. Each of these professions and disciplines is mature enough to provide a picture of the world that is complete, in the sense that every issue raised is taken care of and every question asked is answered within the system of the discipline. Yet each discipline is also inadequate in that it formulates a narrow set of questions and excludes from its view any part of the evidence that would unduly broaden its vision. Each loses its power to convince once the listener's attention strays to some other picture of the world into which the excluded evidence fits better. The three perspectives may be briefly illustrated.

PEOPLE AS NODES IN AN ENERGY TRANSFER SYSTEM

Of the human as of other species the ecologist asks the question, Where does their food come from? Food supplies determine how many can live. With Mexico City's 15 million or Cairo's 10 million in mind, we describe an ecological setting in which food energy circulates in a particularly simple way. Essentially this way of thinking is to be found in writers too numerous to cite; the following type of scenario is implicit in much current expression, though the details vary from writer to writer. It deals with the place in the sun that a large aggregation, say of 10 million people, will require.

Ten million people on a cereal diet of about 1 1/4 pounds per day need one-fifth of a ton of grain each per year. Over any large stretch of country, allowing for houses, roads, and wooded patches, and without imported fertilizer, about one ton per hectare (2 1/2 acres) is the best that can be expected, so the ten million people will require 10,000,000/5 hectares, or 20,000 square kilometers, or less than 100 × 100 miles.

Think, then, of the sun's energy falling on a reasonably fertile temperate or tropical area measuring 100 × 100 miles, a small fraction of the energy converted into carbohydrate and stored in the form of dried grain. When transferred to people, the grain enables them to keep alive and do the work of each day, which is mostly tilling, planting, cultivating, and harvesting grain. With some enlargement of the area, woodland can be set aside to provide fuel for boiling rice or baking bread. With careful tending of the soil—making terraces where the land slopes so as to retain the water and also prevent soil from being washed away—the process can go on forever. Its limiting factor is soil minerals and nutrients rather than solar energy, and indeed only a small fraction of the incident solar energy is drawn on even in the most fertile farmland.

Now what about urbanization? Suppose that the 10 million people are not scattered over the landscape but mostly concentrated in a great city. That increases the energy input required, for now most of the grain has to be transported an average of about sixty miles. With present technology the easy way to do that is with stored solar energy in the form of petroleum. But we cannot count on this if the system is to be permanent, and so some way must be found of using the current solar input for transport. One way is by a mirror field heating boilers which run turbines and produce electricity that suffices for electric railways. A 30 × 30 mile area would gather from the sun all the energy needed for transport as well as for a degree of mechanizing in the tilling, harvesting, and processing of the crop. Here we have a self-contained energy transfer system that would use the solar electric generators now being designed for the 1980s. Such direct use of solar energy requires no rain and no soil, and so could be located in desert areas too dry for farming.

With the inefficient system here described, the United States would easily support half a billion people in cities even more concentrated than we now have. We have some 350 million acres of fertile land, plus plenty of forest and desert, so there would be room for fifty-five such city-hinterland systems, each of 10 million people. The world as a whole could contain many hundreds of such systems. There is no trade-off between amenities and population growth, since desert land abounds, and more area devoted to the collection of sunlight for electricity will not mean less food. A trade-off between amenities and growth is to be found within agriculture: If people wish to eat meat, some of the grain will have to be fed to cows and population will be smaller.

Further details of this engineering utopia can easily be filled in if needed. But it is intended only to show how easily large populations can be permanently provided for on a pure energy calculus. Like many other utopias, this one is empty. It offers no reason why the human nodes in the sun-grain-people energy transfer system should submit to the arrangement. At best it sets some outside physical limits on what is socially possible. Social scientists ask about the human actors: how do they organize production? What economic incentives motivate the production of grain, or what political power compels it? The utopia tells how people relate to the landscape but not how they relate to one another. It omits all the issues related to the surplus that have been implicit in the life of human settlements since the first Neolithic gardeners learned how to produce more than they required for their own sustenance. It was on that surplus that cities, armies, tax collectors, and civilizations were able to come into existence, but not until someone did the organizing. Omission of the social interrelations arouses the sinister thought that would associate the large population and the technocratic utopia with a strong rule to guarantee efficiency and stability. Some at least suspect such a hidden agenda in the engineering model.

ECONOMICS AND CAUSAL ANALYSIS

Economic explanations take the point of view of the individual decision maker, who assesses costs and benefits of a proposed action and moves positively if the latter exceed the former. Evolutionary and historical considerations are subordinated to a calculus of personal advantage by people choosing under scarcity. The test of such an approach is not the moral one—there are worse sins than selfishness—but lies in whether it can explain current happenings and so lead to control.

Consider the loosening of the marriage bond that shows itself in the high divorce rates of the 1970s. Marriage is a part of the division of labor in society; it depends on different endowments of the spouses, in particular the apparent greater effectiveness of men in the work world and of women in the home (G. S. Becker 1960). This difference of capacities provides the basis of exchange; with the restricted market for female labor of past times, a woman was better off sharing a man's income than with any income she could earn independently. When production was largely carried out within the family there were great benefits from the division of labor—men hunted, and women cooked and sewed. Only after production ceased to belong to the home and wages were in some degree equalized did a woman come to have the material possibility of rejecting an unsatisfactory husband.

This economic approach enables one to say that the cause of the high divorce rate (as well as of the low birth rate) is the good state of the labor market. On this calculus of individual advantage, sexual equality weakens the division of labor that held the family together through long ages. That in the last decades women have had increasing access to jobs explains the long-term trend of divorce.

Yet the better position of women in the labor market can only be a partial explanation of divorce and the slackening of family ties. Divorce is partly a relief from the effects of low mortality. Married couples today stay together almost as long as they did a century ago; the change is mostly that marriages that would then have been dissolved by the death of one of the partners are now dissolved by divorce.

Moreover, if the family has become slack, so have other institutions. It is not only that wives leave their husbands; priests and nuns leave their church, soldiers desert their units, students quit school. Temporary or permanent dropping out is a feature of our age. While the institutions of religion, the military, and education may never have commanded the loyalty that nostalgia prompts us to believe, the increasing rate of desertion over the postwar period is a matter of statistical record.

If the general extension of individual freedom at the expense of institutions is a feature of our times, then increasing divorce must be seen as part of this extension. It is gratuitous to elaborate a theory for divorce based only on the choices women can make in the labor market. Some part of the explanation of increasing divorce must derive from the wider phenomenon of institutional change, and part also arises from improved mortality. Not one but at least three causes are operating, and the task is not so much to elaborate and refine a theory based on any one as to find what part each of the three causes plays and how it fits in with the others.

The first-rate minds in economics who have turned their attention to fertility in recent years have produced explanations in terms of decision-making within the family, on the assumption that the family is conscious of what it is doing and deliberately maximizes utility. As Lee puts it, "The new home economics . . . assumes that couples choose or demand the number of children that will maximize their expected utility, where utility is derived from numbers of surviving children, 'quality' of children, and consumption of other goods" (1977:6). Says T. W. Schultz:

> [T]he cost of children increases with the rise in price of human time. . . . [T]he reproductive behavior of parents is in large part a response to the underlying preferences of parents for children. . . . [But there are] sacrifices, measured in terms of opportunity costs, that parents must be prepared to make in acquiring the future satisfactions and productive service they expect to realize from children. . . . [P]arents equate the marginal sacrifices and satisfactions, including the productive services they expect from children, in arriving at the value of children to them. . . . [T]he analytical key . . . is in the interactions between the supply and demand factors that influence these family decisions (1973: 2–3).

In the purely economic response of fertility to the market for women's labor, data on the secular trend show the opposite direction to that shown by cycles. As employment conditions have improved over the long term, childbearing has indeed diminished, but that does not mean that unemployment of women would be an effective pronatalist policy—aside from its other disadvantages. For people defer marriage, and especially defer childbearing, when things are bad in the labor market. Once the low birth rate has been established in a society, women avoid having children in prosperity because of the opportunity cost of their time and in depression because they cannot afford to have children. This irreversibility suggests a historic process of declining fertility not easily influenced by the usual policy instruments.

Any theory that is seriously advanced is supported by some data. Does women's employment reduce their fertility? Of course it does, and a regression can even seem to tell us by how many points per thousand the birth rate will go down for each rise of 1 percent in the female participation rate. Does women's having fewer children on the contrary cause them to seek work outside the home? The same data as before can be made to show that it does; the regression would just go the other way. What we need is data that will discriminate between the two directions of causation. Waite and Stolzenberg (1976) have gone a certain distance toward giving competing models a chance to reveal themselves.

Can the causal direction be found by asking a sample of women whether they are working because they can't have children or don't want them, or whether working dominates and is the reason for their not having children? Probably not; we can have little faith in the answers to such a question, for other experience has shown that people's ability to interpret their own behavior is limited. Questions on childbearing intentions conspicuously failed to anticipate the turning points of the fertility curve; it is as though women reported what they and their neighbors had been doing with regard to childbearing, rather than what they would do in the future.

Not only must data be applied to discriminate between models, rather than just be fitted to one model, but we must be prepared for the answer to come out differently in a different historical and institutional context.

The Institutional Context of Fertility

The new home economics is specific enough to be checked against facts, not so much to find if it is true as to see in what historical circumstances it is applicable. The drop in fertility that occurred in times of bad crops and scarcity in preindustrial Europe usually came not from lower marital fertility rates, but rather from delay of marriage. It was as though a young couple would not marry until there was a farm for it to take over. On this inheritance hypothesis, control of fertility is by age at marriage more than by restraint within marriage. But the decision making of the couple can be very different in other times and places.

In Java marriage does not typically require that the young couple be able to sustain itself independently. If there is any general notion of such a matter in the peasant village it is, on the contrary, that the young couple is entitled to land, and the more children the couple has, the more land it ought to get. Historical memories of land being redivided in each generation, always in proportion to need, are still retold in the Javanese village today, almost as though they were live institutions. Such redivision has not occurred for a long time, and yet as an ideal it influences current behavior.

For the peasant with this redivision at the back of his mind, the European notion of reproductive restraint is reversed: it is not access to land that sets the limit on one's family, but rather the number of children one has that governs the amount of land he should control. Evidently such a relationship could persist only with low densities, and was destroyed during the century and a half in which the population of Java rose from 10 million to 70 million.

What evolved in place of land redivision was a system of wage labor on rented land, growing especially out of the colonial method of sugar production. When there is plentiful employment at miserable rates of wages rather than a fixed landholding, one gains little by postponing marriage; better marry early and have many children, for each of them will earn a little, and in the aggregate they will be able to support their parents. The earlier one marries, and the more children one has, the sooner and the more comfortably one will be able to retire. The logic of the system requires discipline within the family, which Javanese child rearing strongly inculcates. The father and grandfather have a far more exalted status in Javanese than in American society. Lack of family discipline among Americans is one of a hundred reasons why the Javanese system would not work in the United States.

We find then that Javanese parents have their old-age security in the large number of their children, and this has been given as an explanation of their high fertility. No objection, provided one sees it as institutionally limited. European security was based on a small but adequate family property. To have many children, and not turn most of them out as beggars, would have meant dividing up the property and so impoverishing the parents in their old age. Parents had their old-age security in the fewness of their children.

ECONOMIC DEVELOPMENT AND CHILDBEARING

All this has come to life recently in a book edited by historian-sociologist Charles Tilly (1978) which looks in detail at Europe's fertility decline. Before opening the book, one could have safely bet that the demographic transition would not be able to stand up to the barrage of historical facts. Anyone who propounds a demographic transition starting in the nineteenth century, preceded by uniform high birth and death rates, the fall of deaths and of births in the smooth S-shaped curves of the textbook diagrams, is sure to be asked something like, "But have you seen Blaschke's study of rural Saxony from the twelfth to the eighteenth century?" If one has not even heard of Blaschke's massive work (Tilly 1978: 26), he probably does not know that in Saxony the peasants had relatively small numbers of children, while the workers in handicrafts and incipient rural manufacturing had many children.

Tilly has this point (the difference between landowning and wage-labor fertility) in mind when he suggests that such a hypothesis could help account for the gross regional differences in European fertility before the declines of the nineteenth century. "The relatively low premodern fertility levels of Italy, France, Spain, and Portugal could result from the high proportion of peasants to the total. The great block of high fertility in eastern Europe could be a consequence of the early proletarianization of the rural population on great estates." He warns that this needs confrontation with the evidence, but then goes on, "One more question raised by this line of reasoning is how fertility could ever have declined in the countryside. The answer is that the opportunities for rural wage labor declined" (1978:37).

All policy analysis depends on the transfer of relations from one set of circumstances to another. What conclusions can be drawn from the study of nineteenth-century Europe for the Third World in the late twentieth-century? We know that the birth rates of Europe in the nineteenth century were lower than those of Bangladesh today; that marriage was much later; that dependency rates were much lower; that population was less dense; that landholding was much simpler, usually private ownership by the tiller, with rack-renting and share-tenancy relatively rare. We know also that Asia today has some very advanced industry of a kind that would have been inconceivable in the nineteenth century, and that a much larger fraction of the population lives in cities. The list of differences is long, and yet without weighing them and striking a balance we cannot make any transfer of experience from one situation to the other.

Tilly comes close to making such a transfer in his second-to-last paragraph (p. 349), where he describes a possible series running from peasant society to proletarianization to embourgeoisement. Proletarianization tends to raise fertility, and in recent decades we have seen instances, including Jamaica, in which fertility has gone up with the first impact of economic advance. And then, says Tilly, the acquisition of property and the investment in children's futures among all classes of the population checks fertility more decisively than ever before.

Proletarianization in Tilly's sense is occurring in the Third World on an unheard-of scale, in the countryside as well as in the cities. The process includes detachment of individuals and of families from their villages of birth, and the shift from sustenance on the land to a marginal existence in large- or small-scale industry or in service. Apparently urbanization does not bring the automatic fall in the birth rate that one would expect from the Western experience; some Third World countries show little difference in family size between city and countryside.

This by itself would make the prospects for early population control in the Third World very dim. But in many poor countries literacy is more widespread than it was in Europe at a corresponding state. Does not education have an effect that would be superimposed on the other factors? And what about the clear and present interest of governments in cutting their population growth, quite the opposite of nineteenth-century Europe?

So it turns out that in order to draw conclusions from the past, one has to take account of noncommensurable factors that are unlikely to offset one another. Asia today has more population separated from the soil and not yet middle-class than Europe had two centuries ago, and this intermediate condition, this proletarianization, is a bad prospect for population control. On the other hand, Asia has more literacy, governmental pressure in the right direction, contraceptive techniques, and the example of the rich countries. How do these alter the relation between economic advance and the birth rate?

In the end we have to accept Tilly's warning against "the effort to derive a standard sequence for the demographic transition from the experience of single western countries and to apply it directly to the poor countries of today's world" (p. 52). When twenty years ago scholars were confident that the demographic transition gave a simple and complete account of the modern fall of fertility, that theory did not cause much stir in the world at large. Now that scholars have reservations about the theory, and find its simple form wholly inadequate, the world at large has come to hear about it and accepts it as literal truth and takes it as causally operative: economic development, it says, is the best contraceptive.

EVOLUTION AND CROSS-SECTIONAL ANALYSIS

Sociologists had their fling at evolutionism in the writings of Herbert Spencer and his followers. We now see that doctrine as quaint, even ludicrous. The long-term effect of our discipline's experience has been to inoculate us against the subtle forms in which the evolutionary assumption asserts itself. Alert to the bias that things are always going in the one direction called growth, we cannot easily accept some of the inferences that the evolutionary framework makes possible. Whether evolution takes the form of Rostow's Stages of Economic Development, or the increase of Gross National Product by a certain percentage year after year, sociologists find it suspect as a way of understanding social change. As Karl Polanyi said, "Change seems to happen so easily for the evolutionist."

More than one analyst proceeds from a scatter diagram in which incomes of countries and their fertility are negatively correlated to the conclusion that a rise in income will lower fertility over time. This is a complete non sequitur unless one assumes that all are moving in the same direction. If they are, then in Marx's expression the advanced societies show those that are backward the image of their own future. One can accept enough of evolution to believe that all countries will go through the same trajectory, but this is a matter of faith not easily proven empirically.

Choosing Between Causal Schemes

When the citizen of the industrialized country burns more petroleum, or uses more copper or more cocoa, he directly and immediately adds to the money incomes of the producer country, so that Saudi Arabia or Ghana or Chile has more dollars or yen with which to buy the producer goods that will enable it to become industrialized in turn. Our American high level of consumption is the means by which the development of the poor countries can be financed. It is virtually a duty for us to continue our high consumption, if we have any consideration for the poor countries. Their development depends on our rapid economic growth.

The above is an argument that was commonly used during the 1950s. But now, with not much more data, a wholly different argument has come to be heard, expressed not in money terms but in terms of supplies of essential resources. The United States, with 6 percent of the world's population, consumes 30 percent of the world's minerals. Bauxite from Jamaica, petroleum from Venezuela, coffee from Colombia flow into our industrial processes. If these are in fact necessary to industry in fixed proportions, and we use one-third of the world supply of them, then all the remaining countries of the world can have no more than twice as much industry as we have in total. Practically speaking, this would mean no development at all outside of Europe, Japan, and a few small countries already on the road. From this standpoint we harm the poor countries by our profligacy; the way to help them is to economize in our use of materials. Their development depends on our slowing down and would be much aided by an economic depression on our side.

Thus, of the two arguments, fashionable respectively in the 1950s and 1970s, the one proved without any question or doubt that our purchases of their raw materials was what gave the poor countries the capital to industrialize themselves, the other that we are already using so much in the way of raw materials as to deprive the poor countries of these essential ingredients for their development. Both arguments are indeed policy-relevant, only they lead to opposed policies.

Unless there is a way to choose between them, no policy advice on how to help the poor countries can emerge. Plainly the facts must be consulted to see which view is right. Here the decisive fact is whether world supplies of materials are infinite or finite. Those who present the first model deride the talk of exhaustion as imminent. What makes the discussion long and the decision difficult is that it is not the static physical contents of the soil and subsoil that are in question so much as the prospective costs of extraction, whether future changes in technology will multiply resources or whether we will have to live with today's technology. Cheap and abundant energy will release all the materials mankind can ever need. Whether nuclear fusion will furnish cheap and safe energy after the year 2000 is one of the "empirical" questions that must be answered before we can decide whether we are helping or hurting the poor countries by importing half of our petroleum supplies and much of our minerals.

TECHNICAL INNOVATION AND CARRYING CAPACITY

Directly concerned with the support of population is the effect of innovations like synthetic rubber and synthetic fibers. From an overall world viewpoint, they release land formerly producing latex, sisal, hemp, and jute for food production and so directly increase carrying capacity. But they also make the exports of Indonesia, Bangladesh, and other poor countries less than they would be in the absence of the innovations. The producing country loses foreign exchange with which it could industrialize and so increase its carrying capacity. We have a distributional change between countries; the world may be able to carry more people, but we are richer and Bangladesh is poorer. And there is an internal distribution aspect as well, since the rubber and sisal and jute plantations are taken over by peasants for rice cultivation. The returns from the plantations were in the control of the governments of the countries concerned, while the gains from more land to cultivate benefit the squatters and others who convert plantations to rice fields. The resultant effect of invention of synthetics on population-carrying capacity is obviously unfavorable if one takes the economic-development-through-sale-of-raw-materials model; it is just as obviously favorable if one takes a population-resources model.

The life of the researcher and policy consultant is made simpler if he has one single model of the phenomenon in question, from which he can draw a conclusion on what causes what, and from this conclusion make a recommendation for policy to influence the phenomenon in the desired direction. I suggest that whatever the case, clarity, and incisiveness of the procedure, it may come to a wrong conclusion and be worse than no analysis at all. This danger imposes on us as researchers and policy consultants the need to hold in our minds not one but a variety of models incorporating the phenomenon; to seek data that can discriminate which is correct, among the subset of models that seem consistent with the data; to see what differences emerge in the conclusions to which they lead; and insofar as the data do not effectively discriminate, then to suspend judgment. About forty years ago statisticians discovered that a test of significance is incomplete unless it takes account not only of the hypothesis under test, but of the alternatives to that hypothesis. This may or may not be a satisfying methodology, but it is the best that we can honestly use. To concentrate attention on a single model serves more to convince an audience than to ascertain the truth.

Let us consider one final instance of the need to test competing models, reverting to the secular decline of the birth rate, which is perhaps the central problem of demography.

COMPETING THEORIES OF FERTILITY DECLINE

Children were long regarded as producer goods owned by their parents, and parental decisions to have children were determined accordingly. Once children could no longer be regarded as producer goods, it was natural to suggest that they might be consumer goods. They fitted well into the new household economics that provided, among other things, a framework for analysis of family-building decisions.

In either of these models the deciding agent is a person, a fixed self, the occupant of the skin of Mrs. A. The individual so defined appropriates pleasing or useful objects outside of her skin and makes decisions on the basis of utility as to what to appropriate, or more strictly what to trade for what. But in reality the self is both more and less than the contents of someone's skin. Says a well-known textbook of social psychology (Boring et al., 1939:84), "The self early comes to include more than the individual. Cherished toys grow to be a part of the child's personality. He comes to regard an injury to them as an injury to himself." And he goes beyond toys to incorporate in his own ego people he knows and likes.

Thus rather than consider children as either producer or consumer goods, let us think of them as extensions of the selves of the parents. If parents have children in the measure in which they can consider them extensions of their selves, they will have more children when that kind of identification is more feasible. It is certainly more feasible when the children are bound to their parents, either by economic dependence or by family discipline. In the measure in which the dependence is decreased and the discipline relaxed, parents will be less able to identify with their children, will view them as less central to their selves, and so be less interested in having them. They will instead identify with automobiles, second homes, and other goods and put their resources into these.

In this way of looking at the matter, the inability of parents to identify with their children during the 1960s would have reacted on the willingness of couples to have further children. To check out how far this explains the declining birth rate of the 1960s and 1970s, we need independent measures of child discipline, identification with children, and other variables that would seem perfectly feasible to attain. And we could also check the thesis cross-sectionally: are the countries and cultures where children respect their parents, are most thoroughly under their control, and therefore can be considered part of their selves by the parents, the ones where fertility is highest?

Have I proved this theory as against the alternatives? Not on the amount of data that I or anyone else has so far assembled. Is it on its face less convincing than alternative explanations in terms of prices and qualities? I do not believe so.

Conclusion

My intention in the preceding is to draw attention to the strengths of the several disciplines, and in particular to see how sociology can add to its own virtues the incisiveness of economics. The latter is especially valuable for policy, but only where it takes account of the institutional context, gets the direction of causation straight, and effectively discriminates among competing models.

Until the genuine checking of theories against alternatives becomes part of the scientific mores, our policy relevance will be at best merely apparent and at worst downright misleading. Must we be prepared to have competing theories on the social science market, with policy makers choosing among them according to their preferences? To transfer the choice among models from researchers to administrators places the most important part of applied social science outside the boundaries of the profession.

Despite enormous collections of statistical materials, the pertinent facts are extremely difficult to ascertain. Is the world running out of foodstuffs? If it is, then synthetic fibers that release land for cultivation add to the world's carrying capacity and hence to its possible population. If it is not, then our use of synthetic fibers deprives Bangladesh and Indonesia of export markets for jute and sisal and decreases their carrying capacity.

Below all of these issues is a difficulty, a deep and threatening abyss that is a nightmare for empirical social science. This is the danger that a theory not only selects facts which are relevant to its testing, but that the facts which it selects inevitably confirm the theory. Such a condition would make theories self-confirming on the basis of the only evidence suited for testing them. In the worst presentation of this danger, the values of the investigator would determine what policies he wants to recommend; he would look for theory on which these would be based, and the facts by which the theory would be confirmed would be summoned up, as it were, by the theory. The whole of social science would be an emanation of the values of the scientists.

We must not avert our eyes from the danger that a theory can be self-confirming. Social science is more likely to escape the danger if investigators keep it in mind.

Each discipline provides inferences that accord with some of the facts. The solar energy received by the planet sets an upper limit on the population—human and other—that can survive here. We are the continuation of a process of biological evolution, and that frames some of the conditions under which we operate as individuals and as societies. Truth is present in both the energy transfer and the biological model, but immediacy is lacking. Immediacy and policy relevance are to be found in economic models, along with incisive formulations. But the incisiveness is dulled when any of them is compared with competitors. Sociology and history show that relations can be genuinely different in different times and places. And yet out of inadequate and only partly tested models, whose application varies from place to place and time to time, comes the only knowledge that we have of the causes and consequences of population and other change.

CHAPTER **4**

Values and the Ceiling on Population

An Inhabited Satellite and Its Crew

Before this century, it did not occur to anyone that the world of human habitation was effectively finite. Now we have knowledge about man and his habitat in enough detail at least to be sure that no new fertile lands will be turned up by a Columbus of the twenty-first century (White 1965; Clark 1967).

But is not our world infinite in the sense that new knowledge will make it ever more productive? Science and invention have accelerated and their future is open. They seem a modern form of magic, slaves at our elbows to grant all our wishes. Yet even as the wishes in fairy tales are granted each with some unexpected rebound that brings calamity on the wisher, so ecologists are finding that the magic of science can bring an assortment of disasters. DDT kills insect pests but also poisons useful animals; the Green Revolution produces more food but encourages an increase of population and of inequality. Pending the resolution of some major points of ignorance, we have to think of science as limited, at least in the sense that the pace of its useful advance is limited.

Is finiteness of the food supply the ultimate limit on growth, as Malthus believed, or is that limit set by poisoning of the atmosphere or exhaustion of fuels? In almost any of its forms, the ceiling closes in after a time lag. About 120 million babies will be born this year, and their first-year consumption will be small; their demands will grow as they age; a world that can support the babies cannot necessarily support the schoolchildren and adults that they become. Every birth represents a commitment of resources for the following half century or more, not to food only, but to jobs, housing, clothing, transport. Perhaps the environment can stand damage up to a certain point, at which time it suddenly becomes unlivable—because of smog, for instance. Of all the human problems, that of population makes the heaviest demands on foresight.

With separate nations and identifiable races the intergroup competition has taken a demographic form; any groups that were not pronatalist disappeared under the universal high mortality. Once mortality was brought under control, outbreeding one's national, cultural, or racial rivals became functionally obsolete but did not immediately cease. Now most governments have become aware that competitive breeding is destructive for individual countries and for the planet, and they are trying to bring their populations under control. Some changes in the value system are appearing that would permit more determined measures of control. These are the principal topics to be discussed in the paragraphs that follow.

People and Nations

That part of the earth's crust not under salt water is divided among national states, and humanity is allocated among these. International movement for residence purposes is sharply restricted. Eighteenth- and nineteenth-century notions of the state and citizenship, after bringing to an end the unity of the European Middle Ages, have now prevailed around the world.

The disbanding of the colonial empires built up over more than a century occurred mostly in the decade or two after World War II. New national identities were created for which independence was a primary goal. No one can be quite sure why nationalistic movements had such resounding success in so short a time, nor how it was that liberation came about with relatively little bloodshed. Major conflict occurred only where appreciable numbers of European settlers were involved—Algeria and Rhodesia are examples. There were more Europeans in Indonesia than in Ceylon, and the transition to independence was correspondingly harder.

At a certain moment the profits of colonialism dropped below its costs. Part of the reason why the colonial powers did not fight harder was their sense that the tide of history had turned, and that the loss of colonies was inevitable. Yet they must also have recognized the declining usefulness of unequipped labor in production. It was profitable in the nineteenth and early twentieth centuries to recruit hundreds of thousands of Indonesians to produce sugar and rubber. But then beet sugar, grown with labor-saving methods in the temperate zone, came to compete with cane, and synthetic rubber with natural. Nylon cord competed with sisal. The Netherlands in effect replaced its tropical colonies with modern factories in the homeland and attained unprecedented prosperity.

Since World War II no serious thinker has challenged the right of peoples to self-determination—the phrase itself echoes a slogan applied to Europeans after World War I. Indeed enlightened circles everywhere applaud the fierce defense of national rights in the Third World. Former colonial powers are thereby relieved of responsibility for the difficulties of ex-colonies. For the new countries' insistence on standing alone—or in league with other poor countries—enables rich countries, including the former colonial powers, equally to go their own way. Population growth in a world where unequipped people are less and less able to compete with machines can lead to mass tragedy. The time may have come to forget the extreme independence of the 1940s and after, and to deal collectively with the poverty of liberated and increasing populations. The search for a new international economic order, along with heavy indebtedness to western banks, may indeed be the first sign that national independence of poor countries is very workable and that the world will have to find its way back, not to empire, but to some closer cooperation than was thought necessary at the time of decolonization.

Whatever its other consequences, nationalism has given us the benefit of censuses and statistical counting. Present statistical knowledge is an offshoot of the national state, as the word "statistics" itself reminds us. At least we now know more about population and the problems of population than ever before. Is there any hope of policy oriented to what the population *should* be?

WORLD CARRYING CAPACITY AND THE OPTIMUM

The optimal or best population cannot be discussed without first deciding some contentious questions of value. Is the best population the largest possible? Is it the one that has the greatest diversity of culture? The greatest degree of freedom? The optimum depends on what is to be maximized. Three possibilities are numbers, diversity, and freedom; and they lead to very different optima.

The 4 billion people who inhabit the earth in the mid-1970s are a biomass of 200 million tons, increasing at about 4 million tons per year. This increase is about one twenty-fifth of the annual world production of beef and pork, and about one-fifteenth of the annual catch of the world's oceans. It is about one quarter of the combined annual output of wheat, rice, corn, potatoes, and other crops raised as food for men and animals.

If productivity on existing agricultural land were doubled, and if an equal additional amount of land could be brought into use, the population could exceed 20 billion. This depends on higher-yielding varieties, which have the merit that they can feed into the human biomass the stored-up energy of fossil fuels made available through fertilizers. The process would be aided by the shortening of trophic chains—that is, if meat eating declined and men fed themselves directly on the corn now consumed by pigs, cows, and chickens. All this could come about with substantially existent agricultural technology. Whether agricultural systems can sustain such high productivity indefinitely is another question (Ladejinsky 1970; Brown 1968).

With the use of algae and other more efficient primary converters of the sun's energy, and with some quite feasible scientific advances, another doubling, to 40 billion, could well be possible. The globe's carrying capacity might thus be tenfold the present population. Such figures have been given in the literature and have also been widely criticized. Let us accept them here, nonetheless, as suggestive of what might be possible if science and technology were devoted to increasing human subsistence.

But the total effort to maximize the human biomass can arise only from seeing man as a species of domestic animal, and represents a thoroughly inhumane notion of what people are on the earth for. Let us suppose instead that the object is to attain the greatest volume and duration of civilization—not maximization of human biomass, but deepening of culture. The question then is not how many we can have, but how many we need for this peculiarly human objective.

Would a world population of 1 million suffice? This is far more than the 5,040 free citizens that Plato thought ideal for carrying the culture and doing the work of the city, but then we have more specialities than Plato knew about, and even he assumed a number of cities. A world population consisting of 1 million educated and skilled persons could continue the main branches of knowledge and of art for one culture. To provide as well for a wide range of industrial products and consumer goods, the skills and division of labor in a population of the order of 100 million might be required. To go further and preserve a reasonable selection of the world's diverse languages and cultures might require half a billion. Remember that even with our 4 billion people, local cultures and specialized traditional knowledge and occupations are being lost, and good citizens of the world worry about the loss.

A conscious policy of preserving cultures should be able to do better with half a billion than we now do with 4 billion. How that half billion should be allocated among countries and culture groups is a policy question that fortunately no one is pressing us to answer.

The clearest and most enlightened recognition of the issues is to be found in China, where the regime is aiming at one-child families that could reduce the population by as much as 30 percent. Seemingly the authorities are willing to face the awkward age distribution incidental to the transition to a more nearly optimum population. They are also allowing the hill peoples and other minority cultures within China a larger part of the final total population—the one- or two-child limit does not apply to them.

The number of people in the world that would maximize freedom is even harder to assess than the number that would maximize richness and diversity of culture. We know that in most matters more people require more regulation than fewer people. The first automobiles required no traffic lights; regulations on waste disposal would have been out of place on the frontier; in a modern community both traffic lights and waste disposal are indispensable. As each increase of population requires an increase of regulation, it entails a decline of liberty. If freedom were the sole objective, it would make for a very small population, much smaller than maximizing civilization or diversity of culture.

Incentives might well be devised that would bring the world total down to the 500 or so million that would provide a diverse life and a reasonable degree of freedom on the planet over a long period of time. But there is little prospect—and little danger—that population policy will become an instrument for the preservation of peoples and cultures. Considering how hard it has been to attain simpler objectives in international negotiation, we cannot expect much for population. Furthermore, demographers point out that the age distribution of a group that had to drop to one child per couple for several generations would be very peculiar, and the transitional generations would have to carry the burden of large numbers at the oldest ages. The economics of contraction cannot draw the same enthusiasm as the economics of growth.

Given the difficulty of deciding how many people there ought to be in the world, it is no wonder that virtually everyone who has thought about the matter is willing to settle for voluntary control of childbearing.

THE NATURE OF THE CEILING

In times of rapid technical change few useful statements can be made about the ceiling that the environment sets on population. Malthus went out of style partly because his food ceiling on population was repeatedly raised by the discovery of new lands and new techniques. If the ceiling were completely rigid, no sudden tragedy could ever occur. A rigid ceiling would exist if there were a clear and patent division of space, food, and other resources such that no population beyond what resources could sustain at each moment would be possible.

A rigid and visible ceiling to population does exist when resources are appropriately divided up. Births will be sooner checked under a regime of private property than when property is common. We can imagine a division of space, food, and other resources such that the moment when the last sustainable person was born would be clearly recognized. If the absence of support for one more person were unmistakably signaled, that person would not be brought into the world. A birth would be permitted when a death occurred. At all times mankind would be compelled to stay within its food supply. From the moment the limit was reached we could add no further population, except that as individuals died Nature would permit us to replace them. Private property and territoriality are a partial means for making the ecological ceiling more overt and immediately operative.

Without a rigid ceiling, the population problem requires calculation and foresight; Nature is like a moneylender who allows us—even encourages us—to borrow beyond our means and beyond our needs, and then calls in the debt when we are most extended.

Now the calculability of the Malthusian ceiling may be reduced by a new instability (that ecologists have come to fear) which has resulted from man-environment interaction in our technological age. Instead of living with a ceiling over our heads, which is bad enough, we may be on a melting iceberg that can turn over at any moment. This raises the amount of foresight demanded to much higher levels. Let us look into some aspects of the potential instability under which we may now actually be living.

The analogy of our material base to an iceberg that could turn over is not farfetched. As one illustration of the mechanism we can cite the Sumatran or Laotian hill country, where slash-and-burn agriculture has been practiced for centuries. Each year a family burns the trees on about an acre of land, plants with digging stick its cassava, tobacco, and corn or other cereal, and after a year or two abandons the site and makes another clearing in the forest. This neolithic agriculture is perfectly stable as long as people are few.

Above a certain population density, however, each family has to return to the same plot before the forest has had time to reestablish itself. When population increase compels such a premature return, the landscape changes in the course of a few cycles, and instead of forest a tough grass, called alang-alang in Sumatra, comes to prevail. Now no further cultivation is possible and if the inhabitants could not move on they would starve.

We know little about instability in local situations now and can only speculate on its operation on a larger scale in the future. The farmer eliminates species that are not of use to him, including weeds, rats, and other pests, and so increases effective yields. Population again grows on the increased production. One instrument used by the farmer to produce the increased yields is DDT, and DDT turns out to be an active poison. It concentrates in the fat of animals up food chains throughout the world. What happens to the population built up on it when its use has to be discontinued?

Aside from any specific effect of this kind, ecologists fear agricultural procedures that drastically reduce the number of species coexisting in an area. Seed banks can save genetic materials that have for the moment become commercially valueless.

Because the number of inhabitants is set by such considerations, the simple Malthusian ceiling no longer applies. We do not know whether the long-term carrying capacity of the earth is 1 or 5 or 10 billion people, or whether the very notion of a ceiling makes sense.

AUTOMATION

The United States and other industrial countries are now moving into a new phase. The controlled chemical synthesis that enables a modern factory run by a few technicians to produce the same rubber as a tropical plantation with thousands of laborers constitutes a liberation of production from human hands as well as from the natural landscape. A Dutch concern making synthetic fiber now fills much of the demand for Indonesian sisal of colonial times. But synthetics are not the only example of the new industrial power.

A few examples of the directions that industry is taking will serve. Men with pickaxes have not been important in American coal mines for some time; but even men working underground with mechanical diggers and loaders are giving place to strip mining, in which the largest earth-moving equipment ever constructed pushes away the few hundred feet of soil above the coal deposits, and then mechanical shovels take it out several tons at a time. Open strip mining now accounts for a large fraction of American coal production. The extraction of oil and natural gas is even cheaper, and these are moved almost without human effort through pipelines to where they can be converted into electricity in nearly unmanned thermal plants.

The decline of employment in the automobile industry is partly due to numerical control of machine tools, which is spreading rapidly through this and other industries. Instead of craftsmen working with elaborate jigs, we have a library of control tapes (themselves made by computer from engineering drawings), and an operator who mounts whichever tape is required. Makeready time is reduced from days to minutes; inventories may practically be dispensed with when it is possible to make pieces one at a time as cheaply as several hundred at a time. Engineers, no longer held to what a craftsman can produce by hand, can develop more elaborate designs. In electronics printed circuits have reduced the man-hour content of electronic equipment in the same way that numerical control has reduced the labor content of automobiles.

Computers are the most spectacular labor savers. Whether for department store billings, for insurance company records, or for airline reservations, they produce a quality and quantity of work that make previous methods unacceptable.

Internal Labor Displacement

Both economic theory and current experience show that, far from causing unemployment, the worst that automation does is to move people from one occupation to another. The new one is usually more challenging; the work of a computer programmer is incomparably more exciting than that of a billing clerk. It is true that the shiftover cannot always take place in the same generation; many workers in the transition may have to retire younger than they would like unless they can face a change of occupation.

The major discovery has been that the level of unemployment can be kept wherever one wants by adjusting demand. If there is not enough work making automobiles, we can fill the gap by going to the moon. We could equally have filled the gap by planting flowers in the parks, but this has less appeal. We do not want the dull public works of the 1930s; our public works must be cosmic.

External Labor Displacement

The same satisfactory observations cannot be made on the external displacements of labor caused by technical progress. Although these have not ordinarily been spoken of in the same breath, the Indonesian plantation worker dismissed because synthetic rubber limits the market for natural rubber is automated out as decisively as the Detroit automobile worker displaced by numerical control. The difference is that we neither pension the Indonesian nor offer him a way to get back into the system.

Our synthetics attack the economy of the underdeveloped country at the point where the colonial power had put its principal demand for tropical labor, the production of agricultural raw materials. Here the comparative advantages of tropical sunshine and cheap labor are greatest. If these were already being undercut in the colonial period, when Europeans owned the plantations, they will be undercut by Western factory owners even less regretfully when the plantations are in the hands of independent and sometimes unfriendly states. And while the former colonies can sell less, they want to buy more, especially the capital goods needed to industrialize themselves.

But could the ex-colony not turn to what it can now do best, relative to Western capitalized industry? Cannot India make textiles and sell them abroad, using abundant labor and local techniques, and so finance its own industrialization? Japan helped industrialize itself (without the benefit of Western good will) by selling textiles made with cheap labor. It is probably too late for another Asian country to do this.

Suppose Western industry were so mechanized that the competitive wages for unmechanized production would not suffice to enable the worker to buy the food that would sustain him. We are actually at this point in some fields of Western production. An Indian worker with a hand loom produces about three yards of fabric in a long day's work; the value added in a world market whose prices are set by machine-made cloth is barely sufficient to buy him one pound of rice. India has not enough capital to put its redundant population into factories and so make them competitive.

I once calculated that about 50,000 clerks in Calcutta could do the work of a computer of the type common in the United States about 1965. Could they have been organized and trained by someone to take the contract for the computation of the Apollo project? Even if every other difficulty of coordination could be surmounted, it would turn out that the clerks could be paid only about four cents per day each (allowing a computer rental of $250 per hour, or $2,000 for an eight-hour shift), and this would not feed them, let alone feed and shelter their families. Since that time the cost of computation has been reduced by much more than one order of magnitude.

At each point where the West learns to accomplish an industrial process at below what might be called physiological cost, that is, more cheaply than could be done by unequipped labor willing to work for food alone, one more means of sustaining the population of the underdeveloped world is removed.

BEYOND EXPLOITATION

Much concern has been expressed on behalf of the exploited of the world. But now a lower level of the human condition has appeared: the man who is unexploitable. It is not worth anyone's while to use his labor; no one can make a profit by setting him to work, even at starvation wages. This situation could only come about when to the technological leap of the advanced countries is added population density in the poor ones.

Notwithstanding all of this, the poor country can use its labor in conjunction with foreign capital to do those things that are relatively labor-intensive. Electronic components have for some time been made in Taiwan for assembly in Japan. Now Taiwan, Singapore, Hong Kong and South Korea produce goods of increasing technological complexity. The lack of capital in the poor country and the technical advance of the rich one did not prevent cooperation in production between them. The isolation of the poor described in the preceding paragraphs can be overcome, although in many nations politics prevents the unlimited cooperation of poor labor and rich foreign capital. But the more important question is the scale of the process. Can Hong Kong's prescription cure India's unemployment?

CONTROLLING POPULATION SIZE

On the average more children are born to poor couples than to those better-off; this is true both among countries and among individual families within countries. There is no provable genetic or inborn quality difference between rich and poor as such, but the poor command less satisfactory facilities for bringing up children. Children share the standard of living of the home into which they come. The differentials of fertility have been seen as a social problem for at least the past century, which is to say, ever since they came into existence in the now developed countries.

At first those differentials were most conspicuous within countries; it was noted in England and elsewhere that the more urban, the more literate, the better-off generally, in short, those most capable of providing amenities for children, were the ones who had fewest children. The century-old differentials of fertility are now disappearing, and differentials of income are probably less than they were a hundred years ago, although statements on this depend on the method of measurement.

Within rich countries all social groups are converging to about the same birth rates—to something close to a two-child family.

However, birth rates continue at fifty per thousand in some parts of Africa, through forty or so in South Asia, down to fifteen or lower in the United States, Europe, and Japan. An individual family head wants the continuance of his line and in particular enough children surviving to take over his agricultural work and to provide him with whatever old-age security is to be had. (This association of security with large numbers of children is especially close in a regime of wage-labor; with peasant ownership or fixed tenancy, on the other hand, it is in the interest of old-age security to have *few* children.) In a regime of wage-labor where jobs for women are scarce, the interest of fathers in having children who will later support them with their wages often accords with the drive of women to motherhood as the means to securing their marriage and assuming status in the community. The advent of women's careers that provide alternative sources of self-respect also turns women's thoughts away from childbearing.

The fall in mortality drastically reduces the number of sons that one needs in order to have children living into one's old age. In round numbers, eight births would be required to provide two adult sons when over 50 percent of children die before maturity; just over four births will provide the same two adult sons when most live to maturity. Thus the fall in mortality, once it is assimilated into the thinking of parents, is capable of reducing the number of children they want by about half, and four children is a figure often seen in surveys of desired family size in poor countries. The fall in mortality is now reflected in childbearing intentions and ideals in many countries, although not in all. However, four children surviving to maturity are still twice as many as are needed for replacement.

A vulgar Malthusian would think that population control in poor countries depends on high death rates, and he would be against improving health services. He would be wrong; the opposite policy will be ultimately more effective. If people have confidence that a child once born will live, that if they fall sick they will have access to medical services, that some degree of security is possible—in short, if they are in a position to plan their lives—they are more likely to plan their families. Literacy is one of the factors that encourage both general planning and family planning; this we can read in Malthus. It may indeed be true that modern developments in medicine have brought the population problem upon us, but the way to solve it is not to put medicine into reverse, but to push it ahead with all speed. It is the next stages in modernization—more medicine, schooling, and economic advance—that are the best hope of solving the problems that arise in the early phases of modernization. The demographer can in good conscience recommend policies that would be desirable on general grounds as well as for their use in bringing population under control.

This argument is much heard, but it contains some elements of speculation and is true in the long rather than in the short run. The down-to-earth statistical data show that when infant deaths decline the immediate effect is a decline in births, but by a lesser amount, so the net rate of increase goes up. The simplest generalization is that the immediate effect of a decline in mortality is faster population increase, while the longer term effect is slower increase. When the longer term begins is the unanswered question.

OFFICIAL REASONS FOR BIRTH CONTROL

Governments adopting family planning policies advance varied official reasons, among which economic growth of the country is the most frequent. For the United Arab Republic, "This increase (of population) constitutes the most dangerous obstacle that faces the Egyptian people in their drive towards raising the standard of production in their country...." Turkish government statements mention economic development and the capital-income ratio. Kenya emphasizes the problem of providing jobs as the adult male population increases, and the burden of child dependency. Singapore stresses the welfare of the individual family, especially the incapacity of its breadwinners to support many children. Malaysia speaks of its population problem as engendered by lower mortality due to medical and health services and sees it as necessary to complement this health support by family planning if economic progress is not to be inhibited. Indonesia says that "the aim of family planning is in the first place to promote the welfare of the family, especially of mother and child."

Berelson (1969) sums up by saying that in the entire developing world today, about 65 percent of people live in countries with policies favoring birth control. "In Asia and Africa the movement is mainly based on the effect of population growth upon social and economic development.... In Latin America it is based more on medical and humanitarian concern with the prevalence of induced abortion."

The ecological view, that population out of balance with the habitat leads to disaster, is barely hinted at. The closest I see, for instance in the collection of governmental statements on family planning provided by the Population Council (1970), is for India, which does refer to pressure on resources as a subsidiary reason for family planning in its First

Five-Year Plan (1951–1956). Pakistan refers in introducing its population policy for the Third Plan (1965–1970) to the 3.5 acres held by the average cultivator, and hence must be counted as aware of the ecological problem, at least in its gross form.

Although little is said officially about the need to limit population to accord with the finiteness of the environment, much is spoken about vast natural resources. These have been the stock in trade of political discussion of population in Brazil and other countries of Latin America and in Indonesia during Sukarno's regime. Dusty notions about resources that had some substance when a country contained 50 million people become obsolete as it passes the 100 million mark.

If little is said officially about the limits of national resources requiring a limiting of population, the notion of a planetary limit of resources appears not at all. That anyone should curtail his own family because the planetary environment must be protected would seem incomprehensible, if not laughable, to officials of underdeveloped countries, who face pressing day-to-day problems. Yet the finiteness of planetary resources is the ultimate reason for population restraint.

Voluntary Birth Control

The dominant approach is one of providing the means to voluntary birth control, which is to say, offering cheap and effective contraceptives to those parents who feel they have enough children. Some optimists consider that this would solve the population problem—they implicitly assume that the desires of individuals for children and the carrying capacity of the earth's surface are in natural harmony. That such an assumption is gratuitous appears from many studies (Davis 1967).

To cite the most thorough of the investigations now extant, Freedman and Takeshita (1969) found that for Taiwanese wives thirty-five to thirty-nine years old, live births averaged 5.2, living children 4.6, and children wanted 4.2. Availability of birth control to the population under survey would reduce fertility but would still leave it very high. Some assumptions about proportions unmarried and unfertile, as well as about mortality, are required to translate a figure of 4.2 children wanted into a population rate of increase, but even with maximum adjustments for these, a mean of 4.2 births per woman comes out to an increase of over 50 percent per generation.

The groups classified as more modern want fewer children. Professionals in the Taiwan sample, for instance, stated a mean number of children wanted of 3.4, against 4.9 by farmers. Women thirty to thirty-four, moreover, wanted slightly fewer than did women thirty-five to thirty-nine: 4.1 against 4.2; among wives of farmers, those thirty to thirty-four wanted 4.5 children, against 4.9 wanted by wives thirty-five to thirty-nine. That younger women, and those in the modern sector, wanted fewer children is encouraging for any country that is moving rapidly toward modernization. But the number of children wanted by even the most advanced groups is far from suggesting that a stationary condition will follow automatically from present economic trends even in Taiwan, let alone in Nepal or Bolivia.

The birth control movement emphasizes the voluntary approach to family planning. Former Secretary-General of the United Nations, U Thant, in the context of a statement on overpopulation, spoke of "the right of parents to determine the numbers of their children." Is it possible that in a near future this slogan will be taken over by populationists and used to shout down those who initially devised it?

Whether seen on the national scale or on the world scale, the solution of putting safe, reliable, and easily applied contraception within the reach of every couple is only a first stage; it will enable them to have only the number of children they want. The second stage is somehow causing them to want the number of children that the crust of the earth can support. And in view of the urgency of the problem, it would be unpardonable complacency to put off facing the second stage until the first stage is disposed of.

Moral Dilemmas

If voluntary parenthood, the slogan under which contraception has made itself acceptable in wide circles, still leaves a disequilibrium, what is the next step? Must parenthood be administratively controlled? Should we require that couples fill out a form and submit it at the wicket of a government agency, wait several months, and then return to find it stamped as approved or disapproved? This is what we require of anyone adding to the national population in later life as an immigrant. Yet an immigrant entering the United States at the age of twenty-five, his education completed and his working life just beginning, is not the burden that a newborn infant is.

Although our ethics allow officials to make choices among foreigners, we would be repelled by their making choices among natives—deciding which Americans could be parents cannot be left to administrative decision. Should we, then, allow each couple to have two children and no more? This quantitative regulation is analogous to what we now have in respect to marriage: most countries set at one the number of wives a man may have at any moment. And yet his having two wives places less strain on the community than a couple's having four children. The members of the community who support laws against bigamy—presently the majority—ought to support compulsory family limitation if it is true that unrestrained reproduction does more harm than unrestrained marriage as such could do.

Or should limitation be made consistent with market freedom by giving every girl at puberty two coupons, each entitling the holder to a child, as Kenneth Boulding (1964) suggests? Coupons help ration consumer goods in wartime, but here the woman could be allowed to sell the coupons, or buy others, and so the rights to children would drift into the hands of those who most wanted to be the parents of the next generation. Specifically, the coupons would drift into the hands of those who both wanted children and had the financial capacity to give them good schooling and expensive upbringing. It makes all the difference that the payment for the excess over two children would have to be *in advance* of their conception rather than after their birth. Here, as in consumer goods generally, an installment system by which one can make the decision to purchase long before he has to pay encourages improvidence. Of course, the coupon system would only be a test of foresight and saving as a prerequisite for having children if parents were forbidden to borrow to raise the amount needed to buy the coupons. We do have laws restricting purchase of stocks on margin, and such would have to be applied for children.

There are incidental benefits of the scheme. The girl who was poor could sell the two coupons at the high prices that would prevail in the market if children are desired as much as surveys of married couples show them to be. For an upwardly mobile couple, cash from the sale of the coupons could be a dowry, sufficing perhaps to establish the couple in a business.

The children would be born to those financially stronger, and therefore better able to care for them. They would be made comparable to yachts or other expensive consumer goods; those who could afford the high initial cost would be those best able to stand the upkeep. But very drastic changes in values would have to occur before such a proposal could be taken seriously.

The scheme would, in any case, require a new contraceptive technique not under the control of the couple. Guarding the nation's frontiers against illicit immigration would have its counterpart in policing the nation's wombs against unauthorized reproduction. A device would have to be invented to make women temporarily infertile and would be administered to all through the water or in some other way. Only on obtaining permission to have a child would couples be provided with a suitable antidote.

An alternative is a tax, fixed at the level that will just produce the average of two surviving children per couple needed for stability. Taxes are how we discourage the consumption of cigarettes and liquor. This would be going back to an earlier and fairly successful method of population control. When schools had to be paid for by the parents of the pupils, and free lunches were unknown, many expenditures that today are public costs had to be covered privately. In effect, there were heavy charges on children in nineteenth-century England and France, and not even any significant income tax exemption. Can we restore the nineteenth-century arrangement by a tax in the nature of a user charge on schools, similar to the gasoline tax that pays for highway construction and maintenance? People being taxed differentially is not in itself abhorrent; the exemptions at the present time, which are passed down in laws inherited from an epoch of underpopulation, in effect tax couples who do *not* have children. The principle of a tax incentive relative to reproduction is well established in our laws, but heed for the environment would reverse its direction and load the tax burden on the prolific rather than the careful.

This approach of charging parents the full cost of their children has a serious disadvantage: that not the parents alone but in whole or in part the children would pay. We do not want to discourage parents from having children by means that result in poorer food and poorer education for the children that are born. That is why policies perfectly suited to other fields of human behavior are inappropriate for controlling reproduction.

A subsidy for those who do not have children would have more appeal than a tax on those who do. Women would be invited to register for the payment, and to return to the registry office each four months, say, to be inspected for nonpregnancy. After a suitable number of such inspections they could claim their subsidy (Enke 1963). Since a woman may be fertile for over thirty years, and ten years are more than enough to contribute to a dangerous overload on the environment, the subsidy per year of nonreproduction would have to be graduated upward with the length of time. Its administration would offer problems far beyond those known to the U.S. Department of Agriculture, where farmers were long paid for leaving their soil uncultivated on a year-by-year basis.

This discussion is intended only to show the dilemmas posed by the desire of individual couples to have children in the face of the incapacity of the earth's surface to contain more than a certain number of people. The balance in all previous history was maintained by bacterial diseases; now that bacteria have been substantially conquered, we need a moral equivalent to them. But means of control through legal restrictions, taxes, and subsidies that are perfectly acceptable on other matters are offensive when applied to reproduction. No one has yet suggested a suitable way of bringing individual reproductive goals into alignment with the collective need for a stationary population.

CHAPTER 5
Upward Mobility in a Stationary Population

An increasing population facilitates individual upward mobility. One of the consequences of moving toward the inevitable no-growth population is that mobility becomes more difficult.

An equation for the relation between individual mobility and population increase can be applied to determine the age of promotion to a given rank in a stable organization. It will show in what degree the age of promotion depends on the rate of increase of the population under different mortality schedules and other circumstances. The effect will turn out to be numerically substantial—change from the 1½ percent annual increase of the United States a few years ago to its prospective stationary condition implies a delay in reaching the middle positions of the average factory or office of 3 years.

In many organizations the proportion of senior officers to lower-rank personnel is fixed by regulation. The English universities, for example, can have only 7/13 as many senior faculty as junior. In the California system the number of staff is tied to the number of students. Military organizations have relatively fixed ratios of generals, colonels, and other senior officers to lower ranks. Even when there is no staffing table or exact formula, the ratio of supervisors to clerks, or foremen to factory workers, is de facto set by the conditions of the job. A hierarchy may be far from anyone's intention, but it comes naturally into being in many kinds of productive activity; where the convenience of administrators does not create it, the forces of competition set limits to the ratio of supervisors to supervised (O'N. Waugh 1971).

Whether the hierarchy is planned or not, individuals work their way up through the several ranks. They take unequal lengths of time to do so, and by no means all get to the top. Our results may thus be interpreted in three ways:

1. As applying to a system of strict seniority, in which every promotion is determined only by time of entry. Because strict seniority schemes are rare, this is the least interesting application.
2. As applying to an organization in which merit, influence, and other factors determine individual promotion, but in which experience is a factor of some importance. Some kind of age-complementarity must exist in production; old hands generally do different jobs from new recruits. If merit and influence are considered to act at random in relation to seniority, then our results give an average rate of promotion.
3. As showing the pure effect of population increase on promotion, in abstraction from all other circumstances. From this viewpoint, merit and influence that may be determining for the individual are superimposed on the population factor. A person would move up 4½ years earlier if he lived in a population increasing at 2 percent per year than if he lived in one that was stationary; he would have this advantage whether he is above or below average in mobility. He may be brilliant and move up fast in a stationary population; our argument shows that he would move up faster in an increasing population. This seems the most valuable of the three interpretations of the results that follow.

The argument compares populations with different rates of increase, each fixed, rather than one population that slows down its rate of increase. Though the fact will not be repeated each time, the method is always comparative: what is the difference between mobility in a population growing steadily at 2 percent per year and one that is stationary, other conditions being the same? This applies even to derivatives; we want to know how much earlier is the age of promotion as we move from a population increasing at a certain rate to another increasing slightly faster. Our approach is comparative statics rather than dynamics.

The Basic Equation

Consider any particular marker of advance in status, a gateway through which an individual must pass on his upward course, for example promotion to foreman in a factory. Suppose that recruitment takes place at the youngest age and in the lowest status; we want to see how much earlier in the life of the individual the gateway is passed in a growing than in a stationary population.

We must set up some fixed point or observation post on the mobility process, and a convenient one is the ratio of people above to people below in the organization. If the ratio is unity, then we are looking at the point where for each employee of higher rank there is one of lower rank; if it is 0.2, then for each employee of higher rank there are five of lower. This ratio, considered as an observation post, will be designated k in what follows.

Suppose that everyone is recruited at age α and retires at age β, that the lower of two stages in the career from α to β contains v persons and the higher contains u, that everyone passes from the lower to the higher at the same age x, that the probability of surviving from birth to age a is $l(a)$, that the population is increasing uniformly at rate r. Suppose also that either official regulations or the objective conditions of work require in the higher group the fraction k of the number of persons in the lower group (Figure 1).

If a population has been increasing at rate r for a considerable period of time, then a years ago it was e^{-ra} times as large as it is now, and its births also were e^{-ra} times as large as present births. If present births per unit of population are b, then births a years ago, per unit of present population, were be^{-ra}. If the fraction of these births that survived to the present time is $l(a)$, then the number of present population aged a, still per unit of the present population, must be $be^{-ra} l(a)$. Thus, uniform previous increase of population implies that the proportion of individuals between age a and $a + da$ is $b^{-ra} l(a) da$, where b is the birth rate. This is the well-known stable age distribution. Then the number between age x and retirement is proportional to:

$$u = \int_x^\beta e^{-ra} l(a)\, da,$$

and the number under age x to:

$$v = \int_\alpha^x e^{-ra} l(a)\, da.$$

The ratio of those above to those below age x can be expressed as a ratio of two integrals. Our problem requires that this ratio be equal to the fixed and given k:

$$\frac{\int_x^\beta e^{-ra} l(a)\, da}{\int_\alpha^x e^{-ra} l(a)\, da} = k, \tag{1}$$

or for short $u/v = k$, which is the same as $u - kv = 0$.

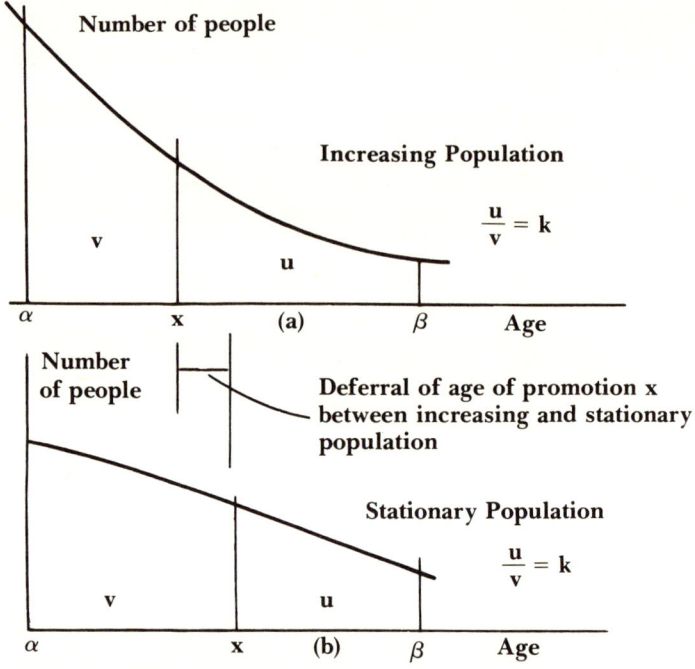

Figure 1: Contrast of Increasing Population (a) and Stationary Population (b), showing age x needed to attain a rank where k persons are higher to each person lower, given promotion by seniority.

The basic equation (1) at which we have arrived implicitly expresses x in terms of r. Everything in it other than x and r is known—the life table $l(x)$, the entering age α and the retiring age β; k is a given gateway on which attention is concentrated for the moment; the dummy variable for age a is integrated out. Hence for any value of r we may solve for x. In accord with the direction of interest of our problem we will regard r as the independent variable, and x as the dependent variable.

The equation has to be translated into finite form, specifically into the five-year intervals in which life table data are ordinarily published. Then it has to be solved numerically; we have to find for each of a series of values of r the value of x. Fitting a cubic through $u - kv$ for four successive quinquennial ages, and then finding the value of x for which the cubic crosses the age-axis, gives an approximation of the value of x for which $u/v = k$ at the given r. By this procedure Table 1 was produced, based on the life table for United States males, 1968, on $k = 3, 2$, and 1, and on $r = 0$ to 0.04 by intervals of 0.01. Age at entry α was taken as twenty years, and age at retirement β as sixty-five years.

Table 1 Age of passing various gateways, from $k = 3$ (at which the ratio of those above to those below is 3:1) up to $k = 1$ (at which the ratio of those above to those below is 1:1); with the rate of increase r from 0 to 0.04 per annum; based on the life table for United States males, 1968

	$r = 0.00$	$r = 0.01$	$r = 0.02$	$r = 0.03$	$r = 0.04$
$k = 3.0$	30.31	28.75	27.45	26.38	25.51
$k = 2.0$	33.79	31.89	30.24	28.84	27.68
$k = 1.0$	40.86	38.55	36.39	34.43	32.71

A number of points stand out:

1. If the population is increasing at the rate of 0.01, a person will pass the gateway represented by $k = 1$, which is to say he crosses into the upper half of the hierarchy, at 38.55 years rather than at 40.86 years of age as he would in a stationary population with the same life table. He saves 2.31 years because the population is increasing at 1 percent per year rather than stationary.
2. The effect of a 1 percent increase becomes smaller as one goes to the higher gateway—for $k = 0.2$ (not shown in the Table) where each person has five others reporting to him the difference between $r = 0$ and $r = 0.01$ is only 1.66 years. Promotion at the top is not as much affected by population growth as promotion at the middle ranks.
3. Some diminishing returns appear with increasing r. The benefit of going from $r = 0.03$ to $r = 0.04$ at the gateway $k = 1$ is to lower the age by 1.72 years as against 2.31 years by going from $r = 0.00$ to $r = 0.01$.

EFFECT OF DEATHS ON THE PROMOTION OF THOSE SURVIVING

Evidently the mortality of one's contemporaries is favorable to one's own promotion, and the hope of advancing by outliving one's colleagues is ancient. It will therefore come as a surprise that the mortality effect is small in comparison with the population growth effect.

Table 2 Effect of mortality. Age of passing through gateway k for $k = 1$, for $r = 0$ to $r = 0.04$, for male life tables of the United States 1968, Mexico 1966, and Sweden 1783–87

$r = 0.00$	$r = 0.01$	$r = 0.02$	$r = 0.03$	$r = 0.04$
		United States Males, 1968		
40.86	38.55	36.39	34.43	32.71
		Mexican Males, 1966		
40.40	38.08	35.94	34.03	32.36
		Swedish Males, 1783–87		
38.44	36.32	34.40	32.70	31.24

To study the relation of mobility to mortality we carry out the same calculation as Table 1, but now with three very different life tables: The United States 1968 with an $\mathring{e}_0$ of 66.1 years, Mexico 1966 with 59.5 and Sweden 1783–87 with 33.6, all males. These represent about the range of human mortality, and 0 to 4 percent increase per annum represents most of the range of human natural increase (Table 2).

This suffices to show that the effect of population increase r is much greater than the effect of mortality. Consider the $k = 1$ gateway, reached at age $x = 40.86$ by United States 1968 males with $r = 0$; promotional age is down 2.42 years to 38.44 for Swedish 1783–87 mortality with $r = 0$, but 8.15 years to 32.71 with $r = 0.04$ and the same United States 1968 mortality. *A rapidly increasing population is more than three times as advantageous as a high level of mortality,* and this is considering only the advantage to those who survive the high mortality.

To analyze the effects on average mobility of population increase and mortality, we simplify by supposing that the death rate is fixed at μ between ages α and β. Then $l(a) = l(\alpha)e^{-(a-\alpha)\mu}$ and the integrand of (1) is just $e^{-(\mu+r)a}$. The fact that μ and r enter the integral only as a sum shows that they have the same effects: a given average increase in the death rate advances the rate of mobility (for those who survive) exactly as much as does the same amount of increase in the rate of natural increase.

This explains why the differences in mobility are smaller as one moves among life tables than as one moves among rates of increase. Death rates at working ages mostly vary within a range of about 0.015 among human populations, while rates of increase vary from about -0.005 to almost 0.04.

Resignations before the age of retirement also have the same effect of hastening the promotions of those who remain. For the promotion of survivors in the hierarchy it matters not whether their associates leave for other jobs or for the other world. Resignations, deaths, and natural increase all tend to push a persisting individual upward through the several steps, and a given change in any has the same numerical effect on his rate of progress. Entry above age α slows down promotion of those already in the system. We have *not* taken account here of either later entry or premature exit.

THE RATE OF CHANGE OF x WITH r

Though we cannot solve (1) for x explicitly in terms of r and the life table, we can find the derivative of x with respect to r. This will be a main result of the present analysis; even if we could find an explicit solution of (1) for x in terms of r, it would be less interesting than to know the difference in x associated with a difference in r. The derivative dx/dr can be expressed as

$$\frac{dx}{dr} = -\left(\frac{1}{1+k}\right)\left(\frac{u}{e^{-rx}\,l(x)}\right)(m_2 - m_1), \qquad (2)$$

where m_2 is the mean age of those aged x to β, and m_1 that of those aged α to x. Differentiation of the implicit function (1) is straightforward.

The three factors of the derivative on the right-hand side of (2) are all positive, whatever the population with which we are concerned, and hence the expression as a whole is bound to be negative. This confirms that the higher the rate of increase r the lower the age of promotion x. They can be approximately evaluated from general considerations:

1. The $1/(1+k)$ depends only on the gateway on which we choose to concentrate our attention. If it is the point where the individual will have as many employees above as below him, then $k = 1$ and the factor is $1/(1+k) = \frac{1}{2}$.
2. The $u/e^{-rx}\,l(x)$ is the sum of the years yet to go until retirement, each discounted at a rate of interest equal in effect to r plus the annual mortality rate. Alternatively, the factor may be thought of as the value of \$1.00 per year to the person if he lives, discounted back to age x at a rate of interest equal to the increase of the population. Hence, it is a number somewhat less than the number of years until retirement from the promotion age considered. If x is about 40, and retirement is at sixty-five, then this factor will be not twenty-five, but about twenty for typical life tables and rates of increase.
3. The $m_2 - m_1$ is the difference between the mean age in the group above age x and the mean age in the group below age x. Each of the

Table 3 Values of derivative 0.01 dx/dr, showing how these are calculated from three factors, for $r = 0.00$ and 0.04, with $\alpha = 20$ and $\beta = 65$, life table for United States males, 1968

Age	$\dfrac{v}{v+u} = \dfrac{1}{1+k}$ (1)	$\dfrac{u}{e^{-rx} l(x)}$ (2)	$m_2 - m_1$ (3)	YEARS OF ADVANCE PER 1 PERCENT INCREASE OF POPULATION $0.01\ dx/dr = \dfrac{-(1) \times (2) \times (3)}{100}$ (4)
		$r = 0.00$		
35	0.361920	26.9043	21.7240	−2.11531
40	0.479708	22.3044	21.9062	−2.34388
45	0.595189	17.7965	22.1303	−2.34410
50	0.707175	13.3960	22.4104	−2.12302
55	0.813780	9.07209	22.7632	−1.68054
		$r = 0.04$		
35	0.564643	16.1174	19.6748	−1.79052
40	0.686030	14.4342	21.2533	−2.10456
45	0.783466	12.4689	22.8888	−2.23599
50	0.860826	10.1860	24.5780	−2.15510
55	0.921119	7.50914	26.3104	−1.81984

mean ages will be near the center of its age interval for a stationary population. If the population is increasing rapidly, both means will be lower than their centers. In either case the difference $m_2 - m_1$ is bound to be about half the length of working life or $(\beta - \alpha)/2$.

These considerations tell us that for $k = 1$, and a typical life table and moderate rate of increase, the first factor will be about 0.5, the second will be about 20, the third will be about 22, so we have

$$\frac{dx}{dr} = -(0.5)(20)(22) = -220.$$

It seems natural to divide this by 100, so that we obtain the number of years by which promotion is earlier for each 1 percent difference in r. That 0.01 dx/dr is −2.20 says that for each increase in growth by 1 percent the age of promotion to the middle level is younger by 2.20 years.

As the more exact calculation of Table 3 shows, the derivative reaches to −2.34 years. It is lower at the beginning of the career and at the

Table 4 Values of derivatives 0.01 dx/dr for $k = 1$, $k = 0.6$, and $k = 0.2$, for $r = 0.00$ to $r = 0.04$, male life tables of three countries, showing advance in age of promotion for each increase of 0.01 in r

$r = 0.00$	$r = 0.01$	$r = 0.02$	$r = 0.03$	$r = 0.04$
	United States Males, 1968			
$k = 1$				
−2.361	−2.255	−2.070	−1.839	−1.594
$k = 0.6$				
−2.308	−2.354	−2.300	−2.159	−1.960
$k = 0.2$				
−1.564	−1.811	−2.017	−2.158	−2.214
	Mexican Males, 1966			
$k = 1$				
−2.376	−2.241	−2.034	−1.790	−1.542
$k = 0.6$				
−2.367	−2.388	−2.305	−2.138	−1.921
$k = 0.2$				
−1.622	−1.877	−2.084	−2.215	−2.254
	Swedish Males, 1783–87			
$k = 1$				
−2.210	−2.031	−1.808	−1.572	−1.344
$k = 0.6$				
−2.312	−2.254	−2.115	−1.924	−1.707
$k = 0.2$				
−1.814	−2.008	−2.136	−2.181	−2.142

end of the career, as it has to be, since we are assuming that everyone starts at the same point and ends at the same point. The effect tends to fall off somewhat as we move to very rapid rates of increase. Table 4 shows the (rather small) variations among the tables in the derivations.

EXPANSION OF INDIVIDUAL ENTERPRISES

So far the rates used have been appropriate to the population of a large country taken as a whole, in which the possible range of natural increase r is between 3 and 4 percent and zero, or to a natural decrease of 1 to 2 percent. But an individual enterprise is subject to a far greater range than this. The air transport and the electric power industries expanded in

Table 5 Rapid decrease or increase. Age of passing successive gateways $k = 1$ up to $k = 0.2$, for $r = -0.1$ to 0.1, United States male life tables, 1968

	$r = -0.10$	$r = -0.05$	$r = 0.00$	$r = 0.05$	$r = 0.10$
$k = 1$	56.96	51.48	40.86	31.23	26.61
$k = 0.8$	58.11	53.30	43.26	33.01	27.73
$k = 0.6$	59.53	55.39	46.31	35.50	29.33
$k = 0.4$	61.33	57.83	50.32	39.26	31.86
$k = 0.2$	63.20	61.16	55.93	45.87	36.77

output at 10 percent per year for most of a generation, and while it is not output but employment that counts for our argument here, even that went up rapidly. On the other hand the numbers of barbers and cinema employees have fallen rapidly as demand for their product has declined.

From the present viewpoint the steady rise of an industry is to be treated in exactly the same way as the growth of a population, with the difference that now the range of interest is much wider, say from $r = -0.10$ to about $r = 0.10$. Table 5 shows how large are the effects on age at promotion of this wide range of rate of increase. With United States 1968 mortality one would reach the halfway point ($k = 1$) at age 26.61 years on the average in a firm increasing at 10 percent per year, and at 59.96 years in one decreasing at 10 percent per year.

A young person is well advised to choose an expanding industry. That advice does not assume that population growth is fully determining, but refers only to the mean age of promotion to a given relative position, around which deviations will be determined by merit, influence, or luck.

THE CHAIN-LETTER ANALOGY TO POPULATION

The purest form of a scheme to take advantage of group expansion, pure because it exists without any pretence of producing anything, is the chain letter. Being honestly based on sheer increase of numbers, the chain letter is well suited to illuminate the populationist argument implicit in the above formulas and tables.

A typical chain letter contains the names and addresses of four people. The recipient sends one dollar to the top name of the list, crosses it out, adds his own name at the bottom on each of the four copies that he makes and sends to four new people. For this small effort, including the investment of one dollar, he is promised a return of $256. The time over which he will obtain this return is only that required for four consecutive letters to be written, mailed, and acted on. (In other versions one sends the letter to five people and obtains $3,125, or to ten people and obtains $10 billion; in general to n people to obtain n^n dollars.)

The four letters that our particular recipient sends out contain his name on the bottom line; each of the 4 people to whom he sends it copies it four times with his name on the second-to-last line, so that sixteen letters go out with him in this position, and so on. If those on the top line are thought of as ancestors, those on the second line as their children, on the third line as their grandchildren, on the fourth line as their great-grandchildren, then the chain letter creates an ordering similar to a genealogy. Each letter contains a part of a table of descent, say for the male sex of a population in which everyone marries and exactly four sons are born to each couple, so that every man has 256 great-grandsons. This corresponds to a net reproduction rate or population replacement per generation of 4, which, though high, is conceivable in a low-death-rate population that made reproduction its primary aim. Note that this is the opposite to the inheritance of property from one's ancestors; here one receives gifts from one's great-grandchildren. When property is passed down from ancestor to children, a declining population is an advantage to the inheritors; when it is passed up the line, an increasing population is an advantage.

Where the chain letter breaks down is that the time for delivery of a letter is less than a week: for a human population the generation time is twenty-five years. The chain letter requires as many addresses per week as the fastest-growing population can produce in twenty-five years. The chain letter is a means by which everyone can become rich as long as new addressees can be found. The addresses must increase in the ratio of four to one per week, while the best the population can do is four to one per twenty-five years. In a very few weeks the chain letter would have caught up with the largest, most cooperative, and fastest growing population.

A rapidly expanding population offers rapid promotion as new recruits come into organizations from the bottom. The economic benefits of both the chain letter and of population growth are limited by extraneous ceilings: for the chain letter the population in existence; for long-term population growth by what the physical environment can support.

Conclusion

If rank of a person is measured by the ratio of the number of persons above him to the number below, and if individuals advance in rank with age and there are no demotions, then one's position is higher the more people there are below one and the fewer there are above. An increase in mortality at ages older than one's own will raise one's rank, as will emigration at those ages. Immigration at lower levels will be similarly beneficial.

Most of the foregoing has dealt with a special case: the way in which rank in this sense is related to population increase. We found that between the rate of increase of the United States at its postwar peak, about 2 percent per year, and the stationary condition that now seems to be approaching, the long-term average delay in age at promotion to middle levels of hierarchies is about 4½ years.

Three possibilities exist for mitigating the depressing effect on personal mobility of a slowdown in population growth.

1. Increase the markers of social status. Differentiation of Foreman Grade 1, of Foreman Grade 2, etc., provides opportunities for promotion, and promotion can be made as frequent as desired for the individual by recognizing sufficient categories. For this to happen people would have to become more sensitive to subtle nuances of status. The rate at which new statuses would have to be interpolated by the authorities, and receive recognition by those concerned, is given by calculations similar to those of the present paper. But at a time when even existing markers of status are scorned, people are not likely to be stimulated by newly contrived finer divisions.
2. Make social status and mobility less important, the opposite of (1). People may be opting out of the mobility race, partly in response to the greater difficulty of ascent as population growth slows.
3. Relate mobility to machines, not to other people. If all manual work were eliminated by machinery, then everyone could start above the line dividing blue-collar from white-collar. Since productivity and hence real income can still be made to increase, people may become more concerned with pay and the goods they can buy than with rank and title. Increasing command over goods may compensate for diminishing command over people.

Part Two
Data and its Limitations

CHAPTER 6
The Use of Censuses for Allocation

INTRODUCTION

Statisticians and demographers use the census to obtain *information.* Approximate numbers, particularly if bounds can be set on their error, serve to guide policy and check theory. Edwards Deming, Morris Hansen, Philip Hauser, Conrad Taeuber, and others associated with the census have shown in their work and writings that exactitude is not possible, but neither is it necessary. We can calmly discuss how much accuracy will meet our information needs.

For *allocation* no uncertainty is permissible; seats in the House of Representatives and dollars of revenue sharing have to be distributed to the last unit. The Treasury Department, responsible for redistributing billions of dollars each year, cannot issue a revenue-sharing check for the expected quantity plus or minus two standard deviations. An indeterminacy of even one person in the population of the United States is indefensible. One missing person in apportionment could deprive a state of a representative and of a certain sum in federal grants. Each additional item of redistributive legislation puts another burden on the census. Exactitude is still impossible, but now it is essential. This situation is embarrassing for our profession vis-á-vis the public and the legislature.

Far from being able to count the population of the United States to the last person, we cannot count it to the last million persons. Omissions in each of the censuses of 1950, 1960, and 1970 are estimated at about 5 million persons despite the effort and expertise applied.

We know all this from estimates made by the Bureau of the Census itself. That agency has explored census error in a series of studies during the past forty years, and its professional competence and integrity have made the fallibility of the statistical collection process a matter of public knowledge. The public understands the fallibility but not the intrinsic character of the error and makes difficulties for the agency that brought the disagreeable fact of census incompleteness to public attention.

For its part, Congress, in its legislative use of the several series, implicitly supposes the statistics to be perfect—an extraordinary compliment to the agency that produced them—but then finds the agency wanting because its statistics turn out not to be suited to this new use.

In response to public concern an unprecedented effort was made in 1980 to get an accurate count. After allowing for inflation, the amount spent on fieldwork was more than double that spent in 1970. Followup enumerators were paid at more generous hourly rates to track down nonrespondents; local offices were kept open months longer than in past censuses. In addition to this paid effort, a great deal of publicity was provided free to the census by public-spirited corporations and media. The equivalent of $50 million in publicity succeeded in catching the attention of varied elements of the population who in the past had not been aware of the census.

The first sign that things were going well was the larger than expected numbers who simply filled in and returned the mail questionnaire. The spontaneous return of 80 percent by mail would have been good; in fact, fully 86 percent of the population was covered by the mail-in/mail-out phase. This freed resources for the more intense follow-up of the 14 percent who did not respond.

One can imagine the census of 1980 being taken at different expense levels. With effective administration, the completeness would be a monotonically increasing function of cost, concave downward. An expenditure of $200 million would probably permit locating and counting 90 percent of the population; $400 million might count 95 percent; $800 million might perhaps count 98 percent. The relation of coverage to expenditure could be established more precisely, but these numbers, and the curve drawn through them in the figure, will serve for the illustration. As one moves toward persons harder to find, the cost per person goes up steeply; measurement of the slope on the figure suggests that another $100 million beyond $800 million would bring completeness up to only 98.5 percent. So at the margin the cost of covering the hard-to-find persons might be as much as $100 each.

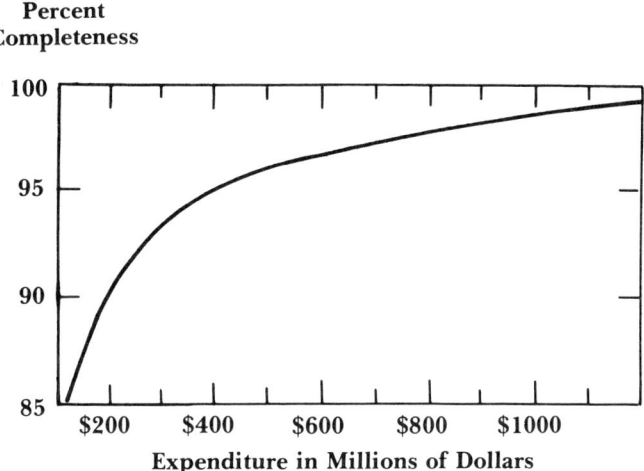

Figure 1: Fraction of Population Counted at Various Levels of Expenditure on the Census: Suggested Relation

The struggle for completeness operates within certain constraints other than financial. If the population could be made to sit at home for a day while the census takers did their work, a higher level of completeness could be attained; the census might even come within 1 million of the true figure. But most Americans would judge this regimentation an unacceptable means of reaching those last persons. The Bureau of the Census has to devise means of counting that do not depend on making this restless nation stop everything for even a moment. (Less democratic nations often take worse censuses than ours but their censuses are bad for different reasons.)

Asking why the census cannot count 100 percent of the population in a free society is like asking why books contain typographical errors, why manufactured products often have defects, or why the police cannot catch all criminals.

RANDOM VARIATION AND BIAS

The exact number needed for apportionment and for allocation of revenue sharing and other funds can be provided in only one way in the face of random variation—by the establishment of a *convention* or agreement before the outcome is known. Establishing the convention includes public announcement of census procedures before the enumeration, response of the Bureau of the Census to objections and suggestions on procedures as fully as possible within cost and other constraints, and education of everyone concerned on the view that the outcome of a particular census is a random variable.

If several censuses were taken independently at the same time and by using the same procedures, the censuses would provide different counts. No such multiplicity of independent censuses is possible, both because of cost and because each census would interfere with the others, but imagining many censuses at one time conduces to a clearer understanding of the unique census that will actually be taken. Once the count is announced in respect of April 1, 1980, the only grounds for contestation would be that the census failed to follow the agreed-on procedure. After the precensus negotiation and with adequate precautions to ensure that the game was fair, all parties would agree in advance to accept the outcome. This agreement is the only way to bring the random component that the census or any other survey contains within the scope of accounting systems that must be determinate to the last dollar. There is no escaping the lottery element, and the problem is to make it a fair lottery.

Purely random and unbiased error, for instance that due to sampling, can be said to be under control. Its expected amount can be estimated as a by-product from the sample information itself; one can reduce it to any desired extent if one is willing to pay for a large enough sample. The larger the population, the smaller the fraction that will serve for a satisfactory probability sample. The smaller size of the sample, as compared with a complete count, permits more care in enumeration of each individual included; hence the apparent paradox that a sample can give a more exact result than a complete count: its sampling error may well be more than offset by greater precision in enumeration.

But it is a misuse of this argument to suggest taking censuses by sampling. There are at least three reasons why we still need counts as full as possible every five or ten years. For one thing, samples are good for characteristics (such as estimating fraction unemployed), but they cannot estimate the total population well; in a sample one cannot urge people who think they have been missed in the enumeration to come forward. Second, censuses are needed in order to draw efficient samples; in one way of looking at samples, they are an updating of a preceding census. Third, data for individual city blocks and other local areas cannot possibly be obtained by a sample.

Unfortunately, it is biases common to samples and censuses, extraordinarily persistent in the face of procedural improvements, that make the allocation problem so intractable. If censuses were taken carelessly, or with restricted funds, then one could sample some areas, ascertain errors, and make corrections in one way or another. But the census of 1980 was in fact taken with great care and with almost unlimited funds.

When a game is biased, in the sense that its expected value is not what a player is told it is, that player has a genuine grievance. The solution to the allocation problem in the face of bias is also a convention agreed on in advance, but devising the convention has to take account of the direction of bias. Before tackling this question, we consider risks associated with legislative transfers.

The Target

Legislative allocations are targeted on problems. These problems may be substandard housing, pollution of waterways, schoolchildren with poor parents, or unemployed youth (Morgan 1978). The statistical variables (including the census) that are used for the allocation are intended as a measure of the problem, but they are at best a proxy for the variable that the legislators have in mind, as Bixby (1977) pointed out. Some entity in the population is in need of assistance; a certain statistical series seems to be correlated with the entity that is in need; the allocation is made according to that statistical series. How much is it worth paying for precision in that series, remembering that the allocation formula itself is only a rough approximation to the purpose of the legislation?

There are random elements in most contracts: how many hours of illumination I get when I buy a light bulb—and hence the cost per hour—has large random variation. We are more risk-averse on large deals; we would like to avoid even a small chance that an automobile will have an expensive breakdown on the first day of ownership, and the supplier cuts off this tail of the probability distribution of cost per mile by a guarantee. Those who are very risk-averse can buy a service contract and pay to shift the risk largely or entirely to the supplier, but the risk remains despite all attempts to pass it back and forth; someone has to carry it. The advantage of having an insurer or supplier carry many risks is that some offsetting will occur. What is an unacceptable gamble for the individual case is a calculable and minor risk for the aggregate of cases.

A state or municipality that is responsible in the management of its affairs is naturally risk-averse; gambling is repugnant to it. Yet it has no way of insuring important components of its income. The state or municipality wants the intentions of the legislature to be implemented, and it wants to know just how much it gets. Protracted disputes, in or out of the courts, are no help in the administration of its affairs. For the state or municipality there are three desiderata: maximum expected value of the payment it receives, minimum variance ex ante, and zero indeterminacy ex post.

The extensive publicity, together with the knowledge that one's town and state benefit financially through each person's being enumerated, engaged civic loyalty in a way that increased the response. But civic loyalty may have been excessive; the awareness by enumerator and enumerated that large payments hang on the result could make for overenumeration. The Census Bureau has checks that limit the sheer addition of imaginary people, what is called "curbstoning"; there is a strict quality control of the individual enumerator's work. There are doubtful cases, however: Jones, who lives in Montana, is found on April 1 in Texas; and what about Cousin Heidi from Dusseldorf, who is staying with relatives in New York for a few weeks? Neither belongs in the census where found, yet a zealous enumerator might include both. The person who died just before the census date, or one who was born just after, if the respondent was not sure of the time, might be included. In the United States there are about 40,000 deaths a week, and about 75,000 births, so any imprecision on the date makes an appreciable fuzziness in the count. It is impossible to push hard for completeness without bringing in at least some people who ought not to be counted. The Bureau of the Census is undertaking matching studies to estimate the number of duplications and persons who for whatever reason should not have been enumerated, but it will be months before results are obtained in this tedious work.

A second group of difficulties concerns the illegal or undocumented immigrants. Estimates of these have run as high as 12 million, though more believable figures make them closer to 4 million. The extracensus calculation of 227 million presumably does not include these people. If a person is not in the birth, immigration, or Medicare records, there is no way of including him in the calculation. The census defined undocumented immigrants as part of the population and made special efforts in the minority areas where they were likely to be found. Its attempts to enumerate them undoubtedly succeeded in a fraction of cases; certainly not all were included, and not all were missed. The undercount is thus improperly reduced by whatever number of illegals were caught in the census. No one knows much about this, and no one will ever know, since the census can hardly ask people whether they are in the country legally.

Though undocumented aliens are the largest, and legally the most interesting, of the groups that give rise to dispute on the part of those who will benefit from a particular definition of population, there are other points on which census practice could be challenged once the door is opened. A college student is to be counted where he lives while attending college, not at his parents' home, even though he may be with his parents when the enumerator calls. On the other hand, a child who is in a residential secondary school is counted in the household of his parents, irrespective of where he happens to be at the time of the census. Could a town like Exeter, New Hampshire, with a large secondary boarding school sue to have the students considered as residents?

Since there is no general definition of resident, the census has to decide where to draw its many boundary lines. The lines should be sharp and objective on the one hand, and suited to the concept of usual residence on the other. These two considerations may conflict. In many instances the sharp definition is not appropriate to the use of the results. A person who has more than one home, and divides his time between them, is to be listed where he spends the largest part of the calendar year, according to the census instructions. It would be sharper to put him where he is actually found at the time of enumeration, but this would be less in accord with the objective of finding the usual population. To the arbitrariness incorporated in the census definitions must be added the errors in implementation by the enumerator. A census is an intricate affair, hedged about by arbitrary definitions, enumerated by people who through human fallibility add their own errors to those provided them by the respondents.

CHOOSING A CONVENTION IN THE FACE OF NONRANDOM ERROR

Census coverage and consequent random error do not offer insuperable difficulties to persons who have experience of risk in such everyday matters as buying light bulbs. Bias is more awkward. If we know in advance that certain groups will be undercounted, and that these contain an undue proportion of the very persons many of the programs were designed to help, then accepting the count as made becomes questionable.

The Bureau of the Census has estimated that of the 5.3 million persons omitted in 1970 some 3.4 million were white and 1.9 million nonwhite. The percentage of whites omitted was 1.9, of nonwhites 6.9. (More males were omitted than females, but that is less important.) That nearly four times as large a fraction of nonwhites as of whites was omitted is recognized by the Bureau of the Census as the major issue of underenumeration, and the bureau is concentrating much of its additional effort in 1980 on the areas where minority persons live.

We need a convention in advance of the census, one that also protects the interests of all concerned. Three conventions among which a choice may be made are:

1. The *census count* as it emerges from the sequence of efforts made in 1980. Such a count was the convention of the past.

2. The *census count as multiplied up by race* to the total for the country as a whole. In particular, the count of blacks in each jurisdiction would be multiplied by the ratio of the number of blacks in the United States (as inferred by demographic methods) to the number counted in the 1980 census. (In practice adjusting for *relative* underenumeration is sufficient.) This synthetic method, as it is called, would not give a number for each locality necessarily more exact than the unadjusted census figure, but it would eliminate the differential undercoverage by race on the average of all areas of the country.
3. The *census count as further modified* by age and sex, individual state corrections, information on differential underenumeration by income, and other indirect and even qualitative evidence. More work would be done on large jurisdictions, and small ones might be left alone. This convention would come closer to the true population of each area than (1) or (2) but would have to be entrusted to a single individual or agency if the outcome were to be unique. If this convention were adopted, no subsequent criticism of the resulting figures would be logically acceptable; the agency would be trusted completely.

The choice among the three conventions cannot be made on purely professional grounds. Between the second and third conventions, for example, the second has the advantage of objectivity, so that once the national totals are agreed on nothing but arithmetic is required to work out the corrected populations for the 39,000 beneficiary jurisdictions. The second convention would, on the average, remove a patent bias, but in particular instances, could take one further from the truth—for example, in a municipality of middle-class blacks where the coverage was essentially complete. The convention's very crudity is an advantage: no one will mistake it for anything other than a means to remove gross bias in allocation of funds.

The third or subjective approach could avoid some of the errors of the second method but would have to do so on an ad hoc basis—taking data where they could be found and applying them with a good deal of judgment. This third approach is subjective, not in the sense that it would guess at the answer, but in deciding which data to use as a guide. The proof that the third convention would be subjective is that two individuals, both highly competent, would choose to be guided by different data and would arrive at different numbers if they worked independently. Thus, (3) is more accurate and (2) more objective, and we have no criteria for a trade-off between accuracy and objectivity.

One who objects to all variants of both (2) and (3) is forced back to (1). The Constitution instructs that the census is to "enumerate" the people, which suggests counting bodies as opposed to making an estimate even at the margins of the count. Of course, the Census Bureau does not actually see each individual in the country personally, but rather accepts various kinds of evidence that he or she exists. The Bureau's preferred evidence is the person's being described on a return-mail questionnaire containing plausible answers. Equally convincing, although more expensive, is being mentioned to an enumerator by self, spouse, or landlady in a follow-up of those for whom no questionnaire is returned. A neighbor saying that he or she is sure that a couple lives in a certain dwelling, even though repeated calls fail to find these persons at home, is another kind of evidence that the Census Bureau accepts. Because such persons could easily have another home at which they are enumerated, there are some risks of overcounting in incorporating them. Even so, these persons are more real (or at least more tangible) than numbers added to the population of a town on the basis of national ratios. As a result of the check of vacant dwellings, the 1970 census added "individuals" whom no one had ever seen. On a sample the census found that about 10 percent of dwellings listed as vacant did have residents, and it imputed a similar degree of habitation to all vacant dwellings. All reportedly vacant dwellings were visited in 1980, however, and no intangible persons were added.

The census count, convention (1), is like the gold standard—a superstition perhaps, but with the positive feature that as long as the superstition holds it provides an absolute measure of value. Under a gold standard, our present inflation and excess of imports could not occur. (Other bad things could occur, of course.) Abandonment of the gold standard or the census count conventions opens up many possibilities. We can adjust for blacks—should we do so in total, or by age and sex? If by age, what age groups should be recognized? We could describe a hundred reasonable ways of making the adjustment, and they would lead to a hundred different answers. Percentage variation might be small, but large enough to confuse whoever has to make out the check in the Treasury Department.

Any of these adjustments would probably be more equitable than the raw census count in the sense that on the average of all jurisdictions they would offset the relative underenumeration of blacks. But such adjustment would be at the expense of the Hispanic population, which is probably equally underenumerated, but on which there are less data. Hispanics have protested vigorously against making an adjustment to the census as long as data for raising their numbers are unavailable.

Thus, anyone who thinks that an adjustment to the census will please all users is mistaken. That person will discover his or her error after an official adjustment is made and promulgated. Public protests may well be louder than the protest now heard about underenumeration.

The Apportionment Problem

It is in connection with apportionment that Congress, the public, and professional statisticians have the longest experience of census incompleteness. Omission of one person from the census could deprive a state of a representative. This possibility is an inescapable property of any method of apportionment that is a function of population. If p is the population of a state and $f(p)$ the number of its representatives, then at some point $f(p)$ must be different from $f(p-1)$. If not, if $f(p) = f(p-1)$ for all p, then $f(p)$ is not a function of p at all but a constant. The only way of preventing an omission of one person from ever affecting representation is to make representation independent of population.

The probability that a state will lose a member by omission of a single person from the census is roughly the reciprocal of the average number of persons per representative, or very nearly 1/500,000. With fifty states this event would be truly rare—to be expected once in each 10,000 censuses. But omission of 100,000 persons in any state would have one chance in five of depriving that state of a representative.

With the House of Representatives fixed at 435 members, only relative underenumeration is damaging. But relative underenumeration of the order of 1 or 2 percent does occur. The 5 million persons not counted are not distributed proportionately among states. A state with 10 million persons (there are six such states) would need a differential underenumeration of only 1 percent (be 3 percent short, for example, compared with a national average of 2 percent) to have one chance in five of being deprived of a representative. Thus, we may safely say that in apportionment after most censuses at least one state is given at least one representative too few. If we use the census estimates for the states in 1970, with a method that allows for the relation of omission to income as well as age, race, and sex, Alabama should have had 8 representatives rather than the 7 it was given, while California was not entitled to 43 but to only 42 (Siegel 1975, p. 13).

Most of the discussion of apportionment has concentrated on the quite different issue of the rounding formula. The census of 1880 applied with the rounding then in use would have given Alabama 8 representatives in a House of 299 members, but if the House total had been raised to 300 members, Alabama's representation would have dropped to 7. This and other paradoxes of apportionment that have arisen during 200 years are described by Balinski and Young (1982). What is needed is a corresponding study of the stability of representation in the face of inevitable incompleteness of census enumeration.

A Minimum Adjustment

No satisfactory way of adjusting the census is available; yet differential completeness of racial groups makes the unadjusted figures unacceptable. We should not pretend that we can do what is in fact impossible—make up by office calculation for shortcomings of fieldwork. One proposal is an unpretentious stylized adjustment of the populations of local jurisdictions according to the number of blacks they contain, applying the relative incompleteness ratio for the United States. If this proposal had been followed in 1970, the number of blacks would have been multiplied by about 1.05 to bring blacks up to the incompleteness of whites. (No one knows how complete the Hispanic population count may be; it may in fact be less complete than the black; perhaps it should equally have a bonus of 5 percent.) Local areas could thus be increased by anything from 0 to 5 percent, but those areas with up to 20 percent blacks would be increased by 1 percent or less.

To adjust by age and sex as well as race is more elaborate and makes little difference. As Siegel (1975, p. 7) said:

> The factors of age and sex have very little impact on the variation in the overall level of underenumeration of States when the synthetic method is used, inasmuch as the sex and age composition of State populations, unlike their race composition, is rather similar. The population corrected only for race composition commonly differs from the population corrected jointly for race, age, and sex composition by 0.1 percent or less.

Worse than making no difference, the use of age and sex has the real drawback of an unjustified pretense to accuracy. Through arithmetical complexity, use of age and sex hides the essential fact that we do not know what is the true population of the 39,000 jurisdictions that receive federal contributions. After all, the census field enumeration is the ultimate source on small-area populations, and working the enumeration over in the office can do little to improve it.

There is no lack of suggestions for improving the census after the count is known. The difficulty is the multiplicity of defensible suggestions. Not only could adjustments be made for each age, sex, and income group, but one could differentiate among states and consider separately the size categories of municipalities within states. One might make the adjustments for large cities and not for small ones. Different adjustments might be made for different purposes—for instance, for separate items of legislation. An apparently valid case could be devised on behalf of any of these suggestions, and an equally valid case against it. Skillful and ingenious arguments will be elicited by the large sums at stake.

CHAPTER 7

How Do We Know the Facts of Demography?

Demographers know that a population that is increasing slowly has a higher proportion of old people than one that is increasing rapidly; and that differences in birth rates have a larger influence on the age distribution than do differences in death rates. They also often claim that a poor country whose population is growing rapidly will increase its income per head faster if it lowers its birth rate.

How do demographers know these things? Many readers will be surprised to learn that in a science thought of as empirical, often criticized for its lack of theory, the most important relations cannot be established by direct observation, which tends to provide enigmatic and inconsistent reports. Confrontation of data with theory is essential for correct interpretation of such relationships, even though on a particular issue it more often generates an agenda for further investigation than yields useful knowledge. This chapter will examine how demographers distill knowledge from observation and from theory. It also will try to show how a reigning theory can be successfully challenged.

Let no one think these questions are remote or purely abstract. The resolution of the major policy issues of our time depends on the answers. How much of their development effort should poor countries put into birth control if they deem their rate of population growth excessive?

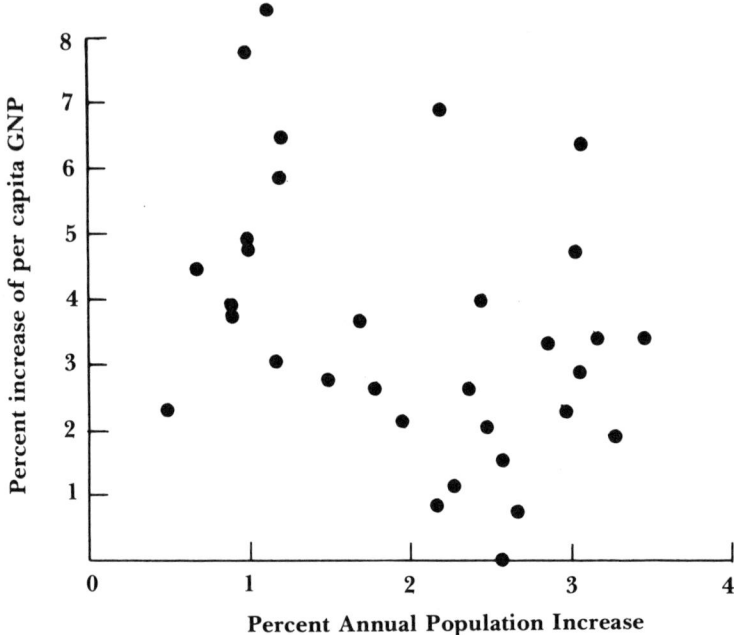

Figure 1: Average annual increase of per capita GNP and of population for countries with over 20 million population, 1960–72

Some would put nothing, in the expectation that rapid increase of income will by itself bring population under control. Once people have automobiles, once their countryside is paved over with roads, once enough air-conditioned houses are built, they will lower their fertility. But is this not an overly circuitous way of getting people to use pills and IUDs as compared with direct intervention aimed at lowering fertility?

Any answer to such questions must take into account the degree to which a low rate of population increase promotes development. That is no simple matter to ascertain. Figure 1 shows the relation between rates of population growth and increase of income per capita. Even the most imaginative viewer would hardly see the strong negative relation that the dominant theory requires. In the pages ahead, the irregularity of empirical data as they appear in charts and tables will be repeatedly contrasted with the clear-cut mathematical relations of theory. Every such contrast presents a puzzle for demographic research.

The theoretical approach can be described as "holding unmentioned variables constant"; the empirical, for example in the form of a regression between measured variables, as "allowing unmentioned variables to vary as they vary in actuality." The difference is introduced with an example in which we think we know the true nature of the relationship between two variables.

GROWING POPULATIONS HAVE SMALLER PROPORTIONS OF OLD PEOPLE

The population of Mexico grows at 3.5 percent per year; its proportion at ages sixty-five and over is about 3 percent. The United States has been growing at less than 1 percent per year; its proportion sixty-five and over is about 10 percent. The relation can be expressed as a linear equation. For 1966 the four numbers are:

	MEXICO	UNITED STATES
Rate of natural increase (percent)	3.44	0.89
Percent aged 65 and over	3.31	9.42

Call the annual percent rate of increase r, and the percent over age sixty-five P_{65+}. Then the straight line from the 1966 information on the United States and Mexico is

$$P_{65+} = 11.5 - 2.3r,$$

which tells us that for each 1 percent by which the rate of increase is higher, there is a decrease of 2.3 percent in the proportion aged sixty-five and over. With zero increase the percent over sixty-five would be 11.5; with 3 percent increase it would be $11.5 - 6.9 = 4.6$ percent.

We should be able to obtain a more reliable result with a larger group of countries, so let us try those of Latin America shown in Table 1. The result is $P_{65+} = 8.45 - 1.6r$. Apparently the more homogeneous group gives a less steep slope than the United States and Mexico. Now each 1 percent increase in r is associated with a drop of 1.6 in P_{65+}—only two-thirds as much. The scatter diagram (Figure 2) shows that we could have chosen two countries that would provide almost any given slope. Moreover, much of what correlation exists is due to three countries of the southern cap—Argentina, Uruguay, and Chile—that are culturally distinct from those farther north, along with Puerto Rico and Martinique. To exaggerate a little, it looks as though countries fall into two groups, those with low r and high P_{65+}, and those with high r and low P_{65+}. In short, much of the pertinent information was contained in the comparison of the United States and Mexico with which we started.

What about taking one country and following changes through time in the two variables? Sweden provides information over nearly 200 years,

Table 1 Proportion Aged 65 and Over and Rate of Natural Increase, 18 Latin American Countries

COUNTRY	PERCENT AGED 65 AND OVER	PERCENT RATE OF NATURAL INCREASE
Argentina 1964	6.05	1.40
Brazil 1950	2.45	2.80
Chile 1967	4.47	1.89
Colombia 1964	3.00	2.85
Costa Rica 1966	3.18	3.44
Dominican Republic 1966	3.57	2.85
Ecuador 1965	3.16	3.25
El Salvador 1961	3.18	3.81
Guatemala 1964	2.77	2.89
Honduras 1966	1.76	3.55
Martinique 1963	4.96	2.50
Mexico 1966	3.31	3.44
Nicaragua 1965	2.90	3.57
Panama 1966	3.57	3.29
Peru 1963	3.42	2.83
Puerto Rico 1965	5.77	2.36
Uruguay 1963	7.81	1.03
Venezuela 1965	2.99	3.65

and also provides a very different regression from any obtained cross-sectionally.

The comparisons and regressions summarizing them are highly inconsistent in reporting how much difference in the proportion over sixty-five is to be associated with differences in the rate of increase. A large research project could be undertaken to see why they fail to agree; it might reveal that the changing mortality over 200 years in Sweden is confounded by the changing birth rate; that the more homogeneous the group, the lower the correlation and the lower the slope of regression. It happens that in this instance no one will undertake such research because a simple theory is available that will provide a better insight into the nature of the relationship between growth rate and age distribution. Let us use this theory to stand back and take a fresh run at the question.

OLDER POPULATION AS A FUNCTION OF RATE OF INCREASE WHEN ALL ELSE IS CONSTANT

For this more abstract consideration we might start with an extreme stylization. Let us imagine a country in which 100,000 births take place

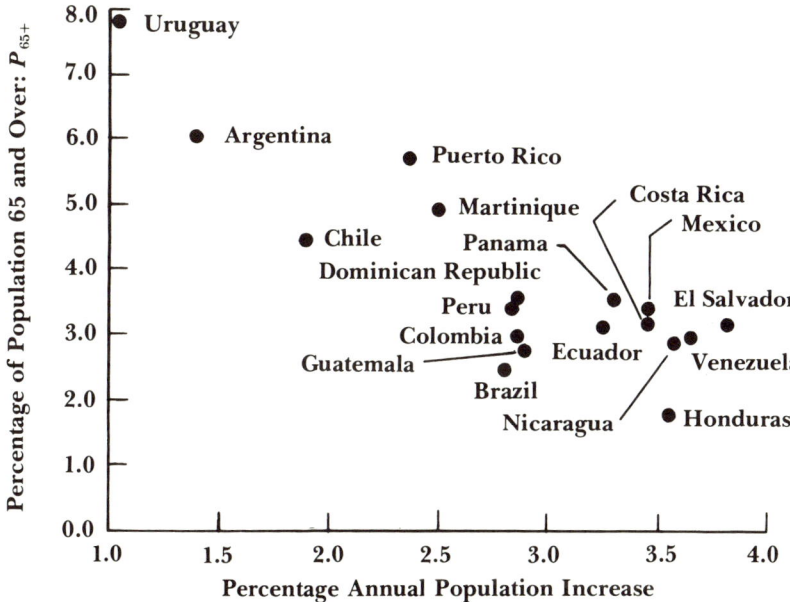

Figure 2: Relation of Proportion of the Population Over Age 65 to the Rate of Population Increase: 18 Latin American countries

each year, everyone lives to age 100, and there is no migration. Then the population at any moment is exactly 10 million, and the fraction over age sixty-five is exactly 35 percent at all times. This contains the essence of the stable population model—a model describing the structure and dynamics of a "closed" population with constant schedules of fertility and mortality. But the assumptions underlying the example just given need generalizing in two directions.

The first is toward a more flexible mortality pattern. To suppose that everyone lives to age 100 is to specify a very special kind of survivorship schedule (or life table), and we can easily improve on it by using the mortality of the country in question. With United States 1972 mortality, taking both sexes together, the life table fraction over sixty-five comes down to 15.5 percent.

Let us now also allow for increasing births. Suppose that the fraction of births surviving to age x is given by a fixed survival function $s(x)$, and the annual percent rate of increase of births is r, so that compared with x years ago the number of births is now $(1 + r/100)^x$ greater. Then for each present birth there were $1/(1 + r/100)^x$ births x years ago, and of these past births a fraction $s(x)$ have survived, the surviving individuals being now aged x. Thus the number of present individuals of age x must be $Bs(x)/(1 + r/100)^x$, where B is the number of current births. This applies for all ages, and suffices to specify the age distribution. Since the expression depends on r, it will tell the relation between any given index of the age distribution on the one hand and the rate of increase on the other.

For example, the proportion aged sixty-five and over is simply obtained by summing up the number of persons at ages sixty-five, sixty-six, sixty-seven, and so on, all the way to the maximum age of life (say 100), and dividing this sum by the total population. The latter is obtained by summing up the number of persons at all ages, beginning at age zero. To express this in percentage terms we must also multiply the result by 100:

$$P_{65+} = 100 \; \frac{B \sum_{65}^{100} \{s(x)/(1 + r/100)^x\}}{B \sum_{0}^{100} \{s(x)/(1 + r/100)^x\}}. \tag{1}$$

If the $s(x)$ is fixed, equation (1) establishes P_{65+} as a function of r and of nothing else. The equation is not very instructive in this form, for we cannot easily see whether P_{65+} increases or decreases with r, let alone by how much. One way to study the matter is to set up model tables of stable populations, in which stable age distributions are in effect tabulated for many combinations of r and $s(x)$.

Another way is to "linearize" equation (1). If r is small, one finds that with good approximation:

$$P_{65+} = 100 \left[1 - \frac{r(m_2 - m_1)}{100} \right] \sum_{65}^{100} s(x) \bigg/ \sum_{0}^{100} s(x), \tag{2}$$

where m_2 is the mean age of those sixty-five and over in the stationary population described by $s(x)$ and m_1 is the mean age of everyone, also in the same stationary population.

Equation (2) can be applied with a minimum of data as it involves quantities that vary little among populations. Thus $\sum_{65}^{100} s(x) / \sum_{0}^{100} s(x)$ —that is, the fraction sixty-five and over in the stationary population described by the survival schedule $s(x)$—is 0.127 for Mexican males and 0.123 for United States males; the means m_2 and m_1 are usually not far from seventy-five and thirty-five, so that $m_2 - m_1$ is about forty. Thus, using information that a demographer carries in his head, the expression (2) comes to about

$$P_{65+} = 100 \left(1 - \frac{r}{100} (40) \right) 0.125$$

or

$$P_{65+} = 12.5 - 5r.$$

A similar expression applies for other ages. For example, the percent 55 and over on the same theory is

$$P_{55+} = 23.0 - 6.9r.$$

These theoretical relations largely escape defects of the data. Another advantage of the theoretical approach is that we know exactly its assumptions. In this instance, our model specifies that comparison be among populations closed to migration, with the same life table but different rates of increase; that each of them has had births increasing exponentially during the lifetimes of persons now alive, or alternatively, has had fixed age-specific birth and death rates over a long past period. Consequently, this model does not tell anything about the change through time from one such condition to another; the trajectory from rapid increase to stability for a given population requires a more difficult kind of mathematics. That the theory here, like the comparative statics of economics, permits the comparison of stable conditions only is both a strength and a weakness.

Instead of supposing fixed rates in a closed population, the empirical regression takes into account migration, in whatever proportion it has been occurring in the populations whose data are included. Insofar as mortality has been falling, the influence of that fall is also incorporated. Thus it is a better description of the state of affairs covered by the data; it is a worse description of the intrinsic relationship between the stated variables. If underlying conditions are the same in the future, the regression will predict better; if they change substantially, the theory is more dependable. If an underlying interference is by some known and measurable variable, the empirical regression can "partial" it out, and in this degree approach closer to theory, while still remaining empirical.

In another aspect the regression inevitably depends on a data base, and that base consists of what data chance to be available. One can hardly apply sampling notions to it, since whatever unit is taken, the number of measured populations that are truly independent is small. Moreover, data on many countries are lacking. Even if each entity describable as a nation could be thought of as providing independent evidence, and if all had good data, the collection of nations is not easy to conceptualize as a homogeneous universe.

This simple introductory example shows how uncertain our knowledge would be if analytical tools like the stable model were not available. One can imagine extensive research projects for describing the various extraneous factors, methodological controversies, and schools of opinion, some perhaps taking the view that the relation was really different for different races or different continents. One who has been thorough the theory would no sooner say that the underlying relation between growth and age composition is different for continents than he would say that the laws of thermodynamics differ from country to country.

Are Births or Deaths Decisive?

The same stable model can help decide whether the age distribution of a population depends more on its births or on its deaths.

Venezuela in 1965 had a greater proportion of children plus old people than did Sweden in 1803–07. To compare a contemporary nonindustrialized country with one in the early nineteenth century shows an aspect of the difference in the process of getting development launched then and now. A high dependency ratio (children under age fifteen plus adults over sixty-five as a proportion of the number of working ages fifteen to sixty-five) is a disadvantage for development; Venezuela's dependency ratio in 1965 of 1.021 is two-thirds greater than Sweden's in 1803–07 of 0.589. One would like to know to what extent this is due to Venezuela's lower death rate and to what extent to its higher birth rate. No such decomposition is even conceivable on the observed rates—they show what they show.

The stable model, in which the number of persons aged x is proportional to $s(x)/(1 + r/100)^x$, allows one to synthesize dependency ratios from various combinations of birth and death rates:

Venezuelan births and Venezuelan deaths	1.021
Swedish births and Venezuelan deaths	0.703
Swedish births and Swedish deaths	0.589

The effect of the birth rate when the death rate is constant is $1.021 - 0.703 = 0.318$; the effect of the death rate when the birth rate is constant is $0.703 - 0.589 = 0.114$; of the total difference of 0.432, the part due to births is about 74 percent, that due to deaths about 26 percent.

Alternatively, we could have used as the intermediate term in the decomposition the dependency ratio with Swedish deaths and Venezuelan births, which is 0.856. The death-effect would have been $1.021 - 0.856 = 0.165$ and the birth-effect $0.856 - 0.589 = 0.267$. Now 62 percent of the difference is due to births, still the larger part. We can say that between 62 and 74 percent is due to births, the interval between these numbers being an interaction that cannot be allocated.

Any other feature of age can be similarly analyzed. Sweden's percent under age fifteen was 31.3, Venezuela's 47.7; the combination of Swedish births and Venezuelan deaths would produce 34.2 percent. Hence, of the difference of 16.4 percentage points ($= 47.7 - 31.3$), the amount of 2.9 ($= 34.2 - 31.3$) was due to deaths and 13.5—over four times as much—to births.

This and other theories show that differences in fertility (birth rates) are more responsible than differences in mortality (death rates) for distinctive features of age distributions. The reader can do a considerable amount of such analysis for himself from the data in Table 2, where

Table 2 Features of the Stable Age Distribution and Rates of Increase Obtained by Combinations of Female Birth and Death Rates from Five Countries: Venezuela 1965, United States 1967, Madagascar 1966, England and Wales 1968, and Sweden 1803–1807

	AGE-SPECIFIC BIRTH RATES OF				
AGE-SPECIFIC DEATH RATES OF	VENEZUELA	UNITED STATES	MADAGASCAR	ENGLAND	SWEDEN
Percent Under Age 15					
Venezuela	47.7	23.9	47.8	23.6	34.2
United States	48.5	24.5	48.6	24.2	34.8
Madagascar	45.0	22.0	45.2	21.8	32.1
England	48.5	24.5	48.6	24.2	34.8
Sweden	43.6	21.0	43.8	20.8	31.3
Dependency Ratio (Percent)					
Venezuela	102.1	58.8	102.4	58.7	70.3
United States	105.4	61.1	105.6	60.9	72.5
Madagascar	91.3	51.5	91.8	51.3	62.8
England	105.2	60.3	105.5	60.1	72.1
Sweden	85.6	46.7	86.2	46.6	58.9
Percent Age 65 and Over					
Venezuela	2.8	13.1	2.8	13.3	7.1
United States	2.8	13.5	2.8	13.7	7.3
Madagascar	2.7	12.0	2.7	12.2	6.5
England	2.8	13.1	2.7	13.3	7.1
Sweden	2.5	10.9	2.5	11.0	5.8
Stable Rate of Natural Increase (Percent)					
Venezuela	3.9	0.5	3.9	0.5	2.0
United States	4.1	0.7	4.1	0.7	2.2
Madagascar	2.2	−1.1	2.3	−1.2	0.4
England	4.1	0.7	4.1	0.7	2.2
Sweden	2.4	−0.9	2.5	−1.0	0.6

age-specific birth and death rates of five countries have been used in all combinations to construct stable age distributions and rates of increase. He will find that fertility differences are always more important than mortality differences.

NO MODEL, NO UNDERSTANDING

A good deal of data is on hand regarding breast cancer. Despite stepped-up efforts to deal with it, including surgery and other forms of treatment, and widespread publicity urging women to examine themselves and to see their doctors at once if there is any indication, the increase of deaths from breast cancer is considerable in North America and Western Europe, just where the most intensive effort is being made. Breast cancer is the leading cause of death for women aged thirty-five to fifty-four and second only to heart disease for older ages. Some of the increase may be due to more awareness and hence more frequent diagnosis now than in the past, and to better diagnosis in America and Europe than in Asia and Latin America, but apparently this is not the whole cause. Women who bear children early seem to have a lower risk of breast cancer, but no one thinks that having children—early or late—is the best or the only way to prevent the disease. Breast cancer is less common in warm climates and among poor populations, but that climate or poverty is a preventive seems unlikely.

Such statistical differentials are merely unsolved puzzles until someone comes along with a model that explains the differences. In the meantime, all that can be done is to continue gathering the data to discriminate among proposed models.

The ratio of male to female births is a similar case, in that there is no obvious model, and no clear-cut result has so far emerged from differentials and correlations. We know that births to young mothers have a higher sex ratio (males to females) than births to older ones, that first births to a mother have a higher sex ratio than later births, and that children of young fathers have a higher sex ratio than children of older fathers. But among age of mother, parity of mother, and age of father, which is the operative cause? The high intercorrelations among the possible causes make it difficult to distinguish. Mechanisms have been suggested involving the relative activity and viability of sperm producing male and female babies, but until some such mechanism is shown to be the operative one, our knowledge has a tentative and uncertain character. Here is just one more question that is unlikely to be solved by any volume of statistics by themselves, although they should be able to discriminate among models based on the biology of the matter, once convincing models are presented.

Too Many Models

India and some other countries have raised the legal age of marriage, partly with the aim of lowering the birth rate. Implicit in the thinking of legislators and others is a theory in which marital fertility age for age is relatively fixed, and the legal minimum age effectively eliminates the part of the fertility curve below that age. Given the curve, the amount of effect is easily calculated. Our sample survey data for India (Keyfitz and Flieger 1968) show that out of 18.14 million births in 1961, some 3.24 million or 18 percent were to mothers under age twenty years. If these could be eliminated, the impact on the rate of increase is exactly calculable.

This seems a potentially powerful argument for restriction of marriage, supposing it feasible to raise the age as high as twenty for women. But before one reaches a firm conclusion, it ought to be noted that on an opposite model raising age at marriage would be wholly ineffective.

Suppose that married couples are not reproducing to the maximum, but that they want a certain number of children, and will have later what the law forbids them to have sooner. After all, the birth rate of India is now under forty per thousand, well below the physiologically possible maximum. Under these circumstances, the only gain from a legal minimum age would be a slight delay—perhaps five years or so—which would lengthen the distance separating successive generations and hence lower the increase, but by a small amount. Illegitimacy is also a problem; it is low in India, but one of the reasons parents want their daughters married off early is to avoid their engaging in premarital sex. If the parents' fears are not all imaginary, there could be some increase in children born outside of marriage.

Yet this argument is in the end unconvincing; one has the impression that couples who lose time before they are twenty may make up some part of the lost ground, but not all, and that extramarital fertility would remain low. To know the net drop in overall fertility as a result of the restriction requires behavioral data. That alone can discriminate among the competing models and predict the quantitative effects of an induced change in age at marriage.

PROMOTION IN ORGANIZATIONS

Everyone knows that in a fast-growing organization promotion is likely to be more rapid than in one growing slowly. Neither elaborate empirical data nor a model is required to demonstrate that bare fact. What one would like to know is the quantitative relation: in a fast-growing organization, does one get to a middle position a few months sooner than in a slow-growing one, or several years sooner?

One can imagine collecting a good deal of data to settle this point. One would have to give attention to the universe of organizations from which one was sampling—perhaps settling on all commercial, transport, and manufacturing firms in the United States. One would have to define the boundaries of each organization, whether it includes all establishments constituting a firm, or whether each establishment is to be considered a separate organization. A lower limit would have to be set to the size of organization considered, say 100 employees. One would want to distinguish family-run enterprises, since the conditions for promotion in these would certainly be different. If a one-time survey were to be made, then the information on promotion would have to be obtained retrospectively, with the errors of recollection that this entails. On the other hand, a succession of surveys that statistically followed careers of individuals would take time and be expensive.

And when the results were in, we would notice that in some organizations there were many resignations, so that promotion would be rapid for personnel that remained; indeed, this effect might be strong enough to hide the effect of growth. We would have to classify organizations into homogeneous groups according to their turnover, or else obtain an index of turnover for each and use regression analysis to "partial" it out. This is only one of many disturbing elements that could be expected to make the results, so painstakingly obtained, uncertain in interpretation in relation to the question to which an answer is being sought.

A simpler approach that would avoid the errors to which a survey is subject (of which sampling error is the least) is through a mathematical model that compares the number of employees ahead of a representative individual—let us call him Ego—in a fast-growing and a slow-growing organization, as if promotion depended only on age. Superimposed on individual ability, assiduity, influence, luck, and all the other elements that determine promotion in the real world, is the pure effect of growth on individual careers, and that is what we want to ascertain. Details of this approach are provided in Chapter 5 above. Here we use the material merely as a further example of the difference between knowledge derived from a model developed for the purpose and the more purely empirical kind of knowledge based on data without a specific model.

First suppose a given schedule of survival—knowing that the deaths of his contemporaries help Ego's promotion, we do not want differences of mortality to cloud the result of our analysis. Then suppose an age distribution that is a function only of this survival function and rate of increase, so that the stable model described earlier is applicable. Finally, take as the arbitrary benchmark for measurement the age at which individuals arrive at a position where twice as many of their fellow workers are below them as are above, say a junior supervisory position.

After that a simple piece of mathematics shows that, for given rates of death or resignation, the age x at which Ego reaches such a position is shortened by two-thirds of a product of two factors: (1) the time from age x to retirement, discounted at the rate of population increase and (2) the difference between the mean age of the group senior to the point of promotion considered and the mean age of those junior to it. This difference cannot be far from half of the length of working life. With an entry age of twenty and a retirement age of sixty-five, the comparison of two populations whose increase differs by Δr percent gives for the difference in ages

$$\Delta x = -(2/3)(15)(22.5)\frac{\Delta r}{100} = -2.25\Delta r.$$

Thus the time of promotion is delayed by 2.25 years for each 1 percent by which population growth is lower. That demographic factor is overlaid on all individual differences of ability, influence, and luck. While the model is based on pure seniority, some such effect will apply if any element of seniority is present. Only if length of service in the organization is wholly disregarded in promotion will the model be irrelevant.

EFFECT OF DEVELOPMENT ON POPULATION INCREASE

Development seems sooner or later to have brought a reduction in population growth in all the instances where it has occurred. All of the rich countries have low birth rates today, and the very richest are not replacing themselves. For example, West Germany had fewer births than deaths in 1973, and in 1974 it had fewer births plus net immigrants than deaths, so that its population actually declined by 2 percent. But the countries of Eastern Europe are much less rich, and they also have low birth rates, while in Britain the birth rate first started to fall almost a century after development was under way. Thus the correlation is not perfect, but still history seems to be saying that with more or less lag, industrialization has led to reduced family size.

In theory this may be due to women finding jobs and sources of prestige outside the home, so they do not need to rely on childbearing for their standing, and to children being on the one hand more expensive and on the other less directly useful to their parents as income increases, both effects being related to the decline of the family as a productive unit with the growth of industry. With easy contraception, relatively weak motivation suffices to cut the birth rate. What we ought to believe in this matter, summed up in the concept of demographic transition (Notestein 1945), is relatively unambiguous because the dominant theories and the most conspicuous anecdotal evidence all point the same way.

Yet even here, the more closely and systematically scholars have looked at the data, the less clear they have found the effect of development on family size to be. Taking income as a proxy for development,

Adelman (1963) makes "an analysis of fertility and mortality patterns as they are affected by economic and social forces." Her materials, based mostly on national statistics for 1953, show a decidedly *positive* relation between income and fertility. Friedlander and Silver (1967) partial out more variables, and find that for developed nations fertility and income are positively related, but for less developed nations negatively related. David Heer (1966) calculated correlations for forty-one countries that suggested that the direct effect of economic development is to increase fertility, and the indirect effects (through education and other influences) are to reduce it. But it makes a difference when the data for the twenty-four less developed countries are separated from those for the seventeen more developed and more than one point of time is introduced, so that changes rather than levels are correlated. Ekanem (1972) used two points of time, the decades of 1950 and 1960, but the effect of his greater care seems to be a less clear-cut result than Heer's. Janowitz (1971; Chesnais and Sauvy 1973; Stockwell 1972) follows five European countries and finds that variables shift enough through time that the longitudinal relations, more likely to indicate causation, are decidedly different from the cross-sectional regressions.

It would be too unkind to say that these efforts constitute raw empiricism. They are oriented to the economic theory that increased affluence causes people to buy more of most things, the exceptions being labeled inferior goods. Since no one considers children inferior goods, many argue that children and income really are positively related, but the relation is concealed by the intervention of other factors. The better-off have access to contraceptives of which the poor are ignorant; the better-off have higher quality (that is, more expensive) children, and so can afford fewer of them (Becker 1960; Leibenstein 1974; Leibenstein 1975).

EFFECT OF POPULATION GROWTH ON DEVELOPMENT

The writers cited above were trying to find the impact of development on fertility where, despite some complications and contradictions, causation seems clearer than in the inverse problem: in which direction and to what extent does rapid population growth affect development? Among all the questions that demographers seek to answer, this is the one that is truly important for policy.

In the classic theory, rapid growth means many children—40 percent or more of the population under age fifteen years. The children have to be fed, clothed, and educated, and however the cost is divided between parents and the state, it requires resources that compete with industrial and other investments. In addition, growth requires that provision be made for *increasing* numbers, in particular to equip a larger and larger labor force with capital goods. Thus a fast-growing population is doubly handicapped.

So much for the static aspect of the demographic-economic relationship. As to dynamics, when fertility falls from an initially high level, the dependency ratio begins to shift immediately in an economically favorable direction. Thus investment can be greater, compared with what it was before. Lagging fifteen or twenty years behind is a longer-run dynamic effect: a slackening of the growth of the population in the labor force ages. When relatively fewer children grow up to enter those ages, there is less competition for productive jobs, and each entrant may have more capital to work with compared to the situation that would exist if the birth rate had not been cut (Coale and Hoover 1958).

All this is based on the view that development is capital-limited rather than resource-limited. But if it is resource-limited, population is an even more serious drawback, although now the absolute level of population is the problem rather than the birth rate; the more people, the less resources at the disposal of each, on a theory running back to John Stuart Mill and ultimately to Malthus. In the most general statement certain ratios of labor to the other factors of production—land and capital—are more favorable than others, and most developing countries are moving away from the optimum with present population sizes and birth rates.

But now try to see how matters would look if no theory had ever been presented. Let us try to wipe theory out of our minds, and look at the data with complete naiveté. Among developing countries, Brazil and Venezuela are not increasing in population less rapidly than their economically stagnant neighbors; indeed, Argentina and Chile, with very low birth rates, may be becoming absolutely poorer. Mexico is advancing economically with an annual population increase of 3.0 percent per year, higher than that in Paraguay or Bolivia, where economic dynamism is absent. On the other hand, sub-Saharan Africa has high rates of population increase and low income growth. Figure 1 depicts the broad array of relationships between population growth and increase in income for large countries in the contemporary world. The relation that theory predicts is not at all evident.

It makes a difference if we compare birth rates rather than natural increase, and for the theory, births less infant deaths might be the best indicator of the demographic impact. But whatever measure is used, the inverse correlation with economic dynamism simply does not appear.

Of course, individual countries can be analyzed, and by making allowance for such nonpopulation aspects as leadership, political conditions, the educational system, religion, the dissolving of patrimonial social relations as expressed in landholding and other ways, along with resource endowment, we need not be at a loss to account for the observed national differences. This explanation a posteriori can be made to sustain the theory, but hardly answers the disturbing question: to what extent would naive examination of population and income data for the poor countries of the world have discovered any clear effect of population on development? Would the effect have been as blurred as the effect of population increase on age distribution?

It is just this incapacity of the raw data to speak for themselves that permits some to argue that population and its growth do not harm development and should be allowed to take care of themselves. One might expect the facts to silence anyone who could utter such opinions, but as presented either anecdotally as above or in simple correlations, they do not. How can the facts be made to speak loudly and clearly to this issue?

How Nature Covers Her Tracks

The reason for bringing these very difficult matters into the present exposition is the hope that their investigation can be aided by going back to some simpler issues, like the relation between age distribution and the rate of increase of a population. There most would agree that theory gives the right answer: the rate of increase determines the proportion of old (as well as middle-aged and young) in the population. Where the relation is obscured by migration or by changing birth and death rates, as it commonly is, these are seen as mere disturbances. Such noise could drown out the relation in the observed data without weakening our conviction that the relation is really as stable theory says it is. Up to this point stable theory has the immutability of the laws of logic: if over a sufficient period of time death rates are the same in two populations, then the one with the higher birth rate will have the lower proportion at ages sixty-five and over. Belief in this is unshaken by El Salvador being higher than Honduras both in rate of population increase and in percent over age sixty-five, or by similar cases that might turn up. The supporter of the theory would convincingly argue that the official data must be wrong (perhaps registration of births is differentially incomplete), or there has been age-selective migration, or some other reason underlies the discrepancy between expected and observed relationships.

Although stable theory can never be disproved, it could be deprived of all interest if in the real world certain things that it assumes constant were in fact steadily changing. If death rates were always falling at a certain pace, then the proportion of old people would everywhere be different from that given by stable theory, and a different theory would be required for interpreting reality. Any steady change that was universal would make us want to replace stable theory with its fixed rates by some other, inevitably more complicated, theory that would have equal force of logic but be more applicable. In fact, change is not so uniform under different real conditions, but is rather erratic, a means by which nature covers up her mechanisms, rendering their interpretation not amenable to a universal theory.

But change, whether steady or erratic, is not the means by which the mechanisms of nature are most effectively covered. More deceiving is the clinging together of variables. Suppose all countries of rapid growth were countries of emigration, so that they lost their young people to countries of slower growth; then the conclusion derived from the application of stable theory would be downright misleading. We would want some other theory, perhaps one on which populations tend to spread out evenly in relation to resources. In fact, such a view is held on internal migration, where free movement occurs and people go to distant places unless they are attracted to intervening opportunities (Stouffer 1940).

THE OBLIQUE USE OF DATA TO CHALLENGE THEORY

In short, challenges to theory have to take the form either of showing that some of the variables assumed fixed move in a systematic fashion, or more importantly, that some variables supposed to move independently in reality cling together; that some of the independent variables are not really independent, but are creatures of other hidden variables of quite different nature.

How then can the classical theory that rapid population growth checks development be challenged? The matter is important because a theory that there is no chance of proving wrong has little value for science.

One way is by declaring that there is a trend toward development everywhere in the world, as well as a trend toward smaller families, and that the latter makes no difference to the former. Suppose the trend to development occurs everywhere sooner or later and nothing can either stop it or hasten it. On this comfortable view of development as immanent in human history no detailed causal theory would be possible, and no policy measures would be sought or needed. Such a view is not entirely absent from contemporary discussion.

A more persuasive direction of attack is to adduce evidence that enterprising personalities are more often born into large families and to show quantitatively that this greater enterprise is sufficient to overcome the capital and land shortage due to large families. Or else that couples with more children will have a greater incentive to save and so increase investment funds. Or else that having many children increases consumption but fathers of large families work correspondingly harder and offset this. All of these are statements on the individual level that there is a sticking together of the variables concerned with development—population growth, motivation to work, motivation to save. Nothing in logic proves that the sticking together does not occur, but it is the obligation of anyone who challenges the theory to adduce evidence.

On the national level, the countries that are developing may be the ones in which the authorities are development-minded and persuade their people to make sacrifices that more than offset the disadvantages of population increase. Again, evidence bearing on this specific point would be required.

What part of the observed phenomena is a manifestation of the underlying causal mechanism, and what part is concealment? Even for the most straightforward matters, this is not an easy question to answer. For national populations, one assumes, age distributions are really determined by the rate of increase, and migration or correlated death rates merely conceal this true relation. On the other hand, density-dependent growth is in evidence for many animal populations, so high birth rates might cause high death rates or out-migration. If the correlation of high births with out-migration is necessary, if it is an intrinsic part of the causal mechanism, then the stable theory of age distribution is downright wrong; if it is a provisional and temporary complication of the observed data, then the stable theory stands. If autocratic regimes produce development and the same autocratic regimes oppose family planning, this may result in a positive cross-sectional correlation between population increase and rise in income per head, and the student who wants to know what is happening must penetrate to the intermediate variable, "autocratic regime."

After discovering the existence of this intermediate variable, the student would have to judge whether its operation is necessary or incidental. Notwithstanding Hume's proof that necessity can never be inferred from finite observation, such judgements are as unavoidable a part of science as they are of common sense. (The difference may be that science makes them tentatively, common sense makes them dogmatically!)

The Psychology of Research

A footnote on the mental conditions in which research occurs may help illuminate the way we get to know the facts of demography. Faced with a variety of data the investigator listlessly surveys them, in the hope of somehow tying them together. He is swamped by the multiplicity of observations and tries to fit them into a scheme, if only to economize his own limited memory. He becomes more animated when he sees that some general connections do subsist in the data, and that a model, however crude, helps him to keep their relations in mind. The model is much more than a mnemonic device, however; it is a machine with causal linkages. Insofar as it reflects the real world, it suggests how levers can be moved to alter direction in accord with policy requirements. The question is always how closely this constructed machine resembles the one operated by nature. As the investigator concentrates on its degree of realism, he more and more persuades himself that his model is a theory of how the world operates.

But now he is frustrated—he has just turned up an incontrovertible observation that is wholly inconsistent with his theory. Such an observation is truly a fact, an exception to the theory that cannot be avoided or disregarded. A struggle ensues as the investigator attempts to force the theory to embrace the exception. As his efforts prove vain he questions the theory, and looks back again at the raw data whose complexity he thought he had put behind him. The intensity of the struggle that ensues is one of the hallmarks of scientific activity and distinguishes it from mindless collecting of data on the one hand and complacent theorizing on the other.

The problem and its possible solutions have now taken possession of the person. In this phase of his research his unconscious is enmeshed and is working on the question day and night. Sleep is difficult or impossible; eating and the daily round of life are petty diversions. He is irritable and distracted. Whatever he does, the contradiction he has turned up comes into his mind and stands between him and any normal kind of life.

During the struggle, the investigator is like a person with high fever. Then with luck he comes on the answer, or his unconscious does. He finds a model that fits, perhaps nearly perfectly, perhaps only tolerably, but well enough to provide a handle on the varied data. His tension subsides, and he goes on with the normal and dull work of establishing the details of the fit and presenting his results. He must indeed revert to a calmer state before he can hope to communicate his finding to an audience that is perfectly normal. An immediate test of his result will be whether it makes sense to his contemporaries; an ultimate test is whether it can predict outcomes involving data not taken into account in the establishment of the model.

Only in exceptional cases will one period of feverish concern produce a final theory and permit immediate relaxation. More often a long series of false starts and disappointments will precede the resolution.

Sometimes the problem turns out to be unsolvable in the existing state of knowledge, or beyond the capacity of the investigator, and then he has the unhappy task of winding himself down without the desired denouement.

None of the psychological accompaniment of scientific production is special to demography, but that field can show it in heightened form. The abundant data of demography cause an inappropriate theory or an erroneous prediction to stand out relatively clearly. Where that possibility of a sharp rejection by hard data is lacking, the game of research loses its seriousness—it is like playing solitaire with rules that are adjustable to the cards that have appeared.

CHAPTER 8
Population Appearances and Demographic Reality

That a country with a higher death rate is less healthy than one with a lower; that overpopulation leads to war; that an excess of births over deaths ensures population replacement: these are some frequently stated propositions on population. They are all common sense, they are all obvious, and yet on closer examination every one of them turns out to be false. I shall elaborate them along with other similar ideas, and show that they pertain to the surface of population phenomena, to appearance rather than to demographic reality. Relations below the surface can be quite different, and we will see how the techniques of demography serve to strip off the superficial relations and, at least in some instances, to produce knowledge of population that has a claim to be called scientific.

MORTALITY COMPARISONS

Taiwan recorded five deaths per thousand population during 1977. The United States in the same year recorded a death rate of about nine per thousand, or 80 percent higher than that of Taiwan. A person chosen at random in the United States is almost twice as likely to die within a year as a person chosen at random in Taiwan. Is Taiwan, then, healthier than the United States?

It is nothing of the kind, as can be shown by comparing people of the same age in the two countries. In Taiwan, the chance that a newborn baby will die in its first year is 0.025; in the United States, it is 0.014. At every separate age, Taiwanese mortality is higher, with no exceptions. The reality, then, is that the United States is healthier than Taiwan, notwithstanding the fewer deaths per thousand population in Taiwan.

For demographers it is crucial that the comparison be made age by age wherever the mix of ages between two countries is different. The ages may be grouped, but then they must be given the same weights for the two countries. If Taiwan had the same age distribution as the United States, its death rate would be thirteen per thousand population. Alternatively, we note that the expected lifetime for males is seventy years for the United States, compared with sixty-five years for Taiwan. It is the fact that greater proportions of the population of developing countries are in the young age groups that gives several of them crude death rates lower than those of developed countries.

Thus, the use of age-specific rates does indeed strip off a layer of appearance and gets closer to the truth. But can we be sure that age is the only variable that has to be controlled in order to make the comparison valid? We cannot, even though age is probably the interfering variable that acts most strongly. That other variables operate as well can be seen by comparing mortality in the states of Arizona and New Hampshire in the United States.

The expectation of life of males at birth in Arizona was 65.38 years in 1967; in New Hampshire it was 67.13. Since population age distribution does not distort the calculation of life expectancy, other factors must be at work to produce this effect. Climate would seem likely to work in the opposite direction; one would think that the Arizona climate would help preserve old people better than the more rigorous temperatures of New Hampshire. That may well be true. A process of self-selection may explain lower life expectancy in Arizona; people in good health may continue to live in New Hampshire, while the less healthy move to Arizona. We would have to go deeper and compare people similar in other respects as well as age to separate out the salubrious effects of climate or other variables of interest. Age-like effects need much more attention.

What is striking in such cases is the ease of drawing a wrong conclusion from statistical data known to be accurate. Without breaking the data down by age, we find Taiwan healthier than the United States; without eliminating the selective effect of migration, we find New Hampshire more salubrious and conducive to long life than Arizona.

This is why demographers are suspicious of comparisons that try to infer the extent to which mortality is governed by environmental conditions. Los Angeles had a death rate of 8.5 per thousand in 1975 compared with Atlanta's 6.9 per thousand. Los Angeles also has greater frequency and intensity of smog. A breakdown by cause of death strengthens the suspicion that mortality and smog are connected; death from lung diseases is proportionally greater in Los Angeles. But the evidence is not conclusive; we must satisfy ourselves that Los Angeles's older age distribution does not account for the difference, and having done so we must look into other variables by which people in the two cities might be different.

Of course to relate mortality to smog, we ought not to stop at two cities but compare a large number of them. But such a comparison is still not conclusive if there is some variable that sticks, so to speak, to the one that we are correlating with mortality. Suppose the data show a negative correlation between the number of days per year with high smog levels and expectation of life at birth, and suppose that the smog is caused by industrial activity (as against employment in trade or government) and that it is the rigorous employment in industry, not the smog, that causes the shorter expected lifetime. If this were true, then pollution controls that would eliminate smog would be a futile attempt to reduce mortality.

Sometimes a variety of evidence, no one part of it very strong, can build up to a powerful case. The effect of cigarette smoking on mortality is the classic instance. The mere fact that smokers had higher death rates than nonsmokers, observed as early as 1938 and confirmed by Doll and Hill (1952), did not prove that cigarettes are harmful. After all, people smoke to relieve tension, and it may be the tension that causes the higher mortality; perhaps smoking even lessens mortality, as people thought in the eighteenth century. But then it was determined that mortality rates increased with the amount smoked—with very high rates for those smoking a pack a day. Again, not in itself conclusive. Men smoke more than women and have higher death rates, but there are far more substantial differences between males and females than the number of cigarettes smoked per day. Animal studies showed clear effects of exposure to smoke, but could these effects be transferred to humans? It was the accumulation of evidence, every part of which taken alone was flawed, that forced the recognition of the causal relation between smoking and death rates (U.S. Dept. of HEW 1964).

Often the true direction of a relation is easily observed, but its size or strength is not. At most ages men have about double the death rates of women. For instance, according to the life table for 1966–67, the chance that an American male of fifty will die in the succeeding five years is 0.059, while the chance that a female of fifty will die during the same time is 0.031. This difference is fairly typical of many other ages as well. Yet women live only seven or eight years longer than men. How can it be that men in the United States have mortality double that of women, but women live only 10 percent longer?

Certainly for a species whose death rates were the same at all ages, double mortality would mean half the length of life. But mortality rates for humans are not the same at all ages, following instead an asymmetric U-shape, a bathtub curve. And on this curve the very high rates at the oldest ages, up to now little affected by medical advance, set an upper limit on the length of life. Because of this upper limit, women obtain only a relatively small advantage from the fact that their mortality rates at any given age are much lower than those of men.

INFERRING CAUSATION FROM HISTORICAL DATA

It is often said that large populations, living in conditions of high density, make democracy impossible; they inevitably lead to regimentation and tyranny. Plato thought so, as did Harrison Brown (1954), and it is true that Bangladesh and China are less democratic than the United States. Concentrating on these cases, we can convince ourselves of the general proposition. But what about Holland, both denser and more democratic than the Soviet Union? This counter-example does not by itself prove that the relation does not exist, for there could be special circumstances in Holland and the U.S.S.R. But at least it proves that the relation cannot be as simple as one would surmise from Plato or Brown. There are bound to be other variables that affect the relation, and until they can be disentangled any statement is as likely to deceive as to enlighten.

Take, for example, the common view that population increase and high density in relation to resources lead to war. A careful examination of the evidence by a political scientist who reviewed scores of cases found density to be associated with war in many historical instances, but not in many others (Choucri 1974; Wright 1965). Even if the data had shown a perfect correlation between population density and frequency of occurrence of war, we could not say that the former caused the latter; it could be just the opposite. It could be that countries of militaristic bent pursue population policies that provide the needed cannon fodder. This is one of many instances in which we have to consider the possibility that the common-sense causal relation may be the opposite of the true causal relation.

STRIPPING POPULATION INCREASE OF AGE EFFECTS

Nothing would seem more certain than that the population of the United States is now increasing, even if we disregard the balance of migration. In 1978 the country had about 3.3 million births, against about 1.9 million deaths. Consider the present native population of the United States as a closed unit. The natural increase of this closed population was 1.4 million in 1978, or about 0.7 percent. In 100 years at this rate the population would double; in 500 years it would multiply by thirty-two and number over 6 billion. Yet the demographer claims that in reality the current levels of fertility and mortality are such that the population of the United States is not even replacing itself. How can such a statement be justified in the face of visible, countable increase?

The answer comes out of a very different perspective from simply noting that births exceed deaths. It does indeed start with such statistics, but it takes them by age and converts them to probabilities. Think of a female child just born in the United States, and suppose that she will be subject to the same regime of birth and death as the United States showed for the year 1978. Then calculate the probability that she will survive to age eighteen and at that age have a baby girl; that she will survive to age nineteen and have a girl; and so on for each year of reproductive age. Adding these up we get the expected number of baby girls by which that baby would be replaced according to the birth and death rates for 1978; it turns out to be 0.9. The expected number of female births a child will have is the same as the ratio of the size of the next generation to this generation, still at 1978 age-specific rates of fertility and mortality. Those rates imply an ultimate decline of 10 percent per generation.

If a baby girl will not in the next generation give birth to at least one baby girl on the average, then the population is not replacing itself, and it will sooner or later decrease if these rates continue unchanged. We can carry the idea of replacement to a per-year rather than a per-generation basis by noting that the average time for a girl to grow up and become a mother is something like twenty-six years; taking the twenty-sixth root of 0.9 we obtain 0.996, a decline of about 0.4 percent per year. This is part of the reality of the present birth and death regime. The reason for the difference between this and the superficial conclusion that the United States population is increasing is the exceptionally large number of women of childbearing age in the present native population—a consequence of the baby boom of the 1950s. We have to strip off the effect of these temporarily large numbers and focus our attention on the amount of childbearing women are on the average undertaking.

WHY BIRTHS WILL REMAIN LOW

During the 1960s and 1970s, the fall in the United States birth rate was accompanied by a sharp rise in female participation in the labor force, an unprecedented increase in divorce, and greater participation of women at higher levels in the education system. Smaller families are thus congruent with other tendencies in the society; for the immediate purpose we do not need to struggle with the difficult question of causality. Do women have few children because they want to be free to work? Or do they go out and take jobs because they have few children and hence less responsibility in the home?

Without answering the question of causation, demographers have noted further aspects of the new context of American fertility (Westoff 1978). The bundle of disparate elements includes later marriage than was previously customary, more cohabitation without marriage, and proportionally more illegitimate births, all paralleling rising divorce rates and increased participation of women in the labor force. If these tendencies are interrelated, then one would not be likely to change without a change in the whole configuration. For the birth rate to rise substantially, women would have to go back to housework—some would say to being domestics in their own homes; they would give up the satisfactions of work and independent incomes in favor of the satisfactions of having many children; they would put up with unsatisfactory marriages rather than undergo divorces. All this is hard to imagine, and that it is unlikely is the basis of the forecast that we will have low birth rates for at least the remainder of the century.

Going still further from the demographic variables, we recall that those who grew to young adulthood in the 1970s have been dubbed the "me" generation. "Look at me" was the quintessential expression of their preoccupation with self. When a "me" person marries an admiring other, the marriage can be stable and satisfactory. But what happens when two "me"s marry? Divorce and resulting single-person households are a likely outcome. Data bearing on such conjectures would help us to understand the demographic configuration.

Labor Force Participation

It was long ago said that as a society becomes richer, agriculture is bound to occupy less of the labor force (Clark 1940); after all, the amount of food we can consume is limited. Economists also saw that the same must apply to manufactured goods—there is a limit to the number of cars, television sets, and other artifacts a society can use. When the society becomes saturated with primary (agricultural) and secondary (manufactured) goods, it moves into a service economy.

Yet in industrial societies, expansion of the services that people once thought they wanted is exactly what has *not* happened (Bell 1973).

Barbers, shoe repairers, taxi drivers, domestics (both live-in and not) are among the occupations that have declined most sharply, both in the number of persons employed and in value of product. Some of these traditional service occupations in the United States dropped by as much as half in the single decade between the 1960 and the 1970 census. What has expanded spectacularly are government, trade, insurance and banking, and education. It is well to avoid stretching the label "services" to cover both these and the traditional service occupations, and to refer to them simply as tertiary. The agency that collects our taxes can call itself the Internal Revenue Service, but its "service" has nothing in common with driving a taxi or repairing shoes.

The forces in the United States economy that are bringing the tertiary sector up to half of the labor force and beyond are not well understood. In the mid-1960s, many economists predicted that with the large number of young people about to enter the labor force, and with increasing productivity of those already working, it would be impossible for married women to find jobs. Yet, in the event, the late 1960s and the 1970s have shown a continued increase in the already large number of married women working outside the home. Only a small fraction of the newcomers have taken jobs in manufacturing; the great majority have tertiary employment.

On the one hand is the puzzle of how the economy has been able to absorb the large number of young people of both sexes, as well as the newly entered married women. On the other hand is the question of why married women want to work outside the home. When women themselves are asked, they tend to reply that they need the money, and common sense is satisfied with this answer. But the answer cannot be correct, since in earlier decades their husbands were earning less, presumably families needed money, and yet wives were content to stay home. Needing money is a universal, a constant, and a first rule of method is that one cannot explain a variable (in this instance, far more women having jobs in the 1960s than in the 1920s) with a constant. Undoubtedly consumption aspirations have risen, but that could be an effect; even if we assume it is a cause of women working, we would need an independent measure of "consumption aspirations" if we are to use this variable to explain women working. Is it that more jobs are now suitable for women? Clearly there are more jobs, and this in turn needs explanation.

Apparently, a huge cultural shift has taken place, but that also is less an explanation than a name for the phenomenon. Once again, it is the responsibility of the scholar to know when the observed phenomenon is an expression of forces working far beneath the surface, and not to be satisfied with brushing the problem of cause aside by giving it a name. To say that women are no longer raising children because of a shift in the culture is by itself merely scholastic. To make the statement useful, we would need some way of independently measuring how the culture is shifting.

In the area of labor force participation, as earlier in fertility, mighty social forces are churning below the surface. The census and vital statistics indicate that deeper changes are taking place, but present data cannot readily delineate them.

ABSTRACT RELATIONS: THE STABLE POPULATION

Age distribution at any moment is a cross-section of the survivors from among previous births. In a population in which there is the same number of births each year and no net migration, the curve tracing the age distribution at any time is exactly the same as the curve showing the probability of individuals surviving to any given age as calculated in a life table. This stationary age distribution is also the same as the distribution traced by the curve showing the attrition of the members of a cohort, that is, showing the attrition of the number of survivors from a group of individuals born in the same year and followed through life. The upper panel of Figure 1 provides a simple illustration of these relationships. The diagram at top left depicts a population with an annual number of births of 1 million, with fixed survival rates—in this instance equivalent to an expectation of life at birth of fifty years. For simplicity, only the survivors of five birth cohorts are shown, each originating twenty years after the previous one. A cross-section of the successive cohorts taken at any given time, such as at $t = 0$, gives the number of persons alive at that time at any given age. Thus, at time 0, the number of 20-year-olds will be the survivors of the cohort born twenty years earlier; the number of 40-year-olds will be the survivors of the cohort born forty years earlier; and so on. The diagram on the upper right shows this cross-sectional age distribution at time 0; its shape, if fully traced, is the same as the survivorship curves of the successive cohorts. (A little reflection by the reader will also suggest what the size of the population in this particular example will be at any given time. The answer is 50 million: the size of the annual number of births times the expectation of life at birth. Since the population is not growing, we also know that the annual number of deaths is the same as the annual number of births—1 million in the example.)

We have seen that the life table depicts the age structure of a population when births just replace deaths. To contemplate the case when births are greater (or less) than deaths, we turn again to the concept of a stable population—one with a constant rate of increase.

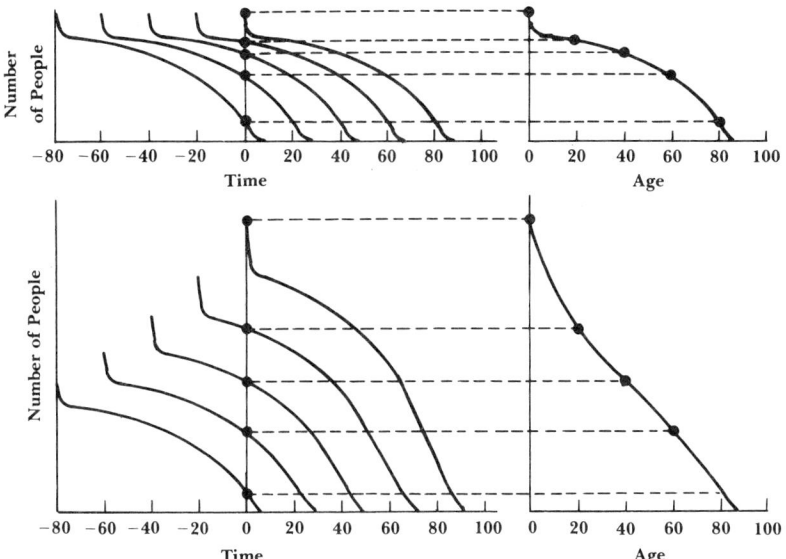

Figure 1: Age Distributions Resulting from Fixed Survivorship in a Stationary and a Stable Increasing Population

Note: Curves drawn from a Coale-Demeny West model life table with life expectancy of fifty years and, in the stable case, growing at 1 percent per year.

Suppose that births are increasing from year to year, always in the same ratio, while the mortality schedule, and hence the table of survivorship, continues unchanged, as in the previous example. The population is still closed: there is no immigration or emigration. The survivorship schedules of the successive cohorts are the same as before, but now the origin of each is raised above the one before by the ratio of increase. This is shown in the lower panel of Figure 1. The illustration assumes that the number of births at time t = −80 (i.e., eighty years ago) was 1 million but increasing at an annual rate of 1 percent. Now when we take a cross-section, say at time t = 0, the proportions at the younger ages are greater than in the stationary population of the life table. The simple reason is that the younger people were born more recently than the older ones, and they are more numerous insofar as births are steadily increasing. This is further illustrated in Figure 2, where the two cross-sectional distributions are drawn so that the total populations in each case are the same size (i.e., the areas under the curves are the same). With higher rates of growth, the

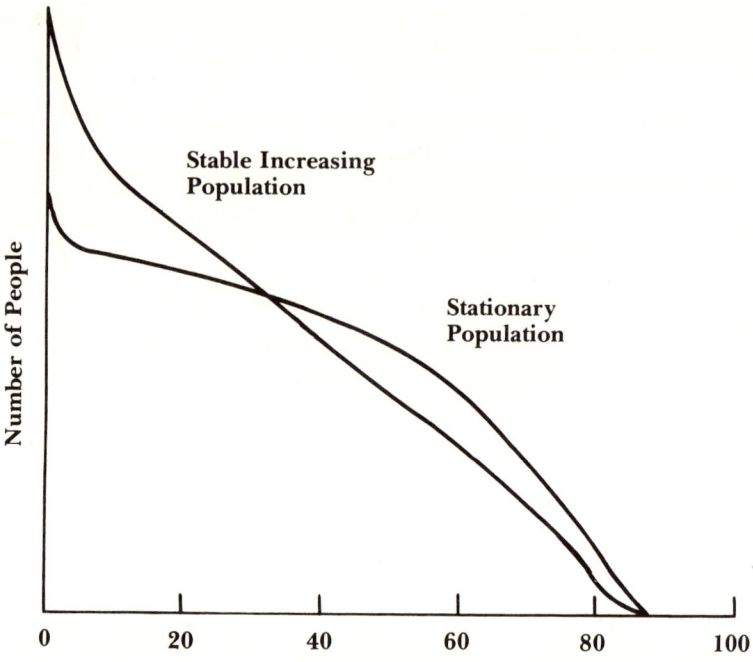

Figure 2: Typical Relation of Stable to Stationary Age Distribution

contrast between the stable population distribution and the stationary population would, of course, be sharper.

Under many circumstances the stable model tells us how fast population is increasing when we have only a census report of the age distribution. We could know from Figure 1 that the steeper the slope of the age distribution, the faster the population must be increasing, but technical theory is required to obtain an actual estimate of the rate of increase based on the observed age distribution and the life table (Keyfitz 1977).

As another application of the stable age distribution to tell us quantitatively what we can surmise qualitatively, think of a country that wants to reduce the population in a region by inducing people to migrate to another region. Indonesia is mounting a major program to take people off crowded Java and settle them in Sumatra and elsewhere in the archipelago. Clearly if the migrants are couples about to enter the childbearing ages, this program will be more effective in holding down the size of the population in Java than if the migrants are predominantly old people who are about to die. But what is the numerical effect of different age distributions of migrants on the subsequent population trajectory? Stable theory can show that having women of about age seventeen migrate reduces growth in Java about 1.5 times as much as the same number of migrants selected at random from all ages; that having women of age thirty migrate helps about half as much as having babies go (if the babies could migrate without their parents). Administrators in Indonesia had thought that the departure of relatively few people in their teens would have a dramatic effect in reducing Java's population growth; it turns out that the difference between migrants in their teens and a random sample of the population is fairly modest.

Also well known to common sense is the promotion that results from the mortality of one's elders and contemporaries. That clearly is favorable (to the survivors), but the effect turns out to be much smaller than the effect of population increase per se. In the highest mortality population of which there is a reasonably accurate record, that of eighteenth-century Sweden, whose expectation of life at birth was thirty years, promotion to a middle-level position would occur about three years sooner than in the low-mortality population of the contemporary United States. (This comparison is made at given rate of increase.) The population increasing fastest among those of which we have records provides promotion about nine years sooner than the one increasing most slowly. Thus, the effect of the highest recorded mortality on promotion (for those who survive) is only about one-third the magnitude of the effect of the highest recorded increase. The argument, based on stable population theory, has been presented in Chapter 5.

THE APPROACH TO STATIONARITY

Population increase cannot go on forever; growth can only be an interlude between periods of nongrowth. This well-founded proposition is commonly translated to mean that some time in the future there will be the same number of births from year to year. But such an interpretation is erroneous. The proposition about the inevitable long-term cessation of growth means that there will be a ceiling to population size, but there is no reason to believe that it will be approached smoothly and that, once attained, population growth will settle down to a steady zero rate. Nothing in the argument proving that population cannot increase forever prevents great oscillations in the number of births from year to year, in short or long waves, regular or irregular. Indeed, such a pattern, with an average nonincrease over extended periods, seems most likely.

Likewise, stationarity need not imply that individual localities will have fixed populations. The population of a country as a whole can be stationary over the long term, and yet in any particular year or decade one of its regions can increase and another decrease. There can be depressed areas and booming areas, in respect of population as well as of income.

The common contrary interpretation seems to have originated in mistaken labeling. We choose a word—stationarity—for the inevitable cessation of growth, and then we are deceived by our own word into accepting something that is far from inevitable: the absence of oscillations. The gap between appearance and reality in this case is not caused by one layer of reality covering up deeper layers; the problem is simply one of semantic self-deception.

Lessons from Failed Forecasts

One of the troubles with common sense is that it so quickly accommodates to what it sees happening, and hence does not know what to be surprised by. In fact it loses the faculty of being surprised at all. That is the advantage of records, including records of past forecasts, especially forecasts that failed. Having these and looking at the present, we know what it is that requires explanation.

Forecasts that do not materialize are objective indicators of the operation of previously unsuspected factors. The fifteen-hour week, forecast by Keynes (1972) and many others, was to be with us by now. In fact the long-term decline of hours worked has slowed since the 1960s, and a projection of the curve looks as though it may level off at about 35 hours. It seemed obvious in the 1920s that with increasing productivity in manufacturing industries, there would be less need for labor. Edward Bellamy's popular *Looking Backward* (1887) forecast a working life from age twenty-one to forty-five. People would work no longer than they had to—increased productivity would be converted to leisure. At least for the United States, this has just not turned out to be so—less than 10 percent of the increase in productivity from 1960 to 1970 was devoted to leisure.

When a knowledgeable person makes what seems a perfectly safe forecast and something quite different materializes, we know that there must be changes, linkages, and variables operating in the depths somewhere that strongly influence what appears on the surface. A methodology for studying the present is derivable from past forecasts.

Part Three
Economic and Social Development

CHAPTER 9

Resources and the World Middle Class

How much economic development is possible? Surely the planet and its materials are finite and not even all its present 4 billion people can live like Americans, let alone the 8 or 10 billion that on present trends will be alive when a stationary world population is established. Indeed, there is doubt whether the 250 million people expected to populate the United States in the year 2000 will be able to live as Americans do today. How far, then, can industrial society spread through the preindustrial world before it reaches a ceiling imposed by space, raw materials, and waste disposal?

That is the wrong question to ask, if human knowledge and capacity for substitution and the resilience of economic systems are unbounded, as they may well be. In that case the right question—and certainly a more tractable and pragmatic question—is how *fast* can development progress, whether toward an ultimate limit or not? What rate of technical innovation can be attained, oriented to allow a corresponding rate of expansion of industry, and how many of the world's people will that expansion enable to enter the middle class each year?

Attainment of the middle-class style of life is what constitutes development in countries as widely separated geographically and ideologically as Brazil and the USSR. In the process peasants gain education, move to cities and adopt urban occupations and urban patterns of expenditure. Changes are involved in people themselves, in their kind of work and in the nature of the goods they consume. These changes can be visualized in terms of a definable line, comparable to the poverty line officially drawn in the United States across which people aspire to move. The pertinent questions then become: how many people are moving across the line each year; what is their effect on resources; at what rate can resources be expanded by new techniques and, therefore, what is the size of the window through which the world's poor will climb into the middle class during the remainder of this century and beyond it?

A main issue of development for many of the people of Asia, Africa, and Latin America is how to enlarge that window into the middle class. If it is middle-class people who limit their families, the rate of movement into that class helps to determine the level at which the world population can be stabilized, and that level in turn will determine the degree of well-being that can be supported by world resources. And if shortage of resources makes the opening into the middle class as it is presently constituted so narrow that the majority will never be able to pass through it, then the sooner we know this the better. The Chinese rather than the Brazilian-Russian pattern of development may be what people will have to settle for.

The questions I have raised are difficult for many reasons, including the lack of statistical information, uncertainty about the capacity of productive systems to substitute common materials for scarce ones, and uncertainty about the directions in which technology will advance. Some data and some pointers are available, however.

Effect of Differential Population Growth

Let us begin with population. The world population, according to the United Nations estimates I shall be following, passed the 4-billion mark in 1975. It had passed the 3-billion mark in 1960. Whereas the last billion was added in fifteen years, the first billion had taken from the beginning (1 or 2 million years ago) until 1825. The growth has been far faster than exponential growth at a fixed rate of increase (as with compound interest); instead the rate rose from something like an average of .001 percent per year through the millennia of prehistory to 1.9 percent through the decade and a half from 1960 to 1975.

Apparently the rate of increase will not rise further. Again according to the United Nations medium variant, by the end of the century the increase will be down to 1.6 percent per year. Other estimates place the peak earlier and make the decline in rate of increase faster. Insofar as the increasing rate of increase constituted a population "explosion," we can draw relief from the fact that we are now down to "only" exponential growth. (This peaking was inevitable because of what mainly caused the rise to begin with: the decline in mortality during infancy and childhood. Mortality improvement after the reproductive ages does not affect increase much and in the long run does not affect it at all. Once the chance that a newborn infant will survive to reproduce itself gets up to about .90, the scope for further rise is limited, and whatever rise takes place will be offset by even a small decline in the birthrate.)

Those who worry about the population explosion can take some comfort in this peaking of the rate of increase, but not very much. Dropping to exponential growth still leaves the world population increasing (on the United Nations medium variant) by about 75 million per year now, with the annual increment rising to 100 million by the end of the century. And the absolute increase, rather than the rate, seems to be what matters. To feed the yearly increment requires nearly 20 million tons of additional grain, about equal to the entire Canadian wheat crop. To look after the annual increment of population on even a minimum basis is going to be difficult enough; the real issue, however, is not how many people can live but how many can live well.

Production of most things consumed by the world's people has been increasing at a higher rate than the 1.9 percent per year of population. During the period from 1960 to 1973 meat output increased at 2.8 percent a year, newsprint at 3.7 percent, motor vehicles at 6.8 percent, and energy consumption at 4.9 percent, and the rise was similar for many other commodities. These numbers can be taken to mean that on the average mankind is year by year eating better and reading more, becoming more mobile and substituting machine power for the power of human muscles. Such a conclusion would seem to be confirmed by worldwide figures on productive activity or income. For example, adding up the gross domestic products of all countries for 1970 yields a gross world product of $3,219 billion, an average of $881 per head. The total has been going up at nearly 5 percent per year in real terms, that is, after price increases. Even allowing for the 1.9 percent increase in population, we seem to be getting better off individually at about 3 percent per year. Projecting on this basis, real goods per head would double every twenty-three years; each generation would be twice as well off as the preceding one. To dispose of twice as much wealth as one's parents, four times as much as one's grandparents, surely cannot be regarded as unsatisfactory; the world, such figures seem to show, is moving toward affluence. That conclusion requires substantial qualification, even beyond the slowdown of the 1970s.

AVERAGES CAN MISLEAD

The division of a total number of dollars by a number of individuals to obtain an average per head has a long tradition; dividing one number by another is an innocent operation and without any necessary implication that everyone obtains the average, and yet it puts thoughts into people's minds. The first thought might be that things are not bad with $881 per head for the entire global population—a conservative conclusion. The second thought might be that things would indeed not be bad if the total were actually divided up—a radical viewpoint that has been voiced often in recent years. Income is an aspect of a way of life, however, and only a trifling part of a way of life is directly transferable.

The fallacy of redivision is encouraged by putting income into terms of money and performing arithmetical division. To say we should divide income so that everyone in the world can have his $881 is to solve a real problem with a verbal or arithmetical trick, because behind the numbers is the fact that Americans live one way and Indians another way. If, starting tomorrow, Americans were all to live like Indians, then their higher incomes would simply disappear. There would be nothing to transfer.

How much is transferable depends on the extent to which Americans could consume like Indians while continuing to produce like Americans. As soon as one tries to plan a transfer the tight bond between production and consumption frustrates the attempt. For example, the cost of travel to work is called consumption, but if people stopped traveling to work, production would fall to zero. What about the cost of holidays and entertainment, which are elements of consumption but which refresh people for further work? What about nutrition, education, and health services? And what about the enjoyment of consumer goods that is the incentive to work and eat? All of these and many other parts of consumption feed back into production. Moreover, to discuss massive transfers of capital would be futile for political reasons even if it were economically practical: the declining United States foreign-aid budget shows how unappealing this path to world development is to the major donor.

Because the world population is heterogeneous, no style of life is in fact associated with the world average of $881. Following that average through time leads to the mistaken impression that things are getting better every year and will do so indefinitely. Even a two-way breakdown of the average is a major step toward realism.

Of the total world population of 4 billion estimated for 1975, 1.13 billion, or nearly 30 percent, live in developed countries. The fraction of the annual increment of population accounted for by those countries is much less, however: only 10 million out of 75 million, or 13 percent. The

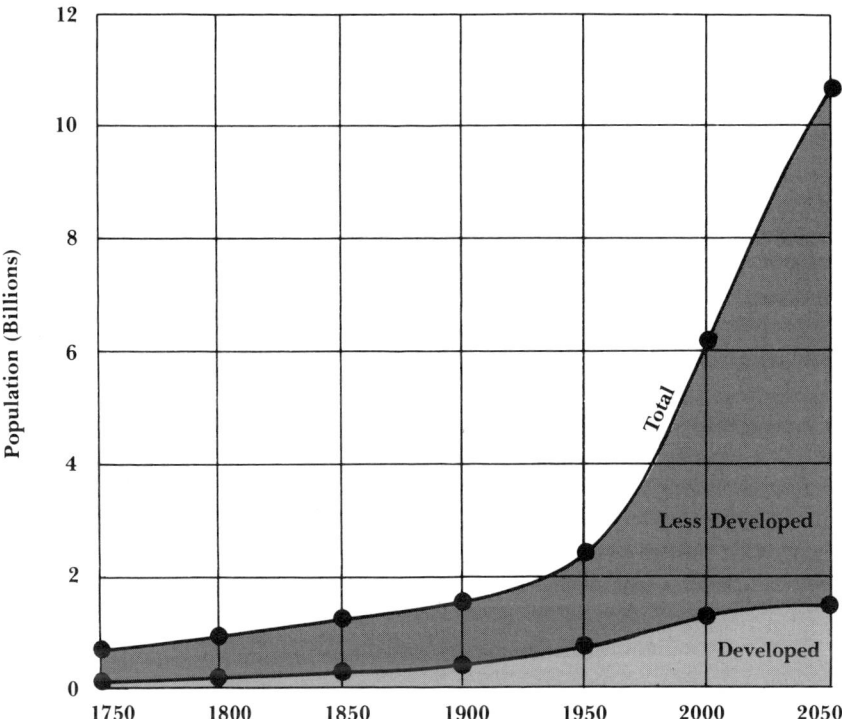

Figure 1: "Population explosion" curve is the result of more-than-exponential growth; the annual rate of increase has itself been rising, most sharply in the past century, largely because of the decline in infant and childhood mortality. In this layer chart the total population (projected to the year 2050 according to the United Nations medium estimate) is given for countries currently classified by the United Nations as "developed" *(light gray)* and "less developed" *(dark gray)*.

annual increment in the less developed countries is more than 65 million, and it will rise to 90 million by the end of the century (again on the United Nations medium estimates). This division of the world into two kinds of countries, rich and poor, or more developed and less developed, has become familiar since World War II. That world 1970 product (or income) of $881 per head is in fact an average of the developed countries' $2,701 and the less developed countries' $208.

Recent fluctuations obscure the long-term rates of increase, but suppose income for the rich and poor countries alike increases at 5 percent per year in the long term. On the population side, suppose the future increase is 0.5 percent per year among the developed countries and 2.5 percent per year among the less developed. Allowing for these population numbers brings the 5 percent annual gain in total product that was assumed for both down to about 4.5 percent for the developed countries and only 2.5 percent for the less developed ones.

The result is a widening gap between the two groups of countries, an exercise in the mathematics of geometric increase. Think of the developed countries starting at $2,701 per capita and increasing at 4.5 percent per year in real terms; after twenty-five years they have risen threefold, to a per capita income of more than $8,000 in 1995. By that time the income per head in the less developed countries has not even doubled: their $208 has risen to only $386. By the year 2020 the grandchildren of the present generation will have, in the one set of countries, more than $24,000 per head, and in the other countries the still very modest $715—one thirty-fourth as much as the rich, and not yet as much as the 1970 world average!

The calculation shows how a heterogeneous population is bound to develop a widening gap between rich and poor if per capita rates of increase are frozen. I have assumed that all national incomes increase at 5 percent per year. Overall national-income growth is not conspicuously different, on the average, for the poor and the rich countries, and so it is the differences in population growth that are decisive.

To speak of developed and less developed countries is an improvement on treating the world as homogeneous, but it has been overtaken by the events of the 1970s. Where two categories of countries once sufficed, we now find we cannot do with fewer than four.

The shifts in raw-material prices have created resource-rich countries such as Abu Dhabi and Venezuela, whose wealth is comparable to that of the developed countries, which by way of contrast can be called capital-rich. Some countries that were poor have actually been developing, including Singapore, Korea, Taiwan, and Hong Kong. Finally there are the many countries that are truly poor, lacking (in relation to their population) both capital and resources. We have, then, the resource-rich countries, the capital-rich countries, the developing countries, and the poor countries. Specifically identifying and classifying all cases to provide numbers for population in these groups is not easy. (Indonesia has resources but not enough so that any likely rise in prices would make its 150 million people rich.) The new categories of resource-rich and developing countries might be defined in such a way that they total 200 million people each; the fact remains that most of the world's people are in countries that have no leverage through either control of capital or control of resources.

No country is homogeneous, however; the poorest countries contain some rich people and the richest contain some poor. Nations and their governments dominate our age so completely that individuals too easily drop out of political as well as statistical view, yet the welfare of governments is not a worthy ultimate objective; it is the people of the poor countries who deserve our concern. And so what follows will deal as directly as possible with people.

MIDDLE CLASS AND POOR

The typical poor person and the typical middle-class person are easy to visualize; the first is a peasant in Java, Nigeria, the Brazilian northeast, or elsewhere in Asia, Africa, and the Americas; the second is a city dweller in San Francisco, Frankfurt, Leningrad, or Tokyo with an office job that puts him well above the poverty line. There are less obvious representatives. Along with the peasant group one should count as poor the wage laborer of Calcutta or the urban unemployed of the United States. And the middle-class group includes the unionized construction worker, the bus driver, the keypunch operator, and the successful farmer in the United States, Europe, the USSR, or Japan; that some of these are considered blue-collar is secondary to their earning a middle-class income.

In survey after survey most Americans, when they are asked where they think they belong, place themselves in the middle class. The self-classification by which most Americans tend to call themselves middle-class and Indians tend to call themselves poor accords with the distinction I have made. Most of those called middle-class in the world live in the cities of the rich countries, but some of them live in poor countries and some live in the countryside. The crucial part of the distinction is that middle-class people are in a position to make effective claim to a share of the world's resources that accords with modern living.

With an income measure of welfare, people fall on a continuum and the location of the poverty line is arbitrary. As a country grows richer its standards rise, so that the same fraction of its population may be defined as "poor" even as everyone in the country is becoming better off. In the case of the United States, however, it has been possible to reach broad agreement on a Social Security Administration definition of poverty based on relatively objective criteria. Chapter 10 will discuss that definition.

"Middle-class" describes a style of life and can cover not only physical necessities but also such conventional needs as power lawn mowers and winter vacations in Florida. It needs to be specified separately for each culture before one can see how many people enjoy it and what the energy and resource consequences of the enjoyment are. Pending such a study I propose to call middle-class those who are above the equivalent of the

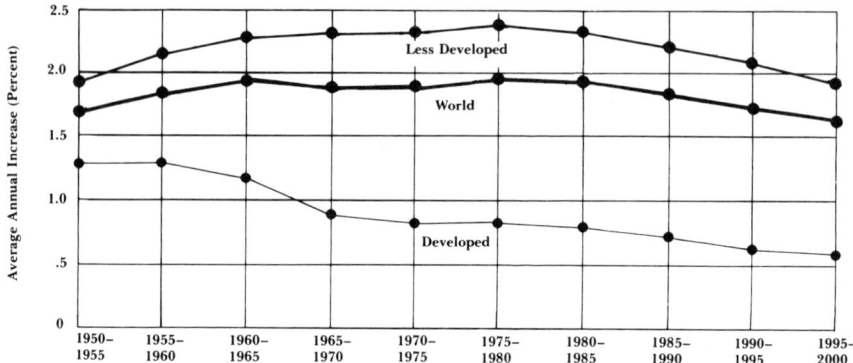

Figure 2: Rate of increase of population is apparently reaching a peak during the present half decade. The average rate of increase per year is plotted for five-year intervals for the developed *(light line)* and less developed *(heavier line)* countries and for the world as a whole *(heaviest line)*. The rate of increase turned down several decades ago for the developed countries and is expected to do the same thing soon in the less developed countries. The "explosion" is ending, in the sense that the growth of the world population will be less than exponential.

United States poverty line, wherever they may live. Cultural differences make poverty in one country intrinsically noncomparable to poverty in another country, but they make average money incomes just as noncomparable. The effort to quantify important notions must not be prevented by some degree of qualitative difference; the fraction under the level of consumption represented by the United States poverty line is not the definitive way of measuring the world's poor, but it will serve for the moment. In the United States that fraction was 11.6 percent in 1974, an increase from 11.1 in 1973 but a decrease from 22.4 in 1959. Of the United States population of 210 million in 1973, some 23 million were poor; call the remaining 187 million middle-class. Let us try to find indexes that will provide a corresponding number for other countries.

Passenger cars in use might be taken as roughly proportional to the middle-class, or above-poverty, population. In the United States in 1973 the number of passenger cars was 101 million and in the world as a whole it was 233 million, a ratio of 2.3. Insofar as the 233 million passenger cars in the world are being driven and ridden in by a world middle class, we can multiply the United States middle class of 187 million by 2.3 and derive a world total of 430 million middle-class people. This number is too low, because automobiles are less a part of daily life even in other affluent countries; we know that trains continue to be used in Europe for much travel that is done in the United States by automobile.

Let us try telephones as the indicator. The world total in 1973 was 336 million telephones and the United States total was 138 million. On this index the world middle class was 187 million times 336/138, or 455 million. With electric energy as the indicator a similar calculation gives a world middle class of 580 million. Each one of these indicators is surely defective. One can nonetheless hope that their defects are more or less constant over the twenty years or so that I propose to apply them to establish a trend.

A slightly different way of doing the calculation is to take it that modern living requires about four metric tons of crude oil a year for heating, air conditioning and motoring, so that the world output in 1973, 2,774 million tons, could cover the needs of 700 million people. (The calculation is approximate because some poor people do use a little oil and large supplies go to military and other government uses.)

Averaging the several approaches gives a world middle class of 500 million for 1970. What is important is that the corresponding average number—indexed on automobiles, telephones, electric energy, oil, and other items—was something like 200 million for 1950. That indicates an average increase of 4.7 percent per year in the middle class: the workers, and their families, who are integrated into industrial society, utilize its materials as the basis of their jobs and apply their incomes to consume its product. In doing so they have an impact on resources and on environment. Just how great is the impact of change in status from poor to middle class, particularly compared with the effect of population change?

EFFECT OF AFFLUENCE ON RESOURCES

Raw materials are used by people, and so, if all else is fixed, the drain on resources must be proportional to the number of people. If each year the world population is 1.9 percent larger than it was the year before and nothing else changes, then each year resources are claimed by 1.9 percent more people, and in the course of thirty-seven years we shall be on the average twice as dense on the land and shall be consuming twice as much iron and other metals and twice as much crude oil. This statement is not true of pollution, where more-than-proportional effects enter. It is true of resources insofar as technology for production and patterns of consumption both remain constant.

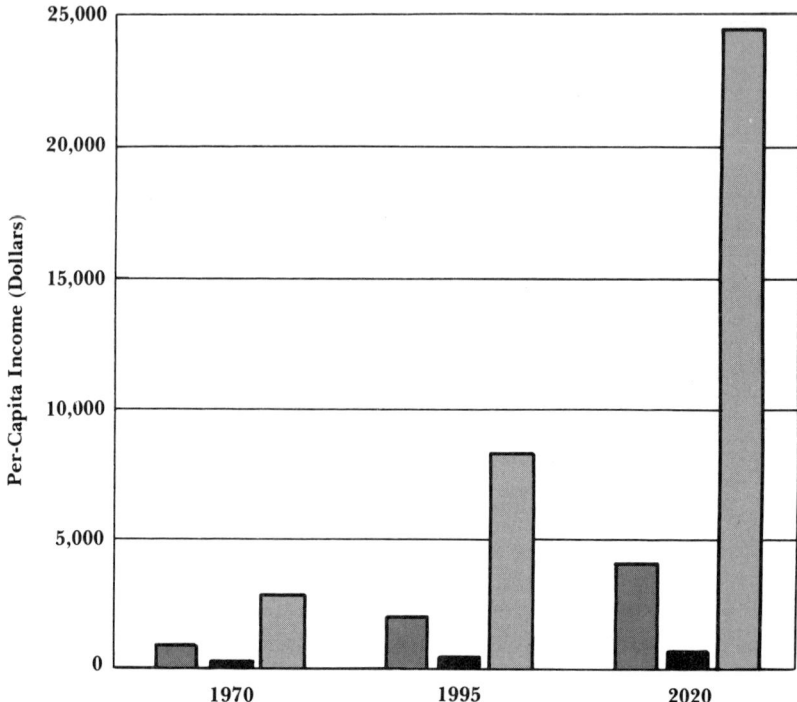

Figure 3: Widening gap between per-capita incomes in the developed and in the less developed countries is caused by the more rapid growth of population in poor countries. United Nations figures for the developed *(light gray)* and less developed *(black)* countries and for the world as a whole *(darker gray)* were projected on the assumption that total income will continue to increase at 5 percent per year in both sets of countries but that the population of the developed countries increases at only .5 percent per year while that of less developed countries increases at 2.5 percent.

Actually they do not remain constant; they exert effects in opposite directions. Technology has been stretching the use of materials. We know how to put the tin on the can more thinly; we can make rubber and fabrics out of coal; we recycle aluminum. The movement, guided by price changes is always toward less scarce materials. As income goes up, however, per-capita consumption increases: more cans are used, albeit each with a thinner layer of tin. Worse still, new materials are invented—detergents, plastics, insecticides—that take a long time to reenter the cycles of nature once we are through with them. It is the net effect of these tendencies that we need to estimate.

One way to get at the net effect of increased consumption per head and of technological improvements is to determine the residual change after population increase is allowed for. Let us try this for energy consumption in the United States in 1947 and 1973. The 1947 consumption was 1.21 billion tons of coal equivalent and the 1973 consumption was 2.55 billion. Meanwhile the population rose from 144 million to 210 million. If the larger population of 1973 had held to the same volume and patterns of consumption and production as the smaller population of 1947, it would have required 1.77 billion tons of coal equivalent. Hence of the total increase of 1.34 billion only .56 billion was due to population growth; the remainder of the increase, .78 billion, was due to affluence. Affluence was more important than population. Similar calculations can be made for metals and other materials, for pollution, for the primary caloric content of food, indeed for any kind of impact that can be measured.

As an alternative way of analyzing the consumption of materials, consider that from 1950 to 1970 the part of the world population that was affluent went from 200 million to 500 million: while total population increases at 1.9 percent per year, middle-class high consumers increase at 4.7 percent. Each high consumer requires the equivalent of three-quarters of a ton of grain, whereas the poor get by on a quarter of a ton. (The consequent ratio of land use is less than three to one, because agriculture is more efficient in rich countries.) The middle-class person requires from fifteen to thirty barrels of oil, whereas the poor person makes do with one barrel at most in the form of kerosene, bus fuel, and fertilizer. The land and energy content of clothing may be in a rich-to-poor ratio intermediate between those for food and for transport. As a kind of average of these several ratios, suppose the middle-class person has five times as much impact on the material base as the poor person. Then the average person on the high side of the poverty line must be taken as being equivalent to five people on the low side in fuel and metals consumed. In considering impact we therefore calculate as though in 1975 the planet had not 4 billion people aboard but 6.4 billion. Of these, 3.4 billion were poor and 3 billion represented the fivefold impact of a world middle class that probably numbered about 600 million.

This would make the average total impact of the small middle class on resources somewhat less than that of the large number of the poor. The middle class has been increasing at 4.7 percent per year, however, and the poor less than half as fast. At the growing edge the increase of affluence has much more effect than the increase of population; the movement of people into the middle class has more effect on materials and the environment than the increase in the number of poor people.

Natural resources account for less than 10 percent of the value of goods and services produced in the United States and other developed

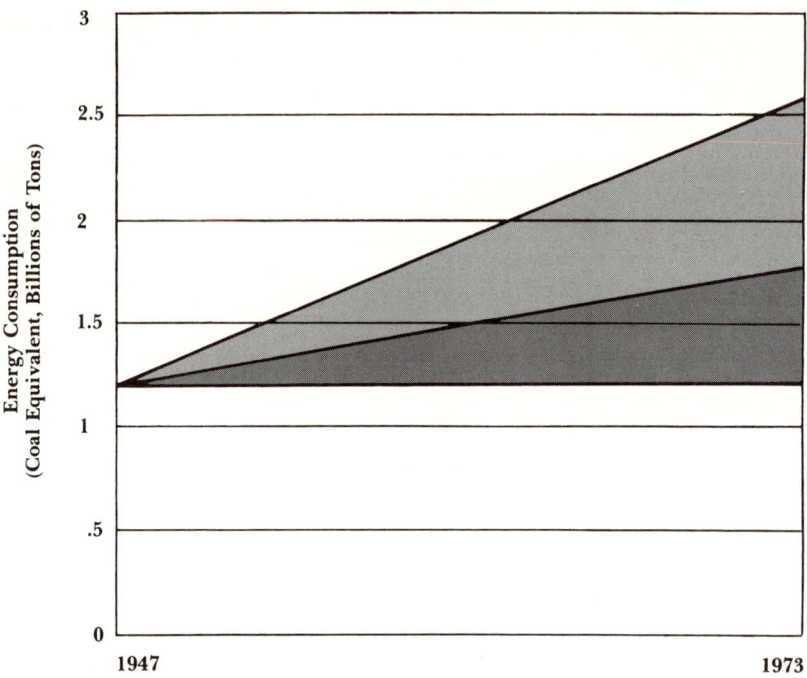

Figure 4: United States energy consumption would have increased from 1.21 billion tons of coal equivalent in 1947 to 1.77 billion tons in 1973 if it had merely kept pace with the rise in population. In fact, however, energy consumption rose to 2.55 billion tons in 1973. The increment *(light gray)* due to a rise in per-capita consumption stemming from affluence was larger than the increment *(dark gray)* attributable to population growth. The same is true of many other materials.

countries. Resources are hence curiously two-sided: extracting them accounts for only a small part of the cost, yet they are the sine qua non of existence, to say nothing of progress. And particular materials do run out. England's Industrial Revolution was in part a response to a firewood crisis: cheap coal had to be substituted for wood, which had become scarce and very dear. In America, on the other hand, wood was cheap and labor was dear, so that houses were built of wood rather than stone, which is more labor-intensive. Now timber is dear here also, and masonry and aluminum are substituted in some products. Plastics take the place of paper in packaging. Cultivated southern pine is used for newsprint instead of the limited pine and spruce of the northern forests.

Thus history shows the resilience of the productive system, its ability to substitute commoner materials for scarce ones. Nevertheless, the extrapolation of this capacity must take account of time. Invention, innovation, and capital replacement can proceed only at a certain pace. It is this pace of innovation that needs to be studied, since it sets the rate at which industrial society can spread in the face of environmental and resource limitations.

Limits to the spread of industrial society under present technology are suggested by the record of trade in raw materials over the past quarter century. To take one example, in 1950 the production and consumption of energy were in virtual balance for the developed countries as a whole. Their deficit amounted to less than 4 percent of consumption. By 1973 production in the developed countries had nearly doubled but consumption had far outrun it and the deficit had swollen to a third of consumption.

The story for metals and other resources is not very different. No country, developed or not, has been provided by nature with a greater quantity and variety of mineral and other resources than the United States. Yet even the United States had become a net importer of minerals by the 1920s, and it now imports all its platinum, mica, and chromium, 96 percent of its aluminum, 85 percent of its asbestos, 77 percent of its tin, and 28 percent of its iron—to select from a long list. Of course, the shortages of some of these minerals are not absolute but are a matter of price. The United States could produce all the aluminum it needs from domestic clay, but bauxite from Jamaica is cheaper. Having virtually exhausted the iron ore of the Mesabi Range, the United States resorts to lower-grade domestic taconite and to imports, in a proportion determined by prices.

The increase of more than 4 percent per year in the number of middle-class people who have come on the scene is too rapid in that these high consumers have to comb the world for resources, but on the other hand it is much too slow to satisfy the billions of people who are waiting in the wings. Whereas Europe, Japan, and the USSR made great gains during the United Nations Development Decades, most of Asia and Africa are dissatisfied with their progress. Moreover, a realistic calculation would probably show a larger gap between the impact on resources of those who have raised themselves from poverty and that of those who are still poor. The weight of a middle-class person is in many respects more than five times that of a peasant. It is to keep the argument conservative that I suppose the ratio is five times and that the world middle class triples every twenty-five years.

The combination of these two modest assumptions produces, as we have seen, a surprisingly high measure of impact for the end of the century, by which time the middle class, which was at 600 million in 1975, would increase to 1.8 billion and have the effect of five times that number, or 9 billion. The total impact projected to the year 2000 is, then, that of 9 billion plus 4.6 billion poor, or 13.6 billion people. This compares with an impact of 6.4 billion for 1975, calculated in the same way. If strains are already apparent in materials and energy, what will happen with a doubling of the rate of consumption?

The accelerating impact that appears from recognition of two categories of people rather than one category is offset in some degree by the decline in the impact per dollar of income once income rises beyond a certain level. People take very high incomes in services rather than in more and more automobiles. Moreover, the relation of impact to income varies from one culture to another, as an anthropologist would point out; an economist would add that the relation can be counted on to change as raw materials, and hence the goods made from them, become scarce and costly compared with less material-intensive forms of consumption. Although the impact on materials may taper off with increased wealth, the impact on air and water may be greater than proportional. There may be thresholds: the air may hold just so much carbon monoxide, a lake just so much fertilizer runoff, without undue effect, but beyond a certain critical point the effect may quickly rise to disaster levels. Such critical points clearly exist in renewable resources. Fishing or cutting timber up to a certain intensity does no damage at all, but continued overfishing or overcutting can destroy the fish or tree population.

In the years since 1973 the pressure of affluence on resources has lessened. That is partly due to increased prices of raw materials, partly due to the economic slowdown. No one can now say whether the future will be more like 1950–73 or like 1973–82.

The rate and direction of development of the period 1950–1970, unsatisfactory though it may be in that the absolute number of the poor would continue to increase until well into the twenty-first century, is still faster than can be sustained on present strategies. The resilience of the economic system, and technical innovation in particular, can be counted on to respond to needs, but only at a certain rate of speed. One can imagine sources of energy, the capacity to dispose of wastes and substitutes for metals all doubling in the century to come, but it is not easy to conceive of such a doubling in the fifteen years that would keep the middle class growing at 4.7 percent per year.

NOT A CEILING BUT A WINDOW

To say that civilization will collapse when oil supplies are exhausted, or that we will pollute ourselves out of existence, is to deny all responsive-

Resources and the World Middle Class

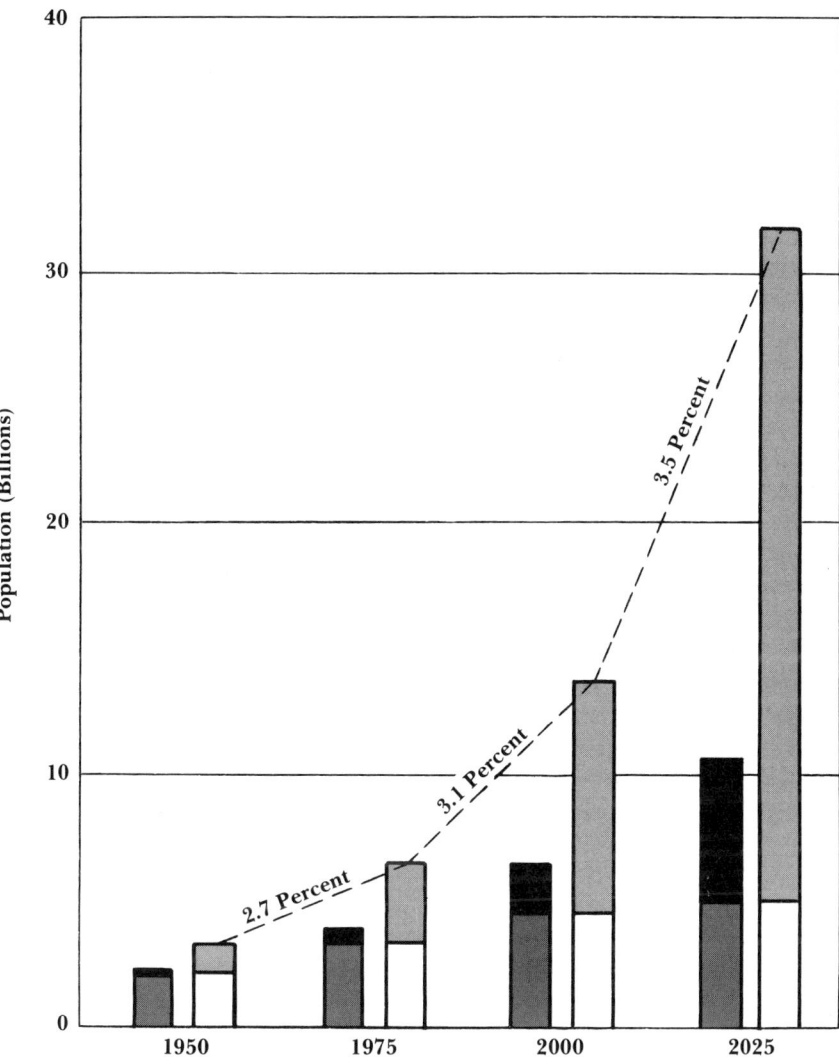

Figure 5: Future impact on world resources is affected by the growth of the middle class, whose members are assumed to consume five times as much as poor people, In population alone the middle class *(black)*, increasing at 4.5 percent per year, would eventually be larger than the poor population *(dark gray)*. When the middle class is multiplied by five, the resulting "consumption population" *(righthand column in each pair)* is seen to grow at an annual rate that increases from 2.7 to 3.1 and then to 3.5 percent. World resources are already strained by the 1975 "consumption population."

ness and resilience to the productive system. The geologist or resource expert tends to focus on the material and technical process he knows and may be less than imaginative with regard to how a substitute might be found to deal with a shortage. On the other hand, the economist may be too imaginative; he may too readily suppose substitutes can be found for anything as soon as it becomes scarce. The ensuing debate between pessimistic raw-material experts and optimistic economists has generated whatever knowledge we have on the subject. The middle ground to which both sides are tending is that every barrier that industrial expansion is now meeting can be surmounted by technological advance, but not in an instant. It is not a ceiling on total population and income that we have to deal with but a window. How large can the window be made?

One conclusion to be drawn from the arithmetic I did above is that a projection in terms of ratios is probably wrong in principle; in the face of natural and human limitations the pace of advance may be determined in absolute numbers rather than ratios. If, for example, pollution effects are proportional to fuel burned, then successive absolute increments in fuel consumption have the same bad effects on the fixed volume of the atmosphere. We should think not of the percent expansion of the middle class but of its absolute increase.

The calculation made in this way starts with the annual growth in world population of 75 million at the present time, gradually increasing to 100 million by the end of the century, and compares that increment with the number annually emerging into the middle class. If the latter went in a straight line from 200 million in 1950 to 500 million in 1970, then the average annual increase was 15 million. My stylized model, wherein industrial society expands through the emergence of people from the peasantry into city jobs as capital expands (while those not yet called remain at their old peasant incomes), goes back ultimately to Adam Smith. This simple application of the Smith model suggests that currently 15 million people join the middle class each year and 60 million join the poor. Even if the middle-class increment could rise to 20 million per year, the poor would still be increasing by 80 million per year at the end of the century. This at least is one reasonable extrapolation of the process of development in the postwar period. Other population estimates are lower than the United Nations, but accepting them would lead to the same result: the large majority of the new generation will be poor.

The natural increase of the affluent population will create difficulties in the years ahead even though birth rates are low. Suppose the window is wide enough for 20 million to pass through it each year. Who will they be? The way the world is made, the children of the currently affluent of America, Europe, and Japan will have first claim. The USSR has found no way of preventing its elite from placing their children in the elite, and neither has the United States. On the basis of 600 million for the

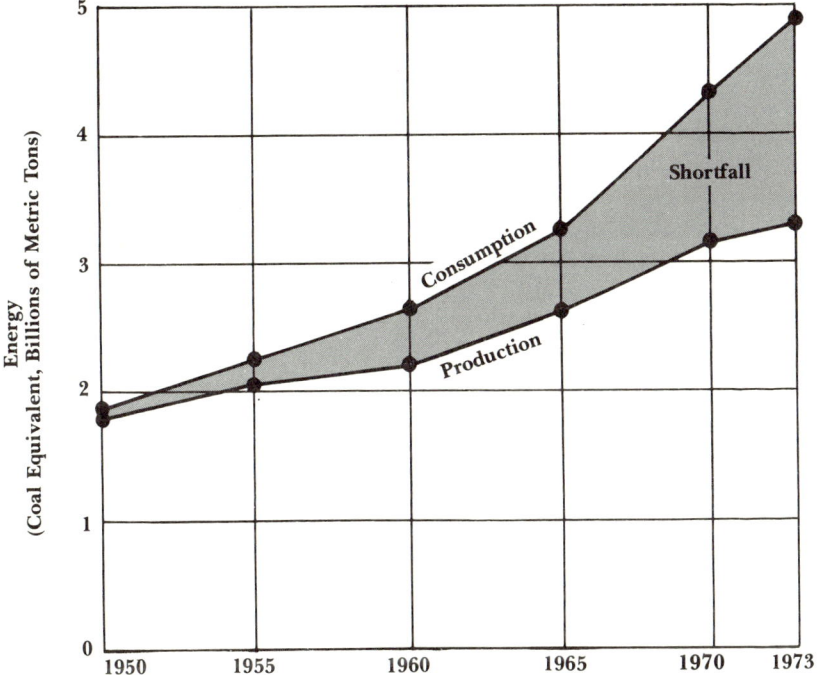

Figure 6: Consumption and production of energy were about balanced in 1950 in the developed countries: they produced the coal, oil, gas and hydropower whose energy they consumed, except for a small shortfall made up by imports from less developed countries. By 1973 rising production had been outstripped by consumption; shortfall amounted to a third of consumption.

middle class in 1975, a net natural-increase rate of .5 percent means 3 million children per year in excess of deaths. Apart from children who simply replace their parents or grandparents, of the 20 million net admissions each year 3 million would be further children of those who have already entered the middle class and 17 million would be new entrants. And these 17 million new entrants would be divided among the poor of the developed countries and those of the less developed countries, with the former having the better chance. Poor people in the poor countries sense that the odds against them and against their children are great.

All of this, it should be noted, can be seen as a critique not of development but of one particular model of development. The distinction between poor and middle class represents the Brazilian and the

Russian direction but not the Chinese. Whether because of China's special culture or the personality of Mao Tse-tung, both the specialization that equips people for middle-class jobs and the durable structures of industry and administration in which those jobs have their place were insistently denied there. Yet the retreat from Mao's philosophy since his death shows how strong are the inherent forces of inequality.

Robert Malthus gave us a land theory of value, Karl Marx a labor theory, and development economists since World War II a capital theory. Land, labor, and capital are plainly all needed (and to assign priority to any one may be as much an ideological choice as a practical one), but a dynamic factor superimposed on all of them is new scientific and technical knowledge. At many points we need to know more in order to even discover the problems we face: only recently have we found that insecticides can be dangerous poisons to organisms other than insects, and that the current worldwide rise in skin cancer may be related to depletion of the ozone layer of the upper atmosphere. Knowledge is needed even to see where the window restricting passage into the middle class is located, and only knowledge can open it wider.

Speeding World Development

Other ways of widening the window have been suggested. One is to raise the price of the raw materials on whose export some less developed countries depend for foreign exchange. Price increases such as those of the Organization of Petroleum Exporting Countries (OPEC) can have little overall effect, however, on the number of middle-class people in the world (although they have some effect on whether the newly middle-class will speak Spanish or Arabic or English). Who ultimately bears the burden of such price raises is not clear. Some of the burden is carried by poor countries that are not endowed with raw materials; when the repercussions have worked themselves out, India may find it has contributed a higher proportion of its income to Saudi Arabian opulence than the United States has. Certainly some United States fertilizer that would have gone to India before 1973 now goes to the Middle East; German chemical-plant investments are similarly diverted. The offsetting of oil price rises by French arms sales to Iran has everything to do with national power and little to do with the total distribution of poverty or even the national distribution. In any case only a small fraction of the world population is in resource-rich areas.

A second way to help more people escape from poverty might be for those who have already entered the middle class to moderate their consumption. If one meat eater cuts his consumption by 100 calories, then five grain eaters can increase theirs by 100 calories. If American automobiles were smaller, more metals and fuels would be available for automobiles in Zaïre and Bangladesh as well as—more immediately—fertilizer plants in those countries. If urban Americans were to live like the equally affluent Swedes, United States energy consumption might be halved. The trouble is that goods, as well as jobs that require materials, fit into other social activities in an interlocking scheme that is hard to change; social configurations are as solid a reality as raw materials. The years since 1973 have seen some real progress toward conservation.

Foreign aid and investment along conventional lines are a third possibility. They have aided in the development of some countries (Canada is a striking example), but for various reasons the volume is inadequate to the magnitude of the problem for most of the world's population. Even where investment is solidly based in economics, some intellectuals argue that it creates dependency, and the politicians of poor countries often respond by expropriation. Ironically the very mention of expropriation is expensive for the poor country because it makes investors demand a higher return.

One can say that better prices for raw materials, reduction of consumption by the rich countries, and conventional foreign aid and foreign investment all ought to be pursued, but the experience of the 1950s and the 1960s shows that they will not make a decisive difference in the size of the window through which escape from poverty is sought.

KNOWLEDGE: THE DECISIVE FACTOR

What will make a decisive difference is knowledge of the following: how to produce amenities with less material, how to substitute materials that are common for those that are scarce, how to get desired results with less energy, and how to obtain that energy from renewable sources rather than from fossil fuels. We have seen some results in the past decade. With the advent of integrated circuits, a calculator that cost $1,000 and weighed forty pounds is now replaced by one that costs $10 and weighs a few ounces. Artificial earth satellites have lowered the cost of communication; they provide television in Indian villages and may ultimately make telephone calls around the world as cheap as local calls. Synthetic polymers have replaced cotton and wool and thus released land. The list of what is still needed is too long to itemize: efficient solar collectors, compact storage batteries to run automobiles on centrally generated power, stronger and cheaper plastics (for automobile bodies, for instance), and so on.

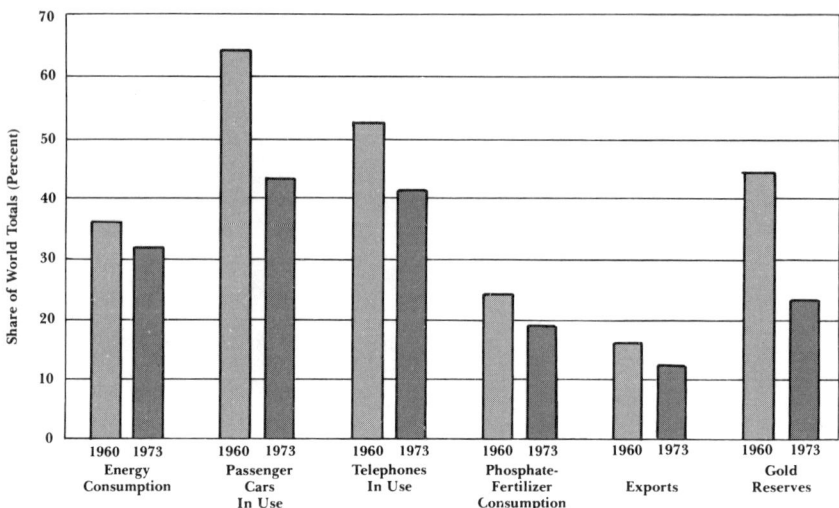

Figure 7: Increase in affluence outside the U.S., particularly in Japan and Europe, has reduced the disproportionate U.S. share of energy consumption, durable goods, and other indicators of wealth. Movement of more people across the poverty line would extend this effect.

If the time dimension in the implementation of these inventions is crucial, then everything that is done to hasten invention will pay off for the world movement past the poverty line. There are many stages, from pure scientific investigation to the translation of science into technology, to the engineering that makes a production model out of a working prototype and finally on to parts contracting and the assembly line, and each stage takes time. The United States, once foremost in the speed with which it could convert knowledge into the production of goods, is said to be losing this preeminence; a slowing down would have bad consequences not only for the American competitive position among industrial nations but also for the world escape from poverty. The need is not confined to scientific and engineering knowledge; prompt solutions are also required to many problems in biology and medicine, climatology and geophysics. The technical and social knowledge for birth control is of special importance; whatever the size of the window through which the poor escape into the middle class, the lowering of births will at least bring closer the day when world poverty ceases to increase in absolute amount.

Some part of American research has been directed specifically to labor-intensive devices suited to poor countries, and that line of investigation ought to be encouraged. Even after the Green Revolution, for example, poor countries still have special agricultural problems. Apart from such specific research, the United States helps all countries when it develops knowledge that makes its own industry more efficient.

Both production constraints and environmental constraints limit the growth of the world middle class. The way the United States can help to open the window is not through schemes for division of the existing product but by contributing knowledge that will expand the product. Solving production and environmental problems starts at home, but any genuine contribution will have value worldwide. Incentives can be devised to direct technology in environment-saving rather than environment-damaging directions. No one can forecast how much time it will take to solve any one technical problem, let alone the complex of problems, but that time—whatever it may be—will be shortened by a larger and more immediate mobilization of scientific and engineering talent.

CHAPTER **10**

Development and the Elimination of Poverty

Why does inequality in poor countries still persist after at least thirty years during which the need for leveling as well as raising incomes has been in the consciousness of all concerned? Why the great expansion of government, with policies that inhibit growth of a native bourgeoisie? Why the handicapping of agriculture through contrived prices and other policies, in countries where many are hungry and the main industry of agriculture is the most obvious basis of a higher standard of living? Why does the educational system almost wholly disregard agriculture, and why is research to improve it neglected?

There is at least one common component of the answer to each of these apparently very different questions concerning inequality, government expansion, neglect of agriculture, the urban bias of education and research. That component of the answer is the drive toward a certain way of living, one so taken for granted that it is not noticed—the style of life that we may call middle-class consumerist, with all the good and bad connotations of those terms.

GROUPS AND CLASSES IN DEVELOPMENT

Development occurs in a context of older institutions, and change of those institutions is a central part of the development process. Everywhere a new leading group has been gaining ascendancy over pre-existing landlords. For the new group development is the means by which it can assert itself, overcome settled landlords, and gain popular support as it achieves development. The traditional culture that gave ideological underpinning to the previous leadership ceases to satisfy, and the new group promises change to something different. In place of religion come goods of hitherto unknown variety and attractiveness, a fully legitimated cargo cult, a vision to be made real by the mastery of modern technique.

The middle class has access to education and can understand the issues, is aware of its interests and able to act politically to further them. Schooling and influence enable it to pass its status to its young, and so it tends to be hereditary. (Nee [1980] shows this even for the equalitarian society of China.) It recruits from the peasantry through the process of urbanization, in highly selective fashion. Its initial task is to defeat the rural landholding class. Once that is accomplished its influence is decisive, for the dispersed, uneducated peasantry are no match for it. The peasant in an economy exporting rice cannot judge the effect on himself of a tariff on flashlight batteries; once it is explained to him that this is a way of getting cheaper batteries in the long run, if only he will be patient, he may well cease to argue. Yet even when he understands well enough to rebel, the government carries on without him, determining national policies in the light of its own (urban) interests while identifying itself with progress and development.

DIFFUSION OF THE MODERN CULTURE

Development has many attributes and may be defined by any one of these. It may be seen as the investments in people that make them more valuable human capital; as the accumulation of physical capital, the rise of income, or the creation of a certain state apparatus, usually with social welfare coloring. Without dropping the other definitions, my discussion regards it as the diffusion of a certain culture, and the dominance of a new class that carries that culture. Like any culture this one exists in people's heads, but its expression depends on material artifacts. My point of view is complementary to the view of development as rising average income per head, and it attempts to place the economics of development in a social and cultural framework.

THE MODERN WAY OF LIFE

The middle-class consumerist style has been taught by the United States and Europe to the Third World. It consists of heated and cooled homes equipped with telephones, television sets, and refrigerators; transport by automobile; procurement of foodstuffs and other supplies in self-service supermarkets. It most typically goes on in cities with paved streets, the countryside between those cities laced with networks of railroads, canals, paved roads, and air transport. Literacy is essential to it, and the daily press and monthly magazines are conspicuous. The content of its press and other media has remarkable similarity worldwide: local, national, and world politics, urban crime, and other problems like the cost of living that arouse its mass public. Whether there is a worldwide culture of poverty one can doubt—poor people seem to retain their indigenous and differentiated ways rather well—but there *is* a worldwide middle-class culture—right down to such matters as when and how to eat one's three meals, what to read, what to do on workdays, and how to spend one's weekends.

Of course, national and regional variants exist. Most obvious is language; the new life goes on not in its language of origin, English, but in Indonesian or Thai or Portuguese. The supermarket in Paris carries better wines, cuts its meat differently, has better bread than the supermarket in Chicago. Automobiles in the United States are heavier than those in Japan. But these differences are smaller than the differences between the middle-class person of any of those countries and his national predecessor, and they are being further reduced.

It is unimaginative to see our way of life as unique, as the only form that our wealth can assume. Plainly we could, like the wealthy Buddhist, consume our productivity in the form of leisure for contemplation. Like the ancient Greeks, we could live simply and spend our time in gymnastics, amateur science, and philosophy. Like an eighteenth-century minor prince, we could indulge in playing and listening to chamber music. We could support gardens that would outshine Versailles. These are not the mainstream activities of the middle-class consumer culture.

What parts of modern living are dictated by man's physical needs and what parts culturally chosen, perhaps as symbols of status? Up to 3,000 calories of food per day, heating in winter, clothing, transport, some entertainment are in various degrees essential; people will seek them as soon as their income permits. However, the food need not include 500 calories of meat, as is proven by wealthy Indians who from time immemorial have eaten no meat at all and lived long and vigorous lives with vegetable sources of protein. Historical cultures show much variation in food, clothing, transport, and entertainment, and only on an arbitrary definition do all of these represent a lower standard of living than the one called "modern."

The one aspect of living in past ages that cannot be reproduced in our age of mass consumption is servants. If the middle-class style of life is to be universal in a community, then by definition it cannot depend on domestic help. Once the wages of those who might be servants approach 10 percent of the incomes of those who might be masters, servants can no longer be afforded.

The American Contribution

Americans have pioneered in the organization of the work place in office, factory, and home. The design of the home, with its kitchen that includes a refrigerator and other electrical appliances, is chiefly of American origin. The three-day weekend spent on the highway and at the beach was first ours.

Cheap land made American society unusually equalitarian from the beginning. Under the constraint that for most of us individual wealth can no longer be consumed in domestic service, we have invented new forms of consumption. Motorboats, record players, along with cigarettes and daily newspapers, that we may or may not have invented but did much to spread, take their place in a culture that has become worldwide. The innovation of telephones about the turn of the century, cheap automobiles and refrigerators in the 1920s, sound films and radios in the 1930s, television in the 1950s, computers and international air travel in the 1960s, has kept our culture moving.

Spread by the development process, this culture is now becoming worldwide. The demonstration effect of films and other media teaches a pattern of consumption that is temporarily beyond the capacity of developing nations to support. Their rapid acquiring of needs causes premature spending and impedes the saving and investment that would bring fulfillment through efficient national production and trade. But the demonstration effect has not had a large impact on economic policies. It forms a very small part of the models of development, mathematical or other, that are used to guide policy. We should take it seriously, both in its negative aspects, and positively, as the motivator of development.

Measuring the Poor and the Middle Class

The usefulness of the concept of the world middle class does not entirely depend upon our being able to measure it. We talk about the hungry, the poor, the managerial class, and many others, even though there is no universally accepted way of drawing a boundary around such categories.

The work of the Social Security Administration has been the major serious effort to count the poor in the United States. Choosing a point on the overall income distribution for individuals or families will not do; one must make specific assumptions about requirements, which will differ according to the respective ages of a couple, and the number of its children. In the United States it is easier to measure poverty, and take the middle class as a residual; when we extend the measure to other countries, it is on the whole easier to measure the middle class, which is the minority, and take the poor as the residual.

The United States Department of Agriculture designed a 1961 Economy Food Plan that forms the basis for the calculation of the poverty income thresholds, recognizing family size, sex and age of the family head, number of children under eighteen, and farm-nonfarm residence. Farm levels are set at 85 percent of the corresponding nonfarm level. Annual adjustments are made on the basis of the Consumer Price Index, but the consumption levels continue to be those established for the base year 1963 *(Statistical Abstract,* 1978, p. 438). The number of families that fall below the poverty line in the United States (ibid., p. 465) was just under 40 million in the late 1950s, and had dropped to 25 million by 1977. Particularly useful are the breakdowns, showing for instance that of white families, 8.9 percent were below the poverty line in 1977; of black, 29.0 percent; of families with male heads, 6.9 percent, with female heads, 32.8 percent. Among Puerto Rican families with female heads, 70.4 percent were below. In New Hampshire 7.9 percent of the population were below the poverty line in 1975; in Mississippi 26.1 percent were below. Among those sixty-five and over, 14.1 percent were poor in 1977.

We note that the proportion of families that own automobiles in the United States in 1974 was 83.8 percent, at a time when the proportion above the poverty line was 88.8 percent. Apparently owning a car is a somewhat more stringent criterion than being above the poverty line. Different individuals are involved; 37 percent of households with in-

Table 1 World Population and Its Division into Poor and Middle Class (Millions). Illustrative numbers.

	POOR	MIDDLE CLASS	TOTAL
1950	2,300	200	2,500
1980	3,600	800	4,400
Increase	1,300	600	1,900
Average Increase per Year	43	20	63

comes under $3,000 have cars, and 3 percent of those above $25,000 do not have cars (*Abstract*, 1978, p. 474).

Thus the Social Security Administration figures, extrapolated to 1980, show 24 million poor, 196 million middle-class, for a total population of 220 million. How can this breakdown be extended to the rest of the world?

A sharp dividing line between poor and middle class is hardly to be expected. It is easy enough to see the difference between the resident of a suburb of Detroit who has a job as office manager with General Motors, and the Javanese peasant with half an acre on which he is trying to grow enough to feed his five children, but it is not easy to draw a sharp boundary through the many intermediate conditions.

If the world population is now 4.4 billion, and of these 800 million are middle class, then 3.6 billion are poor. Let us calculate, however inadequately, the annual increase of the poor (Table 1).

The important matter is that a similar calculation gives 200 million for the middle class of 1950. The entry of Europe and Japan, plus some progress in the Third World, was what brought the total to 800 million by 1980. If the same amount of progress is occurring now as in the years 1950–80, then each year 20 million new entrants join the middle class.

Since the world population increases by about 75 million per year, if 20 million of these are middle-class, then 55 million are poor. (Only a tiny fraction of 1 percent is "rich" in any sense, and our argument does not need to consider them separately.)

This scenario is optimistic in various ways. It assumes that the economic advance of 1950 to 1980 is continuing and applies now. The pace of absolute real income gain in the early 1980s is less than the average of 1950–80, and (omitting the oil price rise) the part of the increase obtained by the poor countries in the present time of recession could well be less than it was in a time of more widespread prosperity.

Hollis Chenery (1974, p. 460) has published calculations of the poor population of the world, using a more austere definition than ours. His definition of poverty is consumption of under 2,150 calories per day per person, which represents the boundary in India, and other countries are taken at the point in their income distribution corresponding approximately to the forty-fifth percentile of the Indian population (ibid., p. 459). He finds 59 percent of the population in poverty in Indonesia, 55 percent in Uganda, 43 percent in Pakistan, 46 percent in India. Our purpose is different; it aims to see how large a fraction enjoys middle-class high energy consumption, based on the United States standard of living.

Production

Being middle-class is not a matter of consumption alone. Certain kinds of work are middle-class, and other kinds (like being a peasant, even a rich one) are not. Office work at a salary that permits owning a car and an adequately equipped house is the ideal; if the salary does not permit buying a car, then obtaining one as a perquisite of office will do. The boundary of the middle class does not coincide with that of nonmanual workers. With contemporary wage scales in advanced countries and in less developed ones, manual and nonmanual wages converge so that all can aspire to middle-class style.

Middle-class workers seek to avoid the hazards of entrepreneurship. The hurly-burly of the early Ford or Carnegie epoch is no longer the ideal either in its native America or abroad. Much better is the job of senior administrator in government, working according to fixed rules and understandings within a framework of law, with no personal capital at stake. Next in desirability to a job in government, and paying better, is being hired by a multinational corporation. Once again there is little in common between the work life of the Thai or Nigerian local executive of Exxon and the life of its founder Rockefeller.

If the multinationals have access nearly everywhere, despite so many words said so loudly against them, it is partly because their kind of steady operation, with administratively determined salary scales and relatively fixed hours of work, is understandable and gratifying. They are seen as offering the right kind of jobs to the right kind of people. But governments offer far more employment than do multinationals.

The entry of cultural preferences into the work world creates a difficulty when government is a large employer. The kind of work people like to do, and which they somehow manage to get jobs doing, diverges from the kind of work that produces the goods on which collectively they want to spend their salaries. In a competitive economy this is no problem: the total production of all concerns is bought by the total of their employees, or by outsiders; any concern that produces things no one wants goes out of business and its employees look for other jobs. But the government employee may be engaged in administering the collection of taxes, or the organization of cooperatives, or the country's foreign policy. These activities make little contribution to producing the groceries he seeks to buy at the supermarket or the plumbing fixtures for his new house. This lack of congruence between what the person wants to spend his work time doing, and the sorts of goods he wants to spend his salary on, could well be the subject of economic study. Elaborate five-year plans involving heavy government expenditure provide little protection against such lack of congruence to which noncompetitive elements in every economy are subject, and which seem to be a special hazard of the less developed countries.

RELIEF OF POVERTY VERSUS A NEW CULTURE

Those sponsoring development, whether in the poor countries as actors, or in rich countries as observers, rarely describe the process as the preceding paragraphs have done. They see its objectives as the relief of poverty, the lessening of hunger and sickness, the spread of education. It is of course all of these things, as well as the creation and spread of a social group that we call middle-class, and this last aspect is stressed here only because the growth of this group received less attention.

Of course the middle-class way is relief of poverty for some. Those who have gained entry into it do have enough to eat, are well-clothed, have adequate medical services, can read and write. Yet such relief of poverty seems to be incidental to the process. For if adequate food and clothing, basic medical services, and literacy were the main objectives of development, it would go on in a very different way from that now pursued. Brazil's national income per capita of $1,700 could provide these amenities for every one of its 120 million inhabitants. Yet in fact the majority of its inhabitants, and conspicuously those in the northeast, lack these altogether, while others in the south have them and much more—television sets, automobiles, air conditioning. After thirty years of formal development effort in seventy-five countries, we do not need to confine our discussion to what development *ought* to be; we can infer the objective of the process from actual observation: the diffusion of the artifacts that support the middle-class way of life. In a poor country only a minority can have these.

While the particular culture of the middle class belongs to the second half of the twentieth century, yet the idea of an urban industrial group with incomes far higher than its rural contemporaries goes back much farther. Adam Smith saw development as taking place in the measure in which material capital accumulated in cities. With each increment of city capital, some jobs would be created. A new textile factory or pin-making concern or steel mill could offer wages high enough to attract people from the countryside. Until the call to city employment came from a productive enterprise, the peasant would remain in his ancestral village, doing what he and his forebears had been doing since time immemorial, in a static society that was no burden to urban industry.

But Adam Smith's path of development is out of ideological favor now, replaced by an alternative offered in its clearest form by Mao Tse-tung. On this equalitarian pattern, which is indeed the relief of poverty, everyone would go up at the same time. It would not be a matter of a few joining the middle class each year, but rather of everyone in the country having a small increase of income each year.

The difference in the distribution of the increment of income between the two ways of doing development appears conspicuously in the physical accoutrements. On the equalitarian path, instead of a few having automobiles in the early stages, everyone would have a bicycle. Instead of college for a few, everyone would learn to read and write. Instead of rags for most and tailored suits for a few, all would wear neat and sturdy, if not very elegant, clothing. Corresponding differences would appear in medical services, in diets, in housing, in entertainment.

The two routes of development can end up at the same place. If 2 percent of the original population enter the middle class each year and have five times their original income, then at the end of fifty years all would have been relieved of poverty. If the income of everyone goes up by 10 percent of its original value each year, then at the end of fifty years all have fivefold their predevelopment incomes on the simple interest basis of this comparison. But though the end point may be the same, the path is different.

Middle-class living is a rounded entity, a lump that seems unstable piecemeal. Those who obtain some part of it want the rest quickly; they are not willing to be held back by the slow pace that raising all of their fellow citizens simultaneously would require. Each element brings a demand for the next. One who obtains a transistor radio wants to grade up to a television set. A kind of standard package is in everyone's mind—including a house, automobile, and the means to do some traveling; within the house must be electric lighting, a refrigerator, and a television set. One can imagine people being satisfied to slow down their progress once they have these facilities, and allowing the rest of the country to catch up, but not before. Lower-level substitutes are unsatisfactory. For those who are well started on this path, a bicycle or even a motor scooter will not do for transport, nor will the services of a barefoot doctor be acceptable.

The consolidation of the less egalitarian form of development is furthered by the institution of the family; the man who has made it to the good life will do everything possible to ensure that his sons have access to the same. The means vary from regime to regime; in the USSR one cannot pass on corporation shares to one's children, but one can exercise influence over their education and subsequent employment.

TEMPORARY INEQUALITY MAY BE THE ONLY WAY

Can the phenomenon of unequal development within a country occur in a free market, or is it the result of governments determining the kinds of goods that are produced and the kinds of jobs provided? That Adam Smith first described this route of development may suggest that it mainly takes place in the free market he recommended, but we cannot be sure. We need comparisons of income distribution between places like Hong Kong, where market freedom prevails, and directed economies like the USSR or Cambodia.

That the tendency to inequality is strong was noted in China, where Mao warned of the danger, giving the USSR as an example to be avoided. The Cultural Revolution was the radical expression of the view that people are intrinsically equal and the masses can do everything. Statistics are needed, but not specialized statisticians—everyone can get into the counting. Forecasting of earthquakes can be provided by the masses, each person making observations near his own house with rudimentary instruments, or by watching the behavior of animals. Plain food, clothing and shelter will do; work as well as consumption can be the same for all.

Yet even China since 1976 has relaxed its insistence that city youths must spend time in the countryside, and that higher education and research wait until all poverty has been relieved.

We cannot pretend to describe the deep social forces that make the unequal pattern of development. It is not enough to say that the mass media, including films, have taught that there is a certain way to live, and everyone wants it. That they want it would not suffice to explain why the Indian factory manager can get it, while more numerous peasants go to bed hungry, when the latter can outvote the former by dozens to one. It can only be that even in democracies, the levers of power are in the hands of the middle class, which determines the policies that make the cities grow and put subways ahead of irrigation schemes.

Rural-Urban Migration

This tendency of the middle class perpetually to enlarge itself acts in various ways to increase first city and then suburban populations. Harris and Todaro, H. Rempel, and others regard the city poor as queued up to enter the protected labor market, which would make them middle-class or close to it. The city attracts people because it is so visibly the place where important things are going on. Its boulevards and great buildings symbolize the nation, the great social organization of our age. If people have a chance of becoming middle-class anywhere, it is here.

Whatever expands city facilities, or lowers the price of foodstuffs, increases the size of the city. Numerous economic measures provide material support to life in the city. We can even suggest a positive feedback that results from legislation and administrative action. The price of rice is, in many countries, fixed well below the world market (translated at a true foreign exchange rate), and a law requires peasants to deliver some part of their crop at this price. Officials go into the countryside to execute the procurement. The unpleasantness and actual loss contribute to causing some of the peasants to leave and go to the city. That increases the need for foodstuffs, including rice, in the city, so that the procurement activity is intensified; the result is to discourage more peasants, and so on. Where the countryside is overpopulated, such feedback can build up city populations rapidly.

One might think that rather than positive feedback there would be an equilibrium point in migration. In a crowded countryside, when some people have left, the remainder should be able to make a better living. When enough have left, the living should be equal to what migrants could get by going to the city, and at that equilibrium point, migration should stop. The reason it does not, as Alfred Marshall pointed out a long time ago (quoted by Lipton, 1977:376), is that there is selection on who comes to the city. While empirical studies show mixed results, on the whole those who come to the city are better educated and have more initiative. Thus, their departure does not make things better, but worse, for the rural areas concerned.

We can imagine policies that would discourage internal migration. Taxes to provide urban services could be levied on urban real estate rather than coming out of the national budget. Inputs to agriculture could be subsidized. Some effort is made in this direction, but it is not enough.

Better than subsidies of farm inputs would be fair prices for farm outputs. Aside from the compulsory procurement at government-established low prices in Burma and many other countries, governments often make market purchases at harvest time in what amounts to a forced sale, as the farmer is pressed by debtors and unable to hold his crop for more favorable markets.

On the other side, the inputs to industry bought abroad tend to be artificially cheapened, most commonly by overvaluation of the local currency. Even if capital goods are cheapened equally for the farmer and the urban industrialist, there is a bias, for capital is a more important part of the productive process in the city. Credit in the city is more available and cheaper than in the countryside. And the output of industry is made more expensive by tariffs, by trade unionization of employees (practically impossible for peasants), and by monopoly practices permitted by the limited number of establishments.

Such are the policies that improve the lot of city people and so increase city size. They help explain the perversity of urbanization, in which a Mexico City of 15 million or a Cairo of 10 million threaten to double by the end of the century. Most newcomers to the city hope ultimately to obtain middle-class jobs. Those who have already attained such jobs and are in power may not be directly trying to expand their numbers, but it is hard for them to avoid doing so. The urban amenities that they introduce—roads, local transport, schools—are available in some degree to the poor. The elite cannot make the city better for itself without in some degree making it better for the newcomers, thereby encouraging more newcomers. It could of course forcibly prevent migration, or expel existing migrants, and this has been tried in Moscow, Jakarta, and elsewhere, but has not been successful. (An exception is Phnom Penh of the late 1970s, where extreme violence caused rapid deurbanization.)

The masses in the capital city are physically close enough to the government to communicate their wishes, as those of Cairo and other cities have done to force the government to cancel an announced increase of food prices. Such an increase would help the peasant and discourage migration.

In the same way, the housing problem is constituted by the pressure of those within the city for middle-class accommodation at something below the equilibrium price. Governments cannot always resist the very reasonable demands of their employees, and other members of the protected segment of the labor force, for decent places to live. And with wages insufficient to buy premises, with a poorly organized mortgage market, the government intervenes and builds houses, with scarce funds that could equally have gone to rural roads, schools, irrigation works, latrines, or other rural investment.

Local transport within the city is often government-run. The cost of the buses it imports, and the fares it charges, are public matters, and very much the business of administrators and legislators. They tend to set the custom duties on imported vehicles, and the fares charged, so as to hold down the cost of transport to users. They do not always set the fares high enough for even their low-cost imported buses, and when the bus operations make a loss, it is covered from general revenues, which often means from the rural sector. The middle class may not partake directly of this benefit, since it uses its own cars. But the middle class benefits indirectly from reducing the cost of transport within the city for subordinate office and factory workers on whom it depends.

The necessity for food supplies to permit the townspeople to engage in manufacturing was understood 200 years ago. Thus, Adam Smith: "... it is the surplus produce of the country only, or what is over and above the maintenance of the cultivators, that constitutes the subsistence of the town, which can therefore increase only with the increase of the surplus produce" (quoted by Lipton, 1977:94). For Cantillon, " ... towns are limited by the product of the land owned by the landowners who live there, net of transport costs" (Lipton, 1977:374).

Some of these points are now being recognized, and efforts are being made on behalf of agricultural output, efforts mostly guided by city people. One would not expect the passive elements of the peasantry to take the initiative. The Mexican government is investing heavily in modernization, and it is stressing the rural use of machinery. "If we do not mechanize our countryside we run grave risks . . . To mechanize the farm is an urgent task." So runs the official message on television and in the press. The man with the bullock is no longer portrayed as a romantic figure, but one to be replaced by a tractor operator, supported by soil chemists, agronomists, irrigation specialists, and bankers advancing rural credit. All this will indeed provide employment, but for specialists and not for the masses in the countryside. It will produce a surplus available for sale abroad and to the cities of Mexico, but will not inhibit movement to the city—indeed, in the degree to which it is successful, it could accelerate migration to the city.

Here much depends on the patterns of consumption and residence of the new classes in the rural areas. If the tractor operator and the soil chemist live in the city and commute to the rural area, or if they live in the village but take out their new incomes in city goods, following the middle-class pattern of life, then unemployment in the countryside will be greater than ever, and cityward migration will continue or accelerate. If they take out their incomes in domestic retainers and live like the caciques of tradition, or if they adopt the style of the English squire with ten or twenty servants, then the countryside will be able to hold its people. But no one expects this—the new agricultural producers want automobiles, refrigerators, television sets. The present policy, sound as it is from the balance-of-payments viewpoint, will do little to check urbanization.

In few fields does the middle-class urban bias reveal itself as clearly as in education. Most schools above the primary level are in cities. The ordinary peasant's children stand little chance of attending. The disparity in numbers of secondary schools between rural and urban areas is matched by the disparity in quality. Moreover, the primary schools that are now to be found everywhere in the developing world, and which are attended at least long enough for most peasant children to learn to read and write, have little to do with peasant life. Rather than being planned to educate and train better farmers, they serve as a selection device by which academic ability is discovered and recruited for secondary schools and jobs in the cities.

INEQUALITY IS INEVITABLE?

Is it possible that creating a middle-class enclave, and allowing that to expand until it covers the country and then the world, is still the efficient way to eliminate poverty? The demographic argument for this view is that to raise the poor a little at a time with the resources available would only encourage childbearing, at the same time as it increased the survivors among children born. Only when people have a quantum leap into the middle class do they control their childbearing. This crude argument does not take into account the spectacular fall in the birth rate in equalitarian China and in Sri Lanka, but it may be valid for some places.

An analogous argument applies to saving and the accumulation of physical capital. If increases in production go to the poor majority of the population, necessarily in small amounts, they will only add to consumption. The family that is on the edge of starvation does not save any appreciable part of its marginal increase of income. Hence, confining the initial benefits of the development process to a minority, each of whom obtains substantial increase of income, will enable a larger part of the increment of income to be saved.

It may also be said that if full development is the ultimate objective, then it is physically more economical to provide it for a small part of the population and then spread out, rather than provide a little bit at a time for all. For the methods of production and the artifacts themselves are wholly different. If automobiles are the only satisfactory means of transport, then why start by making millions of bicycles—better make a few automobiles, and build up the related organization and skills; it will be easier to expand later than to convert from bicycles. The argument is carried further: to produce more food along present lines is to expand the peasant sector, which cannot be development, since it has been going on for centuries. Better start up new lines of activity in manufacturing, which will then later turn out tractors and other agricultural implements, and transform agriculture to more productive forms.

Another reason for depriving the peasant and arranging tariffs, exchange rates, utility prices, and taxes so as to favor city industry is that extreme encouragement is necessary if the new enterprises are to start at all. Imperial Germany's tariffs protected its infant industry against that of England. Japan has used even more drastic kinds of protection, and continued them long after it had attained preeminent manufacturing efficiency. No one can say that the policy was ineffective.

SHORTAGE OF RESOURCES AND THE ZERO SUM GAME

Great resources accord with a generous attitude among individuals and social classes. The gain of one takes little away from others. When the era of planned and assisted development began in the 1950s, the rise of the poor countries seemed to be in the interest of the rich. As a minimum, the developing countries would provide markets for advanced products, and their increase of wealth could not possibly take anything from us. But in the 1970s we were less sure of this. One reason is the competition to our secondary industry from those we have taught—Japan, Hong Kong, Korea. More important is the limit that has now appeared on supplies of certain raw materials essential to industry.

The present pattern of middle-class consumption presents an intractable problem. The number of middle-class people in the world was about 200 million in 1950; it has grown to about 800 million by 1980. The growth was so rapid that it has pressed on oil and other resources. It was too rapid, in that it has not allowed time for the technological progress that will substitute for the materials that are running short.

Yet from the viewpoint of those waiting to join the middle class, growth was much too slow. The world population went from 2.5 billion to 4.4 billion in thirty years. It is true that the increase of the middle class was nearly 5 percent per annum, which seems very rapid indeed compared with the population's 1.8 percent. But percentages are not what count, for nothing can give assurance that this pace of the last thirty years will continue until all of the population enters the middle class. Raw materials limitations throw doubt on whether the pace can be kept up even in absolute numbers. For the short run the absolute figures are in any case more important; if the addition to the middle class was 600 million, and the addition to the world population was 1,900 million, then there were 1,300 million more poor people in 1980 than in 1950.

EXPLANATION RATHER THAN POLICY

The striving for middle-class status is an explanatory variable rather than a variable of policy. It tells us why government has grown, why cities have expanded, why poor countries produce automobiles rather than bicycles, why the import of consumption goods everywhere is a threat to the balance of payments.

This discussion of development tries to look at it from the viewpoint of the citizen undergoing the process rather than of the expert. Citizens of poor countries, under any political regime, see development as the advent of goods that make possible for them a modern style of life. For the typical urban dweller, development is what will enable him to have a pukka house with electrical appliances, above all an automobile, and what will enable him to send his children to college, so that the rise in the world will not have been for himself alone. The goods are of course useful for themselves, but primarily they are symbols that one has attained a certain status. Middle-class status may be something toward which the vanguard of Americans is increasingly indifferent, but it retains novelty and glamor in the poor countries of the world.

This desire of people for middle-class status is an engine of development—it can induce acceptance of the hard work and abstinence that development requires. Yet unlike a tariff or the rate of interest or other readily manipulated variable of policy, it is not a lever in the hands of the administration.

When development as a conscious and controllable process came on the scene in the 1950s, one was free to hold to any ideal one wished about its course. But a quarter century of experience has placed some constraints on our thinking, in the form of facts on how the process has gone. Sometimes these facts are summarized by saying that development has been disappointingly slow: poverty persists and because of population increase is numerically greater than it was at mid-century. Yet from another point of view the process has been a great success. Within each of the poor countries there is an expanding middle class. We need to observe more closely the social mechanisms that cause the spread of the middle class to take precedence over the alleviation of poverty.

PART FOUR
FORECASTING POPULATIONS

CHAPTER 11

The Mechanics of Forecasting

All statistical facts concern the past. The census of April 1980 counted 226 million of us, but we did not know this until November, despite the census emphasis on speed, pursued with ingenuity and with much new electronic equipment. Stock market prices and volumes are hours old before they appear in the evening paper. Statistics of plans or intentions are only an apparent exception. No one can ever gather data directly on the future.

Yet the actions that statistics serve to guide can occur only in the future. The local telephone company wants to know how much a town will grow in population over the next few decades. Its interest is not abstract curiosity, but contemplated construction of new lines out toward a certain suburb. The investment might occur in the next two or three years, and the service given by the investment along with the income derived from it would be spread over thirty years. If the town does not grow as much as expected, the construction would be wasteful. If the growth is in the direction of a different suburb, then lines will be idle on one side of the town and too often busy on the other side. School authorities, the bus company, a textile manufacturer, all similarly need statistics on the future for the conduct of their business, and these are nowhere to be collected until the future has become past and it is too late.

With producers of population statistics all working on the near side of *now* and users all concerned with the far side, it is lucky that even in times of rapid change, some continuities are to be found between past and future. Population projection rests on these continuities.

The continuities are not to be found in simple totals. We know that the number of people in the United States does not increase evenly from year to year, and still less does the population of one town or one age group increase evenly. The age classes especially have fluctuated erratically in recent decades. Today the United States includes an exceptionally large proportion of young people twenty to thirty-five years of age, the result of the baby boom of the forties and fifties. They have crowded the colleges, jobs, and graduate schools across the country. But during the sixties, births fell sharply, and the number of pupils entering elementary schools leveled off.

Yet we can say something about the future. At the end of the seventies, schools and the labor market were reached by the wave of what may be called the nonbirths of the sixties. But, though kindergartens and public schools slowed their expansion in the seventies, they may have to accelerate again in the eighties to accommodate a new generation—children of the children born in the postwar baby boom. How such things can be projected is our subject.

The approach, or model, that we shall build for projection serves purposes other than prediction. It is especially valuable for judging the effects on population growth of a possible change or a proposed policy.

Projection with Constant Birth and Death Rates

To project is to seek elements that remain nearly constant through time. The increase in total population from year to year plainly does not qualify, but certain *rates* do remain more or less the same, and on these we rest our analysis of the future. For example, the proportion of people aged thirty who die each year is likely to remain much the same in 1970, 1980, and 1990. These death rates are constant enough that some fairly reliable predictions can be hung on them, and we proceed to the exploitation of this constancy.

Our projection of a closed population includes three parts:
1. The baseline census from which work starts
2. Effect of death
3. Effect of birth

Demographers ordinarily recognize five-year age groups, to the end of life, for men and women separately, and they have a computer do the arithmetic. To show the procedure without being swamped in numbers,

Table 1 Age Distribution of American Girls and Women Under 45 Years of Age, 1960

AGE	MILLIONS OF GIRLS AND WOMEN
0–14	27.4
15–29	17.7
30–44	18.4

we consider here girls and women only, and these just up to age forty-five. Moreover, we need only consider three age groups, each of fifteen years' width. For purposes of this illustration, three numbers describe the population at any one time.

We can make a fairly complete analysis for these three groups, and show the whole worksheet. The census of April 1, 1960, counted 27.4 million girls under fifteen in the United States. It showed only 17.7 million between fifteen and twenty-nine years. An intermediate number, 18.4 million, were between thirty and forty-four. (This article follows the census in always counting people at their age last birthday.) Those under fifteen, born between 1945 and 1960, constitute the baby boom; the next older group, born between 1930 and 1945, are survivors of the meager crop of depression babies; the oldest, aged thirty to forty-four, were born between 1915 and 1930, when birth rates in the United States were higher than in the thirties, but lower than in the fifties.

Now these three numbers can be written one below another in an array known as an age distribution; see Table 1.

So much for the counts made in 1960, our point of takeoff into the future. We now need to know how death and birth will act on this starting distribution. (Migration is here ignored as is random variation; we present a closed, determined model.)

Let us start with death, but look at its positive side: the people who do not die, but survive into the next period. The question is, how many of the 27.4 million girls under fifteen years of age counted in the 1960 census may be expected to survive to 1975? We have at hand a *life table*, as such collections of survival probabilities are called, that gives the proportion of girls under fifteen who survive for fifteen years as approximately 0.9924. This life table was calculated from deaths in the United States in 1965, and it would not be very different if calculated for any other recent year. Hence the expected number of survivors fifteen years later of the 27.4 million counted in 1960 would be 27.4 multiplied by 0.9924, or 27.2 million. These girls would be fifteen to twenty-nine years of age in 1975.

In the same way the proportion surviving fifteen years among girls fifteen to twenty-nine in 1960 is estimated at 0.9826, and hence the

Table 2 1960 Population of American Girls and Women Under 45, Projected to 1975 at 1965 Death Rates.

AGE	MILLIONS OF GIRLS AND WOMEN	
	1960	1975
0–14	27.4	?
15–29	17.7	27.2
30–44	18.4	17.4

projected number aged thirty to forty-four in 1975 would be 17.7 × 0.9826 = 17.4 million. The projections to this point stand as shown in Table 2. Our next task is to fill the upper cell on the right, which requires an estimate of the number under fifteen in 1975.

All of the girls under fifteen years of age in 1975 will have been born since 1960, and we need to estimate not how many girl births take place in the fifteen years, but how many of these births survive to 1975. We know, also from the 1965 experience, that, on the average a woman fifteen to twenty-nine can expect 0.8498 surviving girl babies by the end of a fifteen-year period. We have counted girl babies only for this purpose because a female model is what we are constructing, and we have deducted deaths among the babies so as to come up with girls under fifteen who will be alive in 1975. There were 17.7 million women aged fifteen to twenty-nine in 1960, and their contribution to the total girls under fifteen in 1975 is expected to be 17.7 × 0.8498 = 15.0 million.

Children will be born also to the women thirty to forty-four years of age; on the average, these women will have 0.1273 girl babies alive at the end of the fifteen-year period. The contribution that these make to the total girls under fifteen in 1975 is expected to be 18.4 × 0.1273 = 2.4 million. (The actual calculation was made to more decimals than shown here.)

Finally, children will be born before 1975 to girls under fifteen in 1960, a large proportion of whom will become of childbearing age during the fifteen years. On the average (again at 1965 rates), they will have 0.4271 surviving girls. This average, like the others above, is taken over many different cases; it includes the girls too young to become mothers, those who will be old enough but not yet married, and those who will marry but not have children. The expected contribution here is 27.4 × 0.4271 = 11.7 million.

To find the total number of girl children under fifteen surviving in 1975, we must add the numbers reached in the three preceding paragraphs; 11.7 + 15.0 + 2.4 = 29.1 million in all. Figure 1 shows schematically what is happening. (Because so few children are born to women over forty-four, we can afford to ignore them. Our simple model will give

The Mechanics of Forecasting

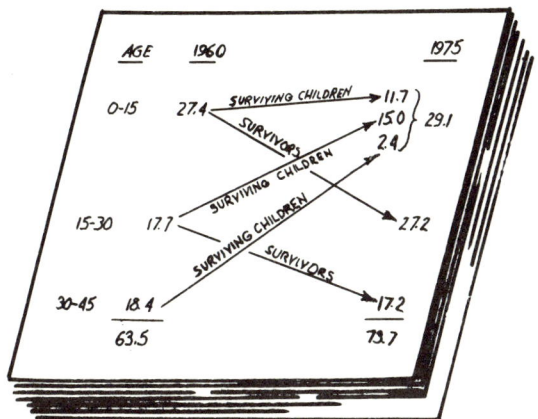

almost the same rate of increase as more elaborate models.)

By repeating exactly the same argument, except that we now start with the 1975 projected population, we obtain the age distribution in 1990; any number of additional fifteen-year cycles may be calculated similarly. Table 3 shows the resulting numbers up to 2065.

To summarize in matrix notation, what we have done is premultiply the vector of ages of 1960, say P_{1960}, by the matrix M to obtain P_{1975}, i.e.,

$$P_{1975} = MP_{1960} = \begin{bmatrix} 0.4271 & 0.8498 & 0.1273 \\ 0.9924 & 0 & 0 \\ 0 & 0.9826 & 0 \end{bmatrix} \begin{bmatrix} 27.4 \\ 17.7 \\ 18.4 \end{bmatrix} = \begin{bmatrix} 29.1 \\ 27.2 \\ 17.4 \end{bmatrix}$$

The only part of matrix theory required is the row-by-column rule for multiplication. The 1990 population would be $P_{1990} = M^2 P_{1960}$, and so on forward. The reader may enjoy reproducing the numbers that follow on his own personal computer.

WAVES OF MOTHERHOOD

The first age group, girls under fifteen, increases less than 2 million between 1960 and 1975, while the women aged fifteen to twenty-nine in 1975 are the babies born between 1945 and 1960, the postwar baby boom, and as these succeed the depression babies in any group we expect its number to rise rapidly. Women thirty to forty-four actually become fewer during this first fifteen-year period, even though the zero to forty-four population as a whole is growing.

Table 3 Millions of Girls and Women Under 45 Years of Age in the United States if Birth and Death Rates Remain at the 1965 Level

AGE	1960	1975	1990	2005	2020	2035	2050	2065
0–14	27.4	29.1	37.7	44.1	54.3	65.0	79.0	95.3
15–29	17.7	27.2	28.9	37.5	43.7	53.8	64.5	78.4
30–44	18.4	17.4	26.7	28.4	36.8	43.0	52.9	63.4
Total	63.5	73.7	93.3	109.9	134.8	161.8	196.4	237.1

Table 4 Increase of Girls and Women in the United States from 2050 to 2065, 1965 Birth and Death Rates.

AGE	2050 (MILLIONS)	2065 (MILLIONS)	RATIO, 2065 TO 2050
0–14	79.0	95.3	1.206
15–19	64.5	78.4	1.215
30–44	52.9	63.4	1.198
Total	196.4	237.1	1.207

Because most children are born to mothers fifteen to twenty-nine years of age, we can expect a new baby boom, an echo of the first one, at the time when the babies of the fifties themselves pass through childbearing age, and indeed the under-fifteens grow by 8.6 million from 1975 to 1990 according to Table 3.

In fact, the depression and boom will keep echoing to much later times, supposing, as we do throughout, that childbearing practices remain fixed. But the table also shows that as time goes on the irregularity of the 1960 age distribution steadily lessens. At the end of 105 years all ages are increasing at very nearly the same rate.

That the several ages ultimately increase at the same rate can be seen by dividing each 2065 figure in Table 3 by the corresponding 2050 figure. In Table 4, this ratio is shown to be about 1.2 for the three age groups and the total. By carrying the projection further, we could have had these ratios as close to one another as we wanted; in fact, further calculation shows that they all would converge to 1.2093.

This ratio may be called intrinsic, or the true ratio of natural increase. It can be shown to depend not at all on the 1960 age distribution with which the process started, but only on the rates of birth and death, and it is the most informative single summary measure of that set of rates. It tells us that any population that is subject to our particular birth and

Table 5 Main Component of Female Population in the United States, 1960

AGE	STABLE EQUIVALENT (MILLIONS)
0–14	25.2
15–29	20.7
30–44	16.8
Total	62.7

Table 6 Departures of Projected Population in Table 3 from Geometric Progression in Millions

AGE	1960	1975	1990	2005
0–14	2.2	−1.4	0.9	−0.5
15–29	−3.0	2.2	−1.4	0.9
30–44	1.6	−2.9	2.1	−1.4

death rates over a period of time will sooner or later settle down to an increase in the ratio 1.2093, which is to say by about 21 percent per fifteen-year period. Under the operation of the projection, applying the assumptions we have made, *a stable age distribution* is sooner or later attained in which all the irregularities of 1960 due to boom and depression have been forgotten. Age distributions tend to forget their past when persistently pushed forward by the method developed above.

Let us find numerically the component of population growth that increases in the same ratio in every cycle, a mode of increase spoken of as *geometric*. If we divide each of the numbers shown under the year 2065 in Table 3 by 1.2093, we get back to an estimate for 2050; if we then divide again by 1.2093 we get back to 2035, and so on. To get back to 1960 we would divide by the seventh power of 1.2093, written $(1.2093)^7$ and equal to 3.78. Carrying out the division gives 95.3/3.78 or 25.2 million for age zero to fourteen, and similar calculations for the other ages provide what we may call the stable equivalent for 1960; see Table 5.

Table 5 shows the set of numbers that, increasing in the constant ratio 1.2093, would sooner or later exactly join the track of our projection in each age group. If we multiply the stable equivalent by the fixed number 1.2093 to obtain the geometric track, and subtract this from the projection of Table 3, we obtain Table 6. For example, for girls zero to fourteen in 1975, we have $29.1 - 25.2 \times 1.2093 = -1.4$. Our analysis has separated the prospective population change into two parts, one a smooth geometric increase, the other a series of waves that are departures from the geometric.

These departures gradually diminish in amplitude. For 1960, we have 2.2 million as a measure of the temporary "excess" of the 1945–60 babies. The -3.0 million are the deficiency of the depression babies, and 1.6 million, again an excess, relate to the twenties. Note that by 1990, each of these has an echo, of the same sign but on the whole of smaller amount.

The tendency of the waves to diminish in amplitude is related to women having their children over a range of ages. If all children were born to mothers of the same age, the waves would steadily *increase* in amplitude. With such concentration any irregularity in the age distribution caused, for example, by a war or depression would not only continue echoing through all later generations, but become magnified. In the United States today, women prefer to have their children around age twenty-five, whereas our grandmothers spread theirs from about twenty to forty-five. The new style, associated with the effective use of birth control, could mean diminished stability.

A More Realistic Forecast

American fertility has dropped since the early 1960s and is now slightly below replacement. Continuance of the 1965 rates is most unlikely; as Table 3 shows, they result in a fourfold increase in the population during one century. It makes more intuitive sense to suppose that births stand at bare replacement from 1975 onward. The matrix corresponding to that condition is obtained by dividing the first row of the M by the net reproduction rate R_0, the mean number of daughters expected to be born to each girl child. That number on the 1965 rates is $R_0 = 1.39458$. With M^* equal to M but with first row divided by 1.39458 applied from 1975 onward, we have for 1990 $P_{1990} = M^*MP_{1960}$, for 2005 $P_{2005} = M^{*2}MP_{1960}$, etc., shown in Table 7. There is still some increase from 1960, but only until age-stability is attained.

In both analyses of the United States population we have gone from the facts of the 1960 census, through various more or less realistic calculations concerning 1975 and even 1990, into a kind of fantasy as we proceed far into the future. The early part of the projection can within limits be useful for practical purposes; the later part is so dependent on various *if's* that one would be very foolish to count on it. The biggest doubt attaches to the birth rate. It may seem that birth is as individual a matter as death, and

Table 7 Numbers of Girls and Women Under 45 Years of Age in the United States if Birth Rates are at Replacement Level from 1975 onward (Millions)

AGE	1960	1975	1990	2005	2020	2035	2050	2065
0–14	27.4	29.1	27.1	28.3	27.6	28.0	27.8	27.9
15–29	17.7	27.2	28.9	26.9	28.1	27.4	27.8	27.6
30–44	18.4	17.4	26.7	28.4	26.4	27.6	26.9	27.3
Total	63.5	73.7	82.6	83.5	82.1	83.0	82.5	82.8

therefore births across the country ought to be independent of one another, yet in fact high and low birth rates spread contagiously across the country.

Why then do we bother with the fantasy of such far-out projections referring to the distant future? The answer is that they help us understand the present. We ascertain the meaning of the present rates of birth and death by calculating what they *would* lead to if they continued for a hundred years or more. Let us see why this is even more important in study of the birth and death rates of developing countries than of a developed one like the United States.

RELIABILITY OF PREDICTION

The techniques presented here and obvious extensions of them are much used for predicting the future. They are used not because they are perfect, but because nothing better is available. Whatever continuities exist in birth and death rates are exploited by the makers of projections. From about 1870 to 1935 in Western Europe and the United States, the birth rate and the death rate were both falling: projections could be made by the method outlined here, except that instead of using fixed rates, the past downward trend in birth and death was projected into the future. Such projections were acceptably accurate as long as the downward trend continued.

But these same countries reached a turning point in the 1940s. People married younger, and births rose rapidly. Moreover, couples varied the timing of their children as well as varying the total number. The fact that in a modern society couples plan their children, both in number and in timing, can be used to strengthen the predictions. Samples of young couples are surveyed to find what their childbearing intentions are, just as we ask intentions on buying houses and automobiles. The official estimates of the United States Bureau of the Census take account of these intentions.

The Census Bureau's projections, which use a vastly elaborated form of the method of this article, can be compared with ours. Theirs are more detailed than ours above have been, and they are also cautious enough to make a variety of projections rather than betting on just one. They end up with four numbers for each age, sex, and future year. For example, for 1990, their four numbers for girls zero to fourteen years of age range from a low of 29.5 million to a high of 41.8 million. Our Table 3 shows 37.7 million.

How well would past application of our model have foretold the 1970 population of the United States? If we had worked forward from the 1920 census total of 106 million, using exactly the procedure of this article, but applying it in five-year age intervals to all ages and to both sexes, we would have found about 185 million for 1970. If we had allowed for immigration less emigration of 200,000 per year, this would have brought us to 195 million against the 205 million actually counted. Something a little lower would have been found starting from 1950; starting from 1960, we would have slightly overestimated the census figure. An error of about 5 percent in estimates made up to fifty years ago is not bad, considering that the Bureau of the Census estimates its own actual count to be subject to nearly 2 percent error.

We would have done much worse starting in 1940, however; the method of this chapter, plus about 6 million immigrants, would have produced a total of only about 160 million. Put another way that sounds even worse: the increase from 1940 to 1970 was about 62 million, and of it, we would have estimated less than 30 million. This is not a good score. The baby boom of the fifties was a historic event about as hard to predict in advance as the war that sparked it. A means of estimating accuracy of forecasts is provided in Chapter 13.

CHAPTER **12**

Forecasts as an Aid to Analysis

The discipline of demography has been greatly influenced by demand for prediction of future population and by efforts of demographers to satisfy that demand. The public expects predictions. When I meet someone who asks me what I do, and reply that I work at the mathematics of population, the reaction is something like: "Great! Then you're the man who can tell me what the population of the world will be in the year 2000," or even: "When, according to your figures, will there be too many people in the United States?" To protest that I and others practicing the profession of demography are interested in *facts* by no means escapes the question; the most interesting facts are those relating to the future.

If the questioner is experienced enough to know that prediction is difficult, he at least supposes, when he hears about demographic models, that the accuracy of prediction is a test of the models. The demographer, he might say, has every right to look into many aspects of past and present population, but he validates this right, and distinguishes himself from the ordinary run of men, by now and again doing a prediction. Our calculations may be esoteric, but everyone can understand a prediction that the census of 1990 will count 250 million persons in the United States, and any layman can check its accuracy when the census total is released about August 1990. By doing this small miracle of prediction we not only help people in their practical affairs between now and 1990, but when that date comes around we will have proved our competence. What needs explaining is how forecasts can be useful despite discouraging departures from the subsequent realization.

THE COMPONENTS METHOD

The work of P. K. Whelpton, described in his own words (1963), will lead to the explanation and also to my main propositions concerning models. Whelpton sometimes refers to his work as projections, sometimes as forecasts, sometimes as calculations, sometimes as estimates. I follow Harold Dorn (1950) in treating these as equivalent. Whelpton was not so innocent as to be unaware that people used his projections for prediction, and calling them projections is a legitimate way of removing some of the burden of responsibility implied by prediction. The main point is that Whelpton cared a great deal how his projections compared with the population counted in subsequent censuses. He developed the method described in Chapter 11 preceding.

"My first attempt to make population projections," he says, "began in 1926. It soon became evident that it would be desirable to project age-specific rates for births, deaths, immigration and emigration, and to compute the resulting population," In this very beginning of his work fifty-five years ago he invented the components method, while his contemporaries were still extrapolating with logistic and other curves. Implicit in his work sheets was the now well-known discrete population model, since expressed in matrix form (Leslie 1945), given a stochastic interpretation, and otherwise elaborated. Before the idea was appropriated by mathematicians, Whelpton was applying what we now know as nonstationary Markov chains. Whelpton's demographic intuition anticipated some higher mathematics, but he paid no attention to that and went on to other population problems.

For his projection did not turn out to correspond very closely to the subsequent performance, and so Whelpton was "led to a desire for birth rates that were specific for parity as well as age, in order to compute better gross and net reproduction rates." The recognition of parity has also led to valuable models. But again more was needed, for the parity-specific rates were not effective predictors either.

The third improvement was "putting together the birth rates for successive ages in *successive* years as well as those for successive ages in the *same* year." And so the cohort approach was born, which has meant other major changes in demography and outside it.

Whelpton's story has now reached 1945; he has gone from the extrapolation by curve fitting used until his time to the components method, to parity, to cohorts—and still the predictions are off the mark. In fact, the results were so bad that Whelpton said he was glad the published report did not mention that cohorts were used, for this might have prejudiced further use of cohort tables. "Cohort tables showed what had happened in the past but not what would happen in the future." Twenty years of labor had not brought him much closer to accurate prediction. Continued discrepancies suggested a fourth approach, which was to be his last.

SURVEY OF CHILDBEARING INTENTIONS

This was "to question a representative national sample of young married couples regarding the number of children they expected to have," an idea that led to the 1955 and 1960 studies of Growth of American Families. Extensive and important results were subsequently produced by surveys based on such direct questioning. "Now," Westoff, Ryder, and others may well say, "the demographer need not depend solely on censuses and vital registrations; these multi-purpose operations serve population analysis only incidentally to many other objectives; sampling permits the demographer to collect his own data."

But has this helped the accuracy of prediction? Ryder and Westoff (1967) are the first to say no. When you ask presently married women their childbearing intentions you cover fairly well the births of the next five years or so, but beyond that time the presently married will for the most part have completed their families. And to ask a girl not yet married, say ten years old, how many children she would have if and when she married is a hypothetical question that can only elicit an arbitrary answer. So this fourth and last phase of Whelpton's search for a dependable method of prediction turns out little better than the first three. Is the whole long effort, forty years' work of one of the most creative of demographers, a failure?

FAILURE AND SUCCESS

Chekhov says, "One must be a god to tell success from failure." Think of the inventors who worked to build perpetual motion machines. No such machine resulted from their efforts, but they and their critics established the first and second laws of thermodynamics; those basic laws of physics emerged from efforts of inventors and mechanics to get something for nothing. The search for a gambling system, destined to failure as surely as perpetual motion and equally animated by the desire to get something for nothing, was a stimulus to probability theory. Optimists tried to trisect an angle in a finite number of operations with ruler and compasses from about the fifth century B.C. Mathematicians of the nineteenth century A.D. proved that it can't be done. A failure? Not at all—one of the outcomes was group theory, an enduring part of both pure and applied mathematics.

Population prediction is our perpetual motion, our trisection. Except when the trends are smooth, it is likely to fail. But the attempt to predict has inspired many of the demographic models that we now possess. Such models permit experiments out of which we obtain causal knowledge; they explain data; they focus research by identifying theoretical and practical issues; they systematize comparative study across space and time; they reveal formal analogies between problems that on their surface are quite different; they even help assemble data.

One immediate use of projection is to explain why the presently underdeveloped countries have much younger age distributions, with higher dependency ratios, than the countries of Europe; indeed they have much younger age distributions than the countries of Europe when Europe was in the condition of underdevelopment in 1800. Is the difference between the high dependency ratio of Venezuela now and the much lower one of Sweden in 1800 mostly due to Venezuela's birth rates being higher or to its death rates being lower? The answer is found by projecting Venezuela with its own rates of birth and death, and then with its own birth rates and Swedish death rates; the difference in the proportion of children under fifteen is due to the difference in death rates. Trying this and other combinations shows that the difference as observed between Sweden and Venezuela is about three quarters due to birth rates and only about one quarter due to death rates (Coale 1956; Keyfitz and Flieger 1971). Whelpton's projection model has permitted a genuine experiment.

Other such experiments come quickly to mind. What is the probability that an American boy will ultimately die of heart disease as against some other cause, on the mortality rates of the United States at the present time? Again a model, this time the multiple decrement life table, an extension of the ordinary life table used for survivorship in population projections, tells us that the overall probability is well over one half. All other causes of death together account for less than half the probability.

Then does it follow that the elimination of heart disease would greatly step up the rate of increase of population? It does not, as we easily find by projecting with a life table in which the deaths from heart disease have been eliminated and all other rates of death and of birth left as they stand. But it greatly changes the age distribution, especially at the older ages: the number of men eighty-five years of age and older would increase twelvefold as a result of heart disease being eliminated, supposing all other causes to persist at present rates. This is decidedly different from the effect of eliminating deaths from cancer alone, which would increase the number of men over eighty-five by only about 50 percent when the age distribution had shaken down.

These are conditional statements, and as such they are true beyond debate, given their assumptions that death rates by age from all other causes and birth rates by age of mother will remain as they are. Because other things will in fact change, they are not the concrete or unconditional predictions so much sought after, and which seem forever out of our reach. Yet when a particular decision is to be taken, do we not want to know what the result of that decision will be by itself, in abstraction from all other changes? There may be circumstances in which the conditional prediction is more helpful than the concrete prediction of what will *really* happen. The main technical difficulty here arises from effects associated with the proposed change—for example, the effect that the elimination of heart disease would itself have on death rates from other causes.

What about the effect of emigration on subsequent population numbers? The authorities in Indonesia have attempted to relieve Java's population problem by outmigration to Sumatra. They know that for this purpose the departure of young couples is more effective than the departure of old men, but how much effect does the departure of young couples have on Java's rate of increase? Again the Whelpton model tells numerically the conditional effect of emigration at one age as against another (Widjojo, 1970). The continuous form of the population projection, pioneered by Lotka (1907, 1939), permits some compact general formulas (Keyfitz 1971). Arranging that all emigrants were seventeen years of age would secure the maximum effect in holding down the rate of increase, but even if this were administratively feasible, well over 1 million emigrants per year would be required to hold Java's population constant.

Models explain data on population characteristics such as age. Coale (1957) shows how a human age distribution is determined by a fertility and mortality pattern. There are five women for every three men at ages eighty-five and over in the United States. The large and rapidly increasing mortality difference between the sexes obviously has something to do with the matter, but exactly how much of the difference between the number of men and of women enumerated does it explain? Amos Hawley (1950) shows how to use the life table to answer such questions. In their systematic study of population characteristics in the United States, the Taeubers (1958, 1971) again and again ask questions of their cross-sectional census data that they can answer only in terms of models. They apply models retrospectively to show how things got the way they are. Even more explicitly, Freedman (1969) explains the falling birth rate in Taiwan by models of conception and birth developed by Potter and others. These are in turn based on mathematical analysis due to Sheps (1967).

Models concentrate the interest of the profession and prevent the scattering to which empirical materials by themselves often lead. Frank Notestein's (1945) demographic transition, a verbal model, has enabled us to concentrate on a host of problems: why was the transition in England different from that in France, and why was the Japanese transition different from both? Merely setting down the ideal form of transition, giving it a name and an existence, has provided a frame in which the demographic process of an individual country can be placed, so that it may be studied in a genuinely comparative fashion. Kingsley Davis (1963) made the transition dynamic—the engine that drives down the birth rate is the fall in death rates.

Models help research by revealing unexpected similarities between problems in different fields. The probability of marriage at successive ages is formally analogous to the probability of dying, and the life table technique applies to both. In fact the same life table technique applies to anything that can happen only once to an individual—it formally unifies first marriage, having a first child, a contraceptive failure that results in the next child (Tietze 1967; Potter 1967), the probability that a given marriage will be broken by divorce (Jacobson 1959).

Paul Glick et al. (1963) have analyzed how in the wake of the baby boom girls seeking husbands somewhat older than themselves encounter a shortage, what he called the marriage squeeze. Following the downslope of the baby boom about 1980, men will experience a shortage of girls of the ages they usually marry. How do ages of brides and grooms adjust to meet such changes in the availability of potential spouses? The problem is analogous to the matching of applicants and jobs; the marriage market and the labor market formally are similar. Since both present difficult problems, it is a help to be able to transfer results in one field to the other.

And finally, models help prediction. Projections by the U.S. Bureau of the Census and other national agencies, as well as the United Nations, based on alternative sets of assumptions, appear conspicuously among official statistics—for example at the very beginning of the *Statistical Abstract*. They leave it to the user to decide which set of assumptions he prefers and hence which future population.

In a similar category are counterpredictions, showing that something cannot happen. Mexico cannot continue with its 1970 rate of increase for as long as the lifetimes of children now born. For if it did, the population would double four times, that is, multiply by sixteen, so that there would be 800 million people in Mexico. Since this is virtually impossible, the argument shows that opposition to birth control cannot be a matter of principle (except for those willing to advocate higher death rates), but that differences of opinion can arise only on whether birth control is to be applied a little sooner or a little later.

As long as a series changes uniformly, extrapolation will give a perfectly good forecast, and this was how reputations for forecasting population could be gained during a long period ending in the 1930s. Since then we have had to live with turning points. To forecast a turning point requires a model incorporating the mechanism that causes the turning point. The line between extrapolation and a model is not always sharp, and an example from the education system may help us draw that line.

Some Turning Points

The difficulty that recent Ph.D.'s in some fields have had in getting jobs could not have been foretold by simple extrapolation. Up to a few years ago the number of universities granting higher degrees was increasing, individual universities were steadily increasing their output of graduates, and everyone with a doctorate was immediately employed. Extrapolation could lead only to the conclusion that every young person in the country would attain the Ph.D. and be hired as a college teacher.

Now consider a model that divides the educational system into just two levels, say college and graduate school. A certain fraction of those graduating from the lower level enter the upper level as students. Teacher-student ratios at both levels are fixed. For each level the supply of teachers in any year is equal to the teachers surviving from the year before, plus a certain fraction of the current graduates of the upper level. This primitive model is sufficient to show that the *absolute demand* for the new Ph.D.'s is closely related to the *rate of increase* of college students, and that a leveling off in the number of entering college students results in drastic declines in the demand for Ph.D.'s for teaching. Such a model could have foretold today's turning point, in which Ph.D.'s in many fields are having to revise considerably their employment expectations.

Extrapolation is bound to miss the turning point, while an appropriate model can reveal it in advance. Thus when a turning point comes along it has the use of telling us whether what we have been doing up to then was extrapolation or the application of an appropriate model. Demographers can be grateful for at least one turning point per decade since the 1930s, for though distinctly unappreciated at the time, it was these that compelled and inspired Whelpton (1963) to devise his successive models. One turning point showed that the demographic calculation was not being correctly made—that it should be arranged in cohorts rather than in periods, a point that Norman Ryder (1964) has developed much further. Joseph Spengler (1966), thinking of other turning points, has insisted that the birth rate is a function of price and income as well as of social values. To predict the demographic future before the future happens requires equations that include more than purely demographic variables.

On a broader front, advanced countries are today up against a far more general turning point, of the puzzling sort that fills one with respect and awe in the face of the future and forces a rethinking of the fundamentals of a discipline. At least four signs of a turning point are described in current literature: deterioration of the environment, the interaction of population and income in causing this deterioration, instability in the ecosystem, and new social attitudes to life and work.

The increasing scale of human activities has begun to overwhelm nature, which heretofore has mostly looked at humans with immutable indifference. Since the Middle Ages men of European descent have multiplied by ten, and in a sudden acceleration at the very end of this second millenium of our era, the total energy at their disposal is multiplying by three each generation. The exploitation of lands and mines, the output of solid, liquid, and gaseous waste, everything that comes under the heading of "conquest of nature," have reached a new level of intensity. Automobile scrap heaps are conspicuous in America and will become so in Europe, just as cathedrals were conspicuous in the Middle Ages. The commercial and technical advantages of disposable containers and disposable vehicles (perhaps in disposable cities) leaves its mark not only on the earth but on the moon, where biodegradation is even less capable of restoring the environment. Technology provides untold benefit; the question is how to secure the goods it produces without what Boulding (1966) calls the bads.

The food ceiling that seemed to limit population in Malthus's day had at least the advantage of stability. Agricultural and other production was so constrained that there was little danger of population rising through the ceiling and then crashing down; I do not recall that Malthus anywhere foretold sudden *ecological* disaster through excess population. For him nature was constant and exercised a severe but steady control over human numbers.

The achievements of modern agriculture, culminating in the Green Revolution, have by-passed the ancient fixity of land and food, and bought a precious ten or twenty years. But soil destruction through overuse, water contamination by fertilizers, exhaustion of minerals, also set ceilings on population, and these lack the one benign feature of the Malthusian food ceiling; they can let population rise temporarily well above its long-term upper limit. The Malthusian ceiling had no waves.

So also can the widespread use of a pesticide. It raises food production by keeping down insects so that population can increase. But then the insects adapt genetically, and the pesticide works its way up food chains and into human fat cells. Once it has become harmless to insects and dangerous to man, the pesticide has to be promptly replaced. The replacement may be another pesticide that goes through the same cycle, and population continues to increase. Highly selected cereal strains that may become susceptible to rust after population builds on them are another source of potential instability, especially critical if the original genetic material from which they were evolved has been lost. Whether we will continue to be capable of meeting successive emergencies is a technical matter on which a demographer as such can have no opinion. If S-shaped curves are more difficult to forecast than exponentials, then the kind of oscillations that may be in prospect are especially difficult.

Tied to the phases of the S-shaped growth curve are personal attitudes and systems of morality. When the population was small and death came early, those who did survive to adulthood had to raise large families if the tribe was to continue, and religion and morality had to encourage childbearing. Once death rates have fallen and correspondingly low birth rates are required, morality has to reverse itself and now discourage childbearing, if equilibrium is to be attained in the new conditions.

The same reversal may well occur in attitudes toward income. In the rising phase of industrial development, when there is much hard work to be done and only primitive capital equipment with which to do it, the prime virtues are diligence and abstinence. Today, we are told, young people are lazy and improvident; they do not work and save as we were taught to. But suppose that excessive diligence scars and bruises the earth's surface, and that excessive abstinence now goes beyond the community's demand for capital, as Keynes (1936) saw that it could. A morality of less diligence may well be functional for the part of the curve in which we are pushing against a resources ceiling. Dudley Duncan (1969) foresees a time when "our assessment of men will not depend so heavily on their ability to 'get ahead.' " Perhaps excessive ambition and income will even come to seem immoral.

Population interacts with environmental, economic and social factors in ways difficult to forecast. Most forecasts do not allow for these interactions. Chapter 13 will assess how well professional forecasts have done.

CHAPTER **13**

The Limits of Population Forecasting

Future population depends on many factors—social, economic, technological—that cannot be taken into account in population projection. However interdisciplinary we become, there are some clear limits to knowledge of the interrelations of the variables whose combined operation will bring about the future population. Demographers can no more be held responsible for inaccuracy in forecasting population twenty years ahead than geologists, meteorologists, or economists who fail to announce earthquakes, cold winters, or depressions twenty years ahead.

What we are reponsible for is warning one another and our public what the error of our estimates is likely to be. Statistics started to approach scientific maturity with the calculation of probable errors (for instance in astronomical observations), and then it went on to confidence intervals and tests of significance. Statisticians are distinguished from other people who use numbers by their effective techniques for dealing with error. The agronomist-statistician not only tells farmers that they will have a higher yield from a new variety of potato, but within what limits that yield will probably fall, with odds nineteen to one, say. The experimental trials are set up to correspond to a probability model, and on the model exact confidence intervals are calculated and promulgated.

The user of a population forecast has no less need to know its error than the user of a yield estimate or of an estimate of unemployment. Unfortunately, population forecasts cannot be framed in a probability model through random allocation of treatments or random choice of units. But demographers have a resource not yet systematically exploited: past forecasts, and the comparison of these with the subsequent population performance. The use of such comparisons for telling the accuracy of a present forecast depends only on finding a set from the past that somehow corresponds to the present forecast. In 1980 we estimate the population of the year 2000. To judge its accuracy we look back at an estimate of the year 1970 made in 1950 by the same method and see how close it came to the 1970 realization. If (1) the method used for forecasting was the same, and (2) the fluctuations of population in the future are similar to those in the past, then the 1950–70 check provides a unit of information for 1980–2000.

One might have thought that population forecasters would be obsessed with eagerness to see how well they have done in the past, and that users would insistently demand reports on the error of current forecasts. No such obsession or demand is to be seen. The only analysis of this kind in print of which I know is that of Louis Henry (1977) on the French Departments. He finds the error to be large, and rests with the modest assertion that forecasts are better than simply assuming that the past population will remain constant.

The total population is the most commonly used single number referring to the future, but in particular application some subgroup is usually of more interest. Males and females at the several ages, the labor force, children at school, people retired, have all been forecast many times. To undertake for each of these an evaluation of past forecasts similar to that made in the following pages would seem to be a useful project for the future.

AGGREGATING PAST EXPERIENCE

To bring the error of past forecasts to bear on present ones, we need to aggregate many previous comparisons. Nothing beyond an anecdote, perhaps a horror story, can come out of one single past error, but a few dozen can provide reliable information.

As in other statistical analysis, the first task here is systematic record keeping. Only after forecasts made in the past have been collected, and compared with the population that was counted subsequently, do questions of inference arise.

I have taken each projection period as a unit, and have gathered over 1,100 such unit forecasts and the corresponding realizations. For example, India's Third Five-Year Plan, published in 1962, gave a 1961 population of 438 million and a 1966 population of 492 million, implying an average annual increase of 2.352 percent. The actual population as subsequently known from later censuses was 447 million in 1961 and 502 million in 1966, that is, a rate of 2.348 percent, lower than the forecast by 0.004 percentage points. In the same document a forecast of 555 million was made for 1971, and this implied an average increase of 2.396 percent, against the performance of 2.352 percent, an error of 0.044 percentage points. These were regarded as separate observations.

What permits taking the projection to each future time as a separate case and then averaging is that the interval over which the projection is made seems to have no effect on its accuracy on this measure. The argument against is that the estimates of error for 1961–66 and for 1961–71 are not independent. Anyone who in 1961 declares too low an estimate in 1966 is likely to declare too low for 1971.

Independence is out of reach in such work as this. The same tendency to be low was shown for a majority of countries and agencies working in the 1940s; the perspectives shared by demographers concerned with the developing world had in common an underestimate of how fast mortality was about to fall. For the developed countries forecasts made in the 1940s were low, in the 1950s high, in the first instance because the baby boom was a surprise, in the second because no one knew that the end of the baby boom was imminent. Even if forecasters were wholly isolated from the common climate of opinion and from one another, the errors of estimate of neighboring countries cannot be independent; when the birth rate of one Western European country unexpectedly falls, that in others is likely to fall.

Lack of independence does not on the whole bias results such as these—no one can say that they would be higher or lower if we confined ourselves to independent observations. But it does a secondary kind of harm in preventing any statement of the error in our estimate of error. To ascertain that would be a further advance, unfortunately requiring data not now available and hard even to imagine.

DIFFERENCES AMONG FORECASTERS

One might be tempted to use the data here gathered to assess the quality of work of the several agencies and individual scholars who have gone into print with the estimates of future population. That is no part of the present objective and as I see it, comparison of individual forecasters is essentially futile. Think of a number of marksmen, all equally competent, facing a target that moves about erratically. Some will do better than others, not because of differences in competence, but because they were fortunate enough that the target stood still when they fired, while others had the bad luck to shoot just before the target moved. It would be pointless to give the several marksmen grades on their accuracy in such circumstances. [The analogy comes from Ronald Lee (1980).] Michael Stoto (1980) has shown that the date when the forecast was made is the major factor determining error.

We will treat the forecasters, then, as competent marksmen aiming at an erratic target, and their errors as measures, not of individual marksmanship but of the intrinsic difficulty of hitting the target at the time. What is important is whether they find it easier to hit a target that is only five years away than one that is twenty years away; whether they come closer in slowly growing or in rapidly growing countries. We are not studying forecasters, but the degree of forecastability of population.

It is well to keep separate questions of accuracy of census counts. This is a big subject and no attempt is made to deal with it here. All official figures constituting the population realization are accepted without comment even though we know that they are themselves subject to error. Any differential error of counting (for example, greater completeness in 1980 than in 1970 in the United States) is incorporated in the error of forecasting as the present calculations are made; it is not believed that the error would be much reduced if this could be subtracted out. In every case the rate of increase was calculated from the same publication, so that at least we have guarded against including data revision with forecast error.

OVERALL ERROR

We can summarize in a single number the 1,100 or so comparisons of forecast with realization: expressed in rounded form for ease in remembering and exposition, the experience of the past thirty years points to a root-mean-square error of 0.4 percentage points for estimates made now.

If one knows nothing more than this, and it is forecast that India will grow at 2.0 percent during the next five or twenty-five years, then the probability is two-thirds that the range of 1.6–2.4 percent will straddle the increase that actually occurs—taking it that our ignorance is normally distributed. If India is now at 690 million, the odds are two to one that its population five years hence will be between 747 and 777 million, and for the year 2001 between 948 and 1,109 million. If it is asserted that India

Table 1 Root-mean-square departure of forecast from subsequent realization, estimates published 1939–1968, expressed in percentage points

	DATE OF FORECAST	FORECASTS FOR YEARS	NUMBER OF FORECASTS	ROOT-MEAN-SQUARE ERROR
Canada[a]	1939–54	1950–70	14	1.123
United States[b]	–1950	1955–75	15	0.907
	1950+	1955–80	92	0.340
Europe and the Soviet Union[c]	1944	1950–70	96	0.949
9 countries of Eastern Europe[d]	1965	1965–80	96	0.219
All countries[e] >1,000,000	1958–68	1960–74	810	0.476
All forecasts	1939–68	1950–80	1,123	0.530

[a]Statistics Canada (1954)   [b]U.S. Bureau of the Census (1975)   [c]Notestein et al. (1944)
[d]U.S. Bureau of the Census (1965)   [e]United Nations (1958, 1966, 1973, 1979)

will grow at 0.7 percent per year over the next century, and attain 1,386 million, then one could bet two to one odds only that it will be between 931 and 2,060 million. In the nature of the exponential, a projection fan calculated in this way widens rapidly. Such use of the exponential is justified by the finding that the departure of the forecast rate of increase from the realized rate is virtually independent of the span of time over which the projection is made.

The practical conclusion, then, is that relatively short-term forecasts, say up to ten or twenty years, do tell us something, but that beyond a quarter century or so we simply do not know what the population will be. That is a consequence of the shape of the projection horn constituted by exponential curves; we repeat that the validity of using exponentials in this way is suggested by the constant error in percentage points in the range from five to twenty years.

Table 1 summarizes various collections of estimates in relation to what subsequently occurred. The three collections prior to 1950 were much less close than those since; there is apparently an improvement with time that appears within the United Nations group as well. One must give somewhat more weight to recent cases, and that is why I have not used the grand average of 0.530 percentage points in the above illustration, but rather 0.4.

In order to investigate forecasting in more detail it seems preferable to take a single large and relatively homogeneous set. The medium variant of the United Nations includes 810 forecasts made on three different occasions for countries of 1 million or more, omitting a very few cases where boundaries changed so that the unit could not be readily identified. This is the set on which I have carried out the most detailed analyses. Not only is it the largest and most varied collection, but it has been developed by a succession of competent technicians, who have been in touch with demographers throughout the world, and much concerned to improve their methods. It is referred to far more often than any other single set of projections.

The first set of supporting figures is the overall average of the 810 United Nations projections made from the late 1950s onward, for countries varying in size and growth rate, some developed and some not, some with good basic statistical data and some not. The measure used in each case was the average annual rate of increase implied by the forecast, r, less the subsequent performance R. Four averages of departure of forecast from the subsequent realization expressed in percentage points are as follows:

Mean departure, recognizing sign	− 0.070
Root-mean-square departure	0.476
Standard error of departure	0.471
Mean absolute value of departure	0.340

The minus sign on the first figure signifies that on the whole forecasts over the 1950s and 1960s were slightly too low, that is, there was a downward bias. The root-mean-square departure includes a component of overall bias in each of the periods when projections were made, plus a component of variance. The standard error is the square root of the variance only and would apply as minimum error even if there were no bias for all countries together. The mean absolute departure is, here as elsewhere, about two-thirds of the root-mean-square.

While none of these is entirely without interest, the basic result is the root-mean-square departure. Strict rounding to the nearest 0.1 percent from 0.476 makes it 0.5 percentage points, but to round down to 0.4 seems justified for current use because the more recent projections show somewhat smaller error. A secondary reason is that projections of lower rates of increase show smaller error, and rates of increase are likely to fall from present levels. The rounding down is a concession to these two considerations.

Table 2 Four measures of error shown for United Nations forecasts made in three jumping-off periods

PERIOD	MEAN DEPARTURE (1)	ROOT-MEAN SQUARE (2)	STANDARD ERROR OF FORECAST (3)	MEAN ABSOLUTE ERROR (4)
	——— Errors of forecast to 4 subsequent periods ———			
1958	−0.266	0.555	0.487	0.417
	——— Errors of forecast to 3 subsequent periods ———			
1963	0.123	0.429	0.411	0.293
	——— Errors of forecast to 2 subsequent periods ———			
1968	0.159	0.357	0.319	0.257
	——— Average of all forecasts ———			
	−0.070	0.476	0.471	0.340

Forecasts Apparently Improving

Table 2 shows our four measures of departure of forecast from realization as they appeared in work published in three different periods. The root-mean-square, the standard error, and the mean absolute error all show steady decline. Forecasts of the late 1960s showed only about two-thirds the error of those of the late 1950s.

One would like to be able to say that methods have been improving, and this is a clear likelihood. An alternative possibility is that sudden changes occurred during the 1960s, including the ending of the baby boom in Europe and the fall of mortality elsewhere, and that the 1970s showed less unanticipatable change. Aside from these, knowledge of the actual levels and rates of increase of population has improved in recent years. To discriminate between the three sources of improvement and know how much is due to each is impossible with existing data.

Given such uncertainties, then, there are at least three ways of treating the results of the table in application to what is now the future, that is, for forecasts being made in 1981:

1. One could argue that the future will be as changeable as the past, and that present demographic methods on the whole are neither better nor worse than those of the past, and average over the entire record, with a root-mean-square of about 0.5 percentage points.

2. One could say that the early work has been improved on, and the current forecasts would at most be subject to the amount of error shown in

the late 1960s. Corresponding to this view, one would take the root-mean-square as 0.00357 or roughly 0.4 percentage points.

3. One could go on to say that errors of the later 1960s are two-thirds of those of the late 1950s and hence those of the late 1970s will be two-thirds of those of the 1960s, a root-mean-square of about 0.24 percentage points. To count on the narrow range derived from this consideration would seem imprudent.

It will require another decade or two to decide among these interpretations, but in the meantime it seems reasonable to place more weight on the more recent evidence.

CONSTANCY OVER DIFFERENT PROJECTION SPANS

Table 3 summarizes the 810 United Nations forecasts as they compared with the subsequent performance, showing forecasting spans of five to twenty years. The departures of forecast from performance are relatively uniform over spans. Note, for instance, the right-hand column. In the first set the lowest root-mean-square is 0.536, the highest 0.589; in the second set the range is 0.408 to 0.465. Some variation appears for the jumping-off point, as we would expect from Table 1, as well as for the rate of increase.

The important conclusion from Table 3 is that the error in estimating the prospective rate of increase is nearly invariant with respect to the time period over which the estimate is made. Extrapolating in the top part of Table 3 would show slightly less error in a one-hundred-year span of projection, but such extrapolation from the second part of the table would show greater error for a longer period. The slight tendencies to decline or rise can be disregarded.

There are some differences in precision on this measure for rich as against poor countries, for large as against small countries, and for the different continents. But all of these seem of secondary importance, and derive ultimately from differences associated with rate of increase. The trials indicate clearly that on the measure used (root-mean-square error of the percentage points of departure of forecast from realization), slowly growing countries are more precisely given than rapidly growing ones.

A rough summary of the basic difference is obtained for the 810 estimates, dividing them into three groups. The 30 slowest growing countries, increasing up to 1.8 percent per annum, showed a root-mean-square of 0.29 percentage points. The middle 30 countries, increasing from 1.8 percent to 2.6 percent per annum, showed a root-mean-square of 0.48 percentage points. The 30 fastest growing countries, increasing more than 2.6 percent per annum, showed a root-mean-square of 0.60 percent-

Table 3 Root-mean-square error of United Nations forecasts for three jumping-off years, percentage points

JUMPING-OFF YEAR	FORECAST PERIOD	RATE OF INCREASE			ALL RATES OF INCREASE
		SLOW	MEDIUM	FAST	
1958	1955–60	0.320	0.555	0.793	0.589
	1955–65	0.338	0.545	0.713	0.553
	1955–70	0.323	0.534	0.698	0.541
	1955–75	0.310	0.538	0.691	0.536
	Total	0.323	0.543	0.725	0.555
1963	1960–65	0.236	0.421	0.527	0.413
	1960–70	0.248	0.447	0.487	0.408
	1960–75	0.250	0.481	0.596	0.465
	Total	0.245	0.450	0.539	0.429
1968	1965–70	0.298	0.359	0.398	0.354
	1965–75	0.245	0.418	0.390	0.359
	Total	0.273	0.390	0.394	0.357
All		0.288	0.478	0.604	0.476

age points. These differences are clearly important. Let us see what they mean in application.

The United States is officially forecast (1980 *Statistical Abstract*) to rise from a 1980 population of 222 million to a 2000 population of 260 million, implying an average annual rate of increase of 0.79 percent. The two-thirds confidence bounds on this will be 0.79 ± 0.29, or 0.50 to 1.08. That means we could bet two to one odds—but no higher—that the population in the year 2000 would be between $(222)(1.0050)^{20}$ and $(222)(1.0108)^{20}$, or between 245 and 275 million. Variants are given in the same official table, a low of 246 million and a high of 280 million. We have thus shown that the officially published low and high variants are slightly wider than the two-thirds confidence intervals—the probability that the official variants will straddle the actuality is slightly more than two-thirds.

We should state our result more carefully. If the forecasts now being made are as good as those of the past and no better, and if the unpredictable twists and turns of the components of population are as great as those of the past but no greater, then we can take it that the error now being made is drawn from the same distribution as past error, so the chance that the 2000 population will fall between 245 and 275 million is two-thirds. There is nearly one chance in three that the 2000 population will be less than the low published variant of 246 million or above the high variant of 280 million.

This result will be disappointing to those who have thought of population as perfectly predictable, but it will hardly surprise those with good memories of past errors, being in fact nothing more or less than a way of averaging those past errors. It tells us that we have some knowledge of the population twenty years ahead, but the bounds on that knowledge are wide.

A similar calculation shows that we know virtually nothing about the population fifty years from now. We could not risk better than two to one odds on any range narrower than 285 to 380 million for the year 2030.

For faster-growing countries we should use not the 0.29 appropriate for the United States, but 0.48, or for most of the developing countries, 0.60.

Distribution of Error

It would hardly be expected that all forecasts are subject to an error of 0.4 percentage points or any other number; the error is to be thought of as a random variable. Some forecasts can be seen after the event to anticipate perfectly the future population, while others are very far out.

The distribution for twenty-year forecasts made in 1958 turned out as follows for ninety countries:

DEPARTURE OF FORECAST FROM REALIZATION	NUMBER OF CASES
More than 1.5 percentage points below	1
Between 1.5 and 1.0 percentage points below	6
Between 1.0 and 0.5 percentage points below	15
Between 0.5 and 0 percentage points below	35
Between 0 and 0.5 percentage points above	31
More than 0.5 percentage points above	2

The distribution has a satisfactory single peak; the whole is skewed downward by the fact that forecasts for developing countries were low through underestimates of the fall of mortality.

Forecasts for Areas Larger and Smaller Than Countries

Subnational data—for states, provinces, countries, departments, cities—are even more plentiful than the national data discussed up to this point, and calculations such as those presented could easily be carried out once the data were assembled.

The states of the United States provide an example. The precensus estimates of population for 1980 of those states can be set against the 1980 counts. When this is done, the root-mean-square with fifty degrees of freedom is 1.164 percentage points, which is to say more than double the error with which national populations are forecast, and this despite the fact that the forecast in this case made use of indicators from the states up to 1979. Evidently unanticipated internal migration is greater than the unknowns of fertility and international migration, but by how much greater remains to be investigated in more detail and for other countries.

For higher level aggregates—continents or the world—there is an intrinsic lack of data. Tomas Frejka (1981) has recently provided a useful history of world population forecasts, but his collection shows that the material available is not sufficient for probability statements. One surmises that the bounds become narrower as aggregation increases, so for the world as a whole the bounds would be narrower than the root-mean-square of 0.4 percentage points that we suggested for all countries together, but how much narrower is hard to say.

Naive Projections

To judge a sophisticated method we need to know more than its error. The effectiveness of a professional forecast ought to stand out in comparison with a naive method like supposing last year's increase to continue into the future. If the error were greater than the error of a naive method, we would have to conclude that the demographic techniques had no value for forecasting. In general we would expect the sophisticated method to show less error than a naive method, and we will want to know by how much it is less. Ronald Lee (1978) has pointed out how close Census Bureau forecasts of fertility are to the actual fertility of the years prior to the forecast, and this suggests the experiment shown in Table 4.

Table 4 Root-mean-square error in percentage points of 1955–75 forecast on two simple methods and that for the forecast actually made: 18 populations in each of five groups of rate of increase

	WITH GEO-METRIC INCREASE FROM ACTUAL 1950–55 (1)	WITH GEO-METRIC INCREASE FROM PROJECTED 1955–60 (2)	WITH METHOD ACTUALLY USED IN PUBLISHED U.N. FORECAST (3)
Slowest growing	0.58	0.32	0.26
	1.03	0.41	0.36
	0.93	0.73	0.63
	0.76	0.68	0.58
Fastest growing	1.18	0.87	0.71
Average	0.90	0.60	0.48

For assessing projections made in the late 1950s, we can take the observed 1950 and 1955 populations, and suppose that the rate of increase that they show will persist into the future. Column (1) of Table 4 tells how good is the resulting forecast; its average root-mean-square error is 0.90 percentage points, while the corresponding figure in column (3) is 0.48. Thus professional work making explicit judgments on mortality and fertility gives a narrower range of uncertainty. Taking the ratio of squares, one can say that the professional forecast contains three times as much information as the projected geometric increase.

Table 4 also shows countries classified into five groups according to their rate of increase. The geometric increase derived from the past is grossly inferior throughout. Column (2) reports on a somewhat less naive method, making a demographic estimate for five years ahead and assuming that rate of increase will continue. It is very much better than column (1), and indeed approaches the accuracy of published forecasts. It shows that what counts is the direction of the initial takeoff; a forecaster does not make much further improvement by explicitly forecasting changes from this initial direction five, ten, and more years in the future. This accords with the fact that only in a very few cases did the forecast curve cross the realized curve; most commonly the two simply diverged from the start. In short, the forecaster was doing something very similar to what was done in column (2).

Conclusion

Forecasting is difficult enough to discourage the most hardy, and for a long time demographers did it under the heading of projection, contending that they merely worked out the consequences of variant sets of assumptions. Yet if demographers cannot judge which variant level of mortality or fertility is likely to be realized, no one can, and in practice users have depended on demographers for such judgment. The interpretation of middle-variant projections as forecasts has been nearly universal among users.

Tables 1 and 2 show that the error is apparently diminishing over time, either because population is changing in more regular fashion, or because forecasters are becoming more skilled. The root-mean-square for United Nations forecasts made in the late 1950s was 0.555; for those of the early 1960s, 0.429; for those of the late 1960s, 0.357. The difference is not due to the fact that we have had a shorter time to check up on the more recent work, since it also appears when we confine the comparison of jumping-off points to forecasts with a ten-year span. In concession to the possibility that there is a trend here, I have suggested rounding down the one-figure summary from the inclusive average 0.530 to 0.4.

Aside from assessing projection methods in absolute terms, I have examined how they compare with naive methods. One way of doing so is simply to find the rate of increase of the preceding five years and carry the population forward into the future with that rate of increase. The departure of that rate from the rate that materialized shows a root-mean-square error of 0.90 (Table 4) as against the 0.48 of actual forecasts. Judgment and the techniques of demography do indeed diminish forecast errors.

The user who objects that the probability set that provided the data for the estimate of error is not the same as the one to which it is to be applied is making an absolutely true assertion. But equally the farmer who trustfully plants potatoes using a variety that came out well in a trial cannot be assured of drawing a random sample from the urn of the trial; he is operating at a later time, in which external circumstances differ in many respects. The kind of logical jump that we make from the past degree of success of forecasts to the prospective success of the one now being made is required wherever statistical data are applied. The agronomist can design an experiment to reduce the error of application but cannot eliminate it.

Note that this is different in fundamental respects from the present practice of showing a number of estimates, calling one high, another low, another medium. Without some probability statement, high and low estimates are useless to indicate to what degree one can rely on the medium figure, or when one ought to use the low or the high. Nor do we derive any help from the notion that each of the projections corresponds to a different set of assumptions and that it is up to the user to consider the three sets of assumptions, decide which is the most realistic, and choose that one. If he actually goes to the trouble and has the skill to reflect on the alternative sets of assumptions and decide which is most realistic, then he might as well make the calculations in addition—that is a relatively easy matter once the assumptions are specified. If on the other hand, as more commonly happens, the user looks at the results and takes whichever of the three projections seems to him most likely, then the demographer has done nothing for him at all—the user who is required to choose on the basis of which of the results looks best might as well choose among a set of random numbers.

SHOULD WE CALCULATE ERROR?

Given the certainty that the future will be different from the past, it may seem wrong to suppose that future fluctuations will be drawn from the same probability set as past fluctuations. Yet the forecasts themselves face this difficulty; however sophisticated they may be, they cannot avoid assuming that the future resembles the past in important respects. Anyone who objects to this assumption ought not to make forecasts. One can respect the view that nothing at all should be said about future population, that our science is too little developed to provide a basis for forecasting. But if it is thought good enough for forecasting, then it is good enough to estimate the errors of forecasts.

It may be argued that projection is professional work analogous to that of a physician. The patient is interested less in fiducial intervals on the outcome of an operation than in the physician doing the best possible job. Just as physicians ordinarily do not discuss error with their patients, so the client who is paying for the projection does not want horror stories of how bad projections have been in the past; all he needs is confidence in the demographer.

This is not the view taken in the present paper. The client I have in mind is not a nervous patient whose calmness and confidence are to be preserved, but an intelligent policymaker who should know the presumed accuracy of information before he proceeds to base a decision on it. There are major difficulties in estimating the error of projections, but so there are also in the projections themselves. If we can usefully extrapolate population from the past, then we ought to use the past to put bounds on the extrapolated population. Demographers realize that there is a limit to the accuracy with which the future can be known, in respect of population as in other matters. The experience of the past tells us something about that limit.

PART FIVE
POPULATION CHANGE AND POLICY

CHAPTER 14
Social Security and Solidarity

INTRODUCTION

Social security presents a continuing and ever more difficult problem. When the United States scheme was patched up by the Legislature in 1977, the commissioner declared that the system would be in good health financially for the next fifty years. Five years later the fund is in trouble again. Other countries are doing only slightly better; a current newspaper headline calls Europe's social programs an endangered species. What makes it a problem is the steady increases of cost that are everywhere experienced, contrary to the popular expectations under which social security had been initiated and expanded. The United States scheme was more optimistic than most; it started with a contribution of 1 percent of wages by employees and another 1 percent by employers, and the public was pleased and surprised that provision for old age could be made so cheaply. Other countries were more realistic at the outset but still face sharply rising costs.

Yet every industrial country has a scheme, and none thinks of abandoning it. All are concerned with costs, yet each of their publics prefers to depend on its children collectively rather than individually, and wants the state to be the intermediary, taking up and disbursing the necessary funds.

The Reagan administration is probing budgets to cut costs, but it has been wary of cutting pensions, the largest item of social expenditure, which account for one quarter of the total federal budget. Like the United States, European countries have come to the point where taxes are seen as a hindrance to investment, as well as a disincentive to work. Sweden proposes to reduce income taxes to a maximum of 50 percent from the present 80 percent; the Netherlands plans to cut public spending by 10 percent each year for the next five years; West Germany, with a cap on present spending, is being pressed by elements in the Social Democratic party to shift money from defense to social areas. All these and other governments are looking hard for savings, but so far they are leaving old-age security severely alone.

Pensions are an example of how quickly a human need can be created and firmly rooted. We are only now celebrating the centennial of the first social security scheme, which was installed by Bismark in imperial Germany in 1881. The United States scheme started to operate only forty years ago. Prior to those dates, people who could no longer work simply expected to be looked after by their children.

In one sense old-age security is the same thing as being looked after by one's children. The generation that works provides the support for the generation that is retired, and mostly the former are the children of the latter. The traditional way of looking after the old is individual, household by household, while the modern way is collective. It was once taken for granted that old people would be part of the household of their children. Now both generations want the freedom and privacy that comes of living apart and of having their maintenance provided in cash rather than in kind. It has taken only a few decades for this desire to harden into an absolute necessity, so that the most determined budget cutter has not dared to whittle away any part of the level of payment so far attained.

In fact the payment becomes steadily greater. This is partly because of the dynamics of politics in a democratic society and partly because of the increase in length of life. During the one decade of the 1970s, American male expectation at age sixty-five has increased by more than one year; female by more than 1 1/2 years. That means that over the period in which they will draw, and quite aside from any changes in the legislation, Americans increase their total lifetime benefits by about 8 percent on the average. This plus the rising cost of Medicare, plus food stamps and other help that is the equivalent of cash—all resistant to budget cuts that are elsewhere merciless—is evidence of the degree to which the collective care of the old, through government, has become fixed in public expectations.

This hardening of expectations that generates rising costs is now opposed by a growing resistance to taxes. Two such strong forces in opposition to one another ensure continuing tension. Social security is not an issue that will be replaced on the public agenda by something else in a year or two just because people get tired of hearing about it. Boring or not, social security will be with us as an increasingly tense issue for another fifty-five years. We will be climbing the *rentenberg*, as Germans call it, the pension mountain. By 2035 the demographic component of costs will have reached a maximum and start to decline, as the baby boom cohorts begin to die off. One cannot guarantee that things will be better after 2035, but at least the demographic factor will start to work for rather than against us.

LEGISLATIVE HISTORY

In the 1935 Congress the original social security arrangement was voted by the Democratic majority; Republicans were opposed, and they carried their opposition to the people in the 1936 election. This was the last serious opposition that social security legislation has had to face from either party; it has been nonpartisan ever since. It is worth recalling that what Republicans opposed in 1935 was a conservatively planned scheme in which payroll taxes collected from 1937 onward would build up a substantial trust fund; they have since gone along with the succession of changes that have departed ever further from conservative financing.

In 1939 the start of benefit payments was advanced from 1942 to 1940, and survivors and dependents were blanketed in with no additional premiums. At the same time as it advanced the increased benefits, Congress postponed a scheduled increase in the tax. That postponement was repeated until 1950 when the tax was raised to a modest 1.5 percent for each employer and employee. But in 1950 Congress increased benefits again, to take immediate effect. It also provided for raising the tax further, but not to start until 1954. Edward Tufte (1978) counts thirteen benefit increases from 1950 to 1976, with proportionately more in election years. These included counting as fully insured any contributors who paid on as little as fifty dollars earnings in each of forty quarters, and from 1972 onward, benefits automatically increased by the price rise of the previous year.

There is a case for protecting sound programs from the arbitrariness of annual appropriations. After all, the constitution of Congress might change, and Democrats especially wanted to make it harder for Republicans to tamper with social security, Medicare, and similar legislation. The formula in several cases, including social security, tied payments to the Consumer Price Index. Often Congress was persuaded to pass the legislation, including the entitlement clause, by gross underestimates of what the cost would be. When more realistic estimates of costs became

Table 1 Estimate of persons 15–64 and 65 and over, U.S. 1980–2060

YEAR	15–64	65+	100× RATIO (65+)/(15–64)
1980	146,212	23,281	15.9
2000	169,734	28,296	16.7
2020	180,233	39,311	21.8
2040	181,853	45,623	25.1
2060	181,281	48,524	26.8

Source: Author's calculation

available, it was very difficult to change the formula. Social security is not the only field in which government expenditures have been subject to cost overruns, and in which rigidities are embodied in legislation.

Such inflexibility is not confined to United States legislation, as Max Horlick (1979:97) points out. Women's equality, for example, ought to include retirement at the same age as men—or even later, if one counts from the end of life backward to give the sexes the same expected time to draw. But many countries have traditionally provided for women to draw from age sixty, five years before men. That means that on the average women are on pension nine years longer than men—an excess of about 75 percent. Yet, reports Horlick, alteration seems politically impossible.

Demographic Analysis

Any analysis of what will happen to social security in the future must start with estimates of future population. The outcome is moderately sensitive to the assumptions for births after about twenty years and for deaths from the beginning.

We begin with a forecast that simply supposes that the population will replace itself and that mortality will be subject to slow improvement. Thus our female expectation of life at age zero rises to 77.7 years by 2075 and male to 72.4, figures that are little above those already attained.

A proxy for the burden of social security is the number of persons sixty-five and over per 100 persons aged 15–64. Our calculation shows a climb, slow at first but rapid after about the year 2010, and a leveling off at about 2030. An excerpt from a more detailed table is given as Table 1 above. If we had been more generous in respect of mortality, we would have shown a climb of the ratio to a higher plateau. Thus the U.S. Bureau of the Census finds an even steeper rise in the twenty-first century (1980 *Statistical Abstract* p. 338), showing over 30 percent by 2030 against our 25 percent.

Partly because of the initial restrictions on the disbursement of benefits that 2 percent of payrolls did at first serve the purpose and even sufficed to build up an appreciable trust fund. Aside from the restrictions on benefits, demography was kind to the scheme in its first years. The ratio of the number of persons sixty-five and over to those eighteen to sixty-four was 0.11 in 1940; each 100 men and women of working age had only eleven people of retired age to support.

To illustrate such matters a Lexis diagram, drawn in the age-time plane, will be found useful. It represents each individual of a population as a diagonal line, corresponding to the fact that every year a person grows one year older. A figure that sketches the evolution of the American population into the twenty-first century shows how the baby boom of the 1950s comes into the labor force about now, and how it works its way through and enters the pensionable group by the first quarter of the new century. We should be surprised that the fund is having difficulties now when the ratio of old to working people is increasing slowly if at all; the real difficulties are still three or four decades ahead of us.

On the surface it appears that the troubles of social security are caused mainly by improved mortality at older ages. To show what has happened to mortality, it could be argued, we need to look at advances in the expectation of life. That expectation at age zero could have been as low as forty-five years in 1880; it had risen to about sixty years by 1930; now in 1980 it is nearing seventy-five years. The improvement is about thirty years during the century, about fifteen years since 1930. As the expectation goes beyond sixty-five, the burden of old-age insurance increases rapidly.

Such reasoning in terms of expected lifetime is almost entirely erroneous. The expectation of life at age zero is much influenced by the drop in infant mortality, as well as by the virtual disappearance of many infectious diseases of later childhood and young adulthood, of which tuberculosis is a prime example. A study of the survivorship curve is what is wanted, rather than of the expectation of life; the probabilities of living have risen most *prior* to the age of retirement. Evidently the tendency since the beginning of the mortality record has been for an increasingly larger fraction of people to live into adulthood, while extension of the span of life has been slight. The effect of mortality change as such has been mostly to increase the working population by reducing mortality at younger ages. We can examine the ratio of sixty-five and over to twenty to sixty-five in successive life tables to demonstrate this.

What has raised the ratio of those sixty-five and over to those twenty to sixty-five from 0.11 in 1940 to 0.18 today, and will increase it by about

Table 2 Ratio of population 65 and over to that 20 to 64 at last birthday for various rates r of increase, given U.S. mortality of 1978, under stability

r	STABLE RATIO $(65+)/(20-64)$
0.00	0.239
0.01	0.172
0.02	0.122
0.03	0.088
0.04	0.059

50 percent subsequently, is above all fertility change. The high and increasing cost of social security is in most periods caused not so much by old people living longer as by the relative lack of increase in the population of working age. If the peak mortality and fertility rates of 1957 had continued, and population had increased at nearly 2 percent per year, the ratio of those over sixty-five to those twenty to sixty-four would have been much lower than it now is. Table 2 shows this ratio for various rates of increase with present mortality rates. Such an exercise in comparative statics is useful if one wishes to separate out the pure effect of natural increase from the influence of mortality (Keyfitz 1977, p. 168).

Countries vary greatly in the degree to which the ratio of persons at retired ages to those at working ages changes over time. In both Germanys and in Austria, France, and the United Kingdom, the increase is small; in Japan it is very large, going from 11 percent to 24 percent in fifty years. This means that the cost per worker of provision for old age in Japan will rise by 12 percent for demographic reasons alone. Rises nearly as substantial are shown for Canada, Poland, the Netherlands, and Finland.

A stationary population is near in industrialized countries and will extend to the world as a whole. The comparative statics of Table 2 show double the cost for zero increase as for 2 percent increase. Rapid increase of population, which has made possible the low costs of social security in the past, is transitory; stationary rather than increasing population is the normal condition, and it now becomes clear that we have been playing a chain-letter game. Like all such games that depend on ever more participants, this one sooner or later had to come to an end.

LABOR FORCE PARTICIPATION

We need more knowledge of the factors influencing retirement. People in their late sixties have never been in better health than today, nor have they had more retired years in prospect. Yet the age of retirement has been dropping. The more generous social security improvements provided add not only their own costs to the budget but also the additional cost arising from the earlier retirements that result from these improvements. For Swedish men (Artle 1980:10) we have the participation rates

AGE	RATE
63	66.3
64	62.7
65	19.3
66	15.7

which make clear the effect of the age sixty-five social security benefit. Any doubt about this is resolved by the great drop in participation that occurred when the pension age was lowered from sixty-seven to sixty-five in 1976. Experiments on various participation schedules for the future will show how influential is this variable compared with mortality.

There is clearly a limit to the degree to which older people will be supported, and one suspects that raising the pension age will be more and more discussed. The mortality drop, a gift to the old, means a rise in life expectancy $\overset{\circ}{e}_x$. In 1940 $\overset{\circ}{e}_{65}$ was twelve years in the United States; in 1980 it is about sixteen years. Thus in 1940 the person of pensionable age could expect to live to seventy-seven; in 1980 he could expect to live to eighty-one. Should we not count backward from these ages and say that social security is just as generous in 1980 as in 1940 if it provides twelve years of benefit on the average? On that condition the pension age would go up as expectation does and would be $81 - 12 = 69$ in 1980. Or perhaps a compromise could be provided, by which half of the increased expectation would be taken out in work, half in social-security-funded leisure.

No one argues that healthy men and women in their sixties and seventies are incapable of working, or that their efficiency in many jobs would not be high. (The minority not in good health is a different case.) The question, then, can be stated more broadly: how much leisure does society want for its members, or more precisely, how much is it willing to pay for? Once this is determined, it would seem a clear gain to allow individuals to choose the ages at which they would like to take that leisure. A person might take a year at age forty-five for learning a new occupation; there is no reason to deprive him of that option, of course at the cost of deferring his retirement (say by a year and a half to allow for interest, sickness, and mortality).

Two Ways of Providing for Old Age

Enough for the legislation and demographic preliminaries. We need now some theory of the two ways in which social security can in principle

be provided. These are illustrated by the two principal perspectives of the Lexis diagram on which contributions and benefits may be portrayed.
1. Each cohort looks after itself. The method obtains the advantage of interest to reduce cost; the working people who save through the scheme obtain a share in the economy aside from their jobs; that one cohort is large and another is small is in principle indifferent (though we shall have to justify this last assertion). The method cannot easily protect against inflation; it requires some stable repository of value. The unit is in the group of people on each diagonal strip of the Lexis diagram.
2. Each time period looks after itself. Interest does not come into the matter; no fund is built up; changes in cohort sizes make for awkward changes in cost; cost becomes great with the approach of a stationary population and stationary economy. Transfers are along horizontal lines in the diagram. This pay-as-you-go method is inflation-proof since the contributions of each moment are paid out to the old people of the moment very soon after collection. Just after a baby boom the method is cheap, since contributors increase sooner than beneficiaries.

An objection to funding is that it is impracticable to place the large sums involved (over $1 trillion at any one time in the United States) in the hands of the government. How could it choose impartially among the concerns in which it might invest? Would it single out declining sectors of the economy for rescue rather than stimulating the more dynamic ones? Does not government ownership of the shares of private concerns constitute socialism? And would the total amount of shares and bonds, indeed total wealth, be adequate to the size of fund that would accumulate (Bourgeois-Pichat 1978)?

Most such doubts and fears are shown to be groundless by the Swedish experience. No one proposes complete funding; a funding of one-fifth of the scheme avoids most of the objections. Sweden has had an earnings-related pension program, a second tier on top of the flat amount that everyone was entitled to, since 1959. By 1978 it had accumulated 131.5 billion kronor (some $30 billion), over one-third of annual Gross National Product. That fund is now a major source of capital formation in Sweden.

As far as capital markets are concerned, it does not make much difference whether the government runs a budget surplus of 1 percent of the national income, or individuals save 1 percent of the national income. Either way the same amount is available for investment. The government's budget surplus would be used to pay off the national debt, and the individuals whose bonds were called for repayment would seek a new investment of the funds. But though the economic effects of the two kinds of saving—governmental and private—are similar, they are seen very differently by the citizen. The money that he sets aside is his own nest egg; the money he pays in taxes is gone. It is vain to tell him that the effect on the economy is the same; he looks with a kinder eye on an accumulation in his own name, even one made under compulsion. Inflation qualifies this, and troubles pension policy as many other matters.

Different Bookkeeping in Free Enterprise and Socialist Societies

The changing ratio of people of retired age (say, sixty-five and over) to those of working age (18 to 64) is bound to affect all countries.

The ultimate effect of this is everywhere the same—fewer workers to support each retired person—but it shows itself in different ways, depending on the bookkeeping system. In the United States the successive threatened bankruptcies of the Social Security Trust Fund, built up by a special tax, are the aspect with which the public and legislators are all-too familiar.

Some countries have no specific tax but simply take payments out of the national budget. This means that the demographically engendered crisis can be covered over a considerable time at the cost of other items in the budget. In a socialist state where the budget covers all of the nation's productive activities, this capacity to disguise the immediate effect is especially great. Yet somehow the issue must be met, and making the costs explicit and separate helps sound and quick decisions.

If one goes to the extreme of an economy in which the product is divided equally among the entire population, and if then we abstract from other changes, a larger number of nonworkers will mean a falling standard of living. A society facing this would want to even things out and might well accept more savings ahead of time so as to increase its capital stock and prevent the fall. Typically a society has many opportunities for investment of savings, and the return on investment would help support the old people. With even 3 percent return each dollar or ruble of saving would provide two dollars or rubles twenty-three years later.

Different countries have different ways of keeping the accounts, and bookkeeping has much effect on the way the problem is perceived. With a funded scheme the future old people *as a cohort* set aside money resources equivalent to physical capital. The society is then doing what an individual does when he builds a house durable enough to live in through his old age. Everyone has some such physical saving—clothes or other goods if not an automobile or a house.

Yet because we all require nondurable goods as well, physical saving is not a complete solution for the individual. Samuelson (1958) shows that perishable goods require some kind of social solution. If working life is in two or more periods, an old person can bribe younger workers to support him. If it is only one period even that is not possible, and only a fiat of the community can ensure the continuing consumption of the old (Samuelson, 1958).

Yet this solution, embodied in the social security legislation of most advanced countries, plants the seeds of intergenerational discord. In past populations, which grew quickly with high mortality, the young might have been supported by their parents for fifteen years, with the parents later requiring support for ten years. But today the young might be supported for eighteen years and the old (at higher cost per person-year) then for twenty years, a very different ratio. Moreover, the care of the young is decentralized into families; the collectivization of the care of the old makes it seem a heavier burden.

Intergenerational transfers present the problem of time in its most acute form. Insofar as goods have no keeping qualities, one is driven to a social solution; each time period must balance its books; the old can only live off current work.

Limits on the Independence of Cohorts

Since a main argument for the funded scheme is that it makes each cohort independent of the others, we need to look more closely into the degree to which this can be so. It would be possible if the working population produced the actual physical goods on which they would live in their old age—if they could make the clothing, build the houses, bake the bread that they would use when they were past sixty-five. Insofar as they cannot do this, they will have to depend on those currently in the labor force. This dependency is inevitable for bread, avoidable for houses.

Yet still keeping the discussion close to real goods, that must be qualified. A man during his working years can build a house that is more durable than he currently needs and that will last him into his old age. But in an exchange economy he does not need to build the very house in which he will live; he can perform services for those who build while he is of working age, or he can otherwise come into the purchase and control of a house. Nor need the facility be a house or other object that directly serves for his personal use; he can save the money and invest it in a company that builds a steel mill, and so at second remove be said to build a steel mill to produce steel that will be sold to pay his rent and buy his groceries when he is old.

Thus seemingly unanswerable cases can be constructed to support two opposing contentions: (1) that on a funded scheme each cohort independently provides for its own old age, and (2) that whether or not the scheme is funded, each cohort when old must depend on the goods produced by the cohort that is then of working age. The first case is built by thinking of the saving and investment of money or of physical saving of durable consumer goods like houses. The second case is made by thinking of perishable goods like bread that have to be produced from day to day, and excluding the possibility of saving.

The extent to which the cohorts can be independent of one another is limited: if the society collapsed there would be nothing for anyone, including the old. If the society does not collapse but suffers wild inflation, the possession of pensions resulting from saving, however fully funded, will do no good.

It is important to draw a distinction between this discussion and a similar problem that arose during the war. It was said that a war has to be fought in real terms, that there is no way of putting the burden on a future generation. Borrowing seems to do this, but that is an illusion, for borrowing is no more than a financial rearrangement; the tanks and planes have to be made while the war is going on, and they might just as well be paid by taxes then as by taxes later. Borrowing merely redistributes claims subsequent to the war. Fighting a war differs in many ways from supporting people in their old age, but most importantly in that once it occurs a war cannot be prepared for in advance. Old age is different in being perfectly predictable, and it is ridiculous to say that an individual or a cohort cannot save up for it. The general principle is that one cannot draw on future production for today's needs, but one can certainly draw on past production if one has had the foresight to increase production with old age in mind.

I have given examples in physical terms by which individuals and cohorts can provide for their old age, but that may not be adequate for a complex money economy. If for instance individuals save but no one wants to invest, the Keynesian problem, then notwithstanding any number of physical examples, the society as such cannot provide in advance for its old age. Again, if money is not a stable repository of value, then any transaction across time is frustrated, including saving for old age.

A full fund would be of the order of magnitude of the national debt, now approaching a trillion dollars. This refers to the amount on hand at any given moment in an operating scheme. (It is somewhat less than half of the expected claims of individuals, their social security wealth.) If the

United States scheme had been funded from the start and the fund invested as the national debt was successively increased, then the interest now paid on the debt would be available for social security. That interest now amounts annually to about $80 billion, so it would cover almost half the cost of current pensions.

This would be no mere paper difference from the present arrangement. We now tax ourselves ($80.4 billion in fiscal 1981) to pay the interest on the debt, and we separately tax workers and employers to pay pensions of $163 billion in 1981. We would of course still need taxes to cover the interest payments on the debt; since these are half of the social security burden, they could be applied to relieve the wage earner of the entire half of the social security tax that he now pays.

It is true that people and institutions would have to adjust if government bonds and treasury notes were not publicly available. Insurance companies and others whose investments are now determined by law would have to be released from at least some of their present restrictions. They would be pushed out into financial markets that would channel their funds into productive use.

The view that there is no difference between pay-as-you-go and funding is expressed with most energy and enthusiasm by Nicholas A. Barr (1979). Spending by the retired has to be matched by nonspending by the workforce. Suppose that the workforce does not want to spend less; suppose that it simply repudiates the bonds or other assets into which the old have put their savings. For Barr that possibility is to be taken as seriously as the refusal to pay social security taxes in the next generation.

Barr very correctly says that "the choice of pay-as-you-go or funding is completely irrelevant unless the method of finance is the *cause* of an increase in national output" (Barr 1979: 50). But under most conditions savings do cause an increase in output. Unless capital has entirely ceased to be productive, more output follows from more saving, and the claim to that extra output would be in the hands of those whose nonspending has been responsible for it.

The problem of the increasing costs of pensions on the present scheme will not go away, but one can try to dodge it. One way to dodge it is to combine it with other questions. It can be said that we should not worry about the costs of pensions in the year 2030 because our children's children will be so rich that the price will be easily borne however high it may be. Or else we can compare pension costs with child upbringing costs, and take one as offsetting the other. These are alternatives to the basic way of concealing the cost, which is to pay it out of the national budget, without a separate tax.

One can make the question of intergenerational equity as complex as one likes. If we save less and spend more, our children will not be as rich as they otherwise would be—though they will in any case be richer than we are unless things go very badly. The issue can be expressed in physical terms—if we build more solid but smaller houses, we can spread the same utility over a longer time. On the other hand, our efforts to help our children by bequeathing them more durable artifacts may be vain if tastes change greatly. Certainly we help our children by consuming a smaller amount of nonrenewable resources, all other things being equal.

But it seems better to keep the issue of pensions simple by taking it in a narrower context, and especially by focusing on the right of contributors to interest on their premiums and the need of the American economy for investment funds.

SOCIAL SECURITY AND SOCIAL COHESION

When social security was initiated in the 1930s, with a 1 percent tax on the wage earner and 1 percent of payroll from the employer, the public was in favor of and, indeed, enchanted by the idea that the problem of old-age security could be solved at so little cost. No longer would it be necessary for old people to be dependent on their children individually; they could be looked after collectively. Where once they had been a burden on their children, they would now be only a small cash outlay for the community as a whole.

It must have been realized by those who thought about the matter that the shift from individual support to collective support of parents could not possibly lighten the financial burden, whatever its other advantages. It is more expensive to support people in cash and independence than in kind within the family. Now they would have separate dwellings and live independently of their children, where previously they had typically lived in the homes of their children. When aged parents moved from a separate room to a separate apartment, someone had to pay the added rent.

Note that social security is distributionally different from depending on one's children. The support from children offered by social security is the same for old people who have many children and those who have few or none. Yet the same intergenerational transfer is involved, with the main difference that social security removes the incentive for individual couples to have children. It is also distributionally different in that the better-off workers contribute more in taxes per dollar later received—although this analysis is complicated by the better-off having more favorable mortality.

From a sheerly rational perception of self-interest, as Samuelson (1958) pointed out over twenty years ago, the right thing for any generation to do is to repudiate the implicit "debt" to its elders. As he says, inflation does this in respect of personal savings tied to nominal dollars. A generation faced with a particularly sharp rise in tax could even repudiate without in any way breaking its word, since the promise to pay pensions had been given not by it but by a generation long past, if it had been given by anyone. It might admit that it received its upbringing and education from its parents but deny the existence of any contract for a quid pro quo. It might argue that the ratio of old-age costs to upbringing costs has risen so greatly (especially medical expenses) that if there ever was a contract its terms have so changed that no one can be held to it.

Social security can be regarded as a way of countering the diminished cohesion within the family in a modern industrial society. When firm bonds exist among the several generations within a family, governments are hardly expected to take funds from individual workers and hand them over to the aged parents of those workers. The intermediacy of government only comes to be offered and welcomed as the family loses its centrality. When the family was society's main unit, working people would no sooner see their helpless parents go into an institution for the aged than they would send their children out to be looked after in an orphanage. No matter how it is described, the advent of social security marks a stage in the loosening of family bonds.

Yet social security itself requires bonds, though of another kind. Individuals must replace their loyalty to parents within the family by loyalty to the state, if they are to continue to pay taxes.

A generation or two ago people were expected to prepare for their old age individually; they might prepare by saving or by having children or both. If they did neither, or if their children were unable to look after them, they had to resort to other relatives; failing that, they suffered the punishment of being looked after by charity, private or public. The incentive to save and to have children was strong.

Many things have changed since that time only fifty years ago. The birth rate is down, so families have fewer children. Those children they do have want to lead their own lives; they typically leave home long before marriage and, having lost the habit of living with their parents, they do not usually welcome them back into their homes forty years later. It is true that sometimes parents are inexpensive babysitters. In Eastern Europe old people have the very important use of queuing in stores for luxuries and even for necessities. Yet everywhere dignity is lost for old people who have no other option than to return and live with their children. Even the faithful single daughter whose mother is living with her, probably the circumstance in which the parent is best off, appreciates the extra income provided by the mother's social security check, and the check increases the mother's options and dignity.

Thus the constituency for social security goes far beyond the old people who are drawing it. It includes their children, other relatives, indeed virtually the entire electorate. The young want their parents to be independent, and in the past they have only loosely identified the parents' social security check with the tax they are paying. But one can expect that the connection will be made more and more often as the burden increases. The strong forces in support of social security will clash with equally strong forces opposed to high taxes, and the outcome is unpredictable.

Summary

After a certain age, selected by convention rather than by nature, the old have done their work and will offer no further contribution to production in exchange for their keep. This was so in the days when they depended on their families for support; it is so in the present where they depend largely on the state, and it will be so in whatever new arrangement can be devised. We have shifted from support by the family to support by the state as the cohesion of the family has diminished. But now doubts are expressed as to whether the social cohesion of the state is strong enough to guarantee the continued support of the old. The question becomes more urgent as population growth slows and longevity increases.

For part of their keep, the old can use the physical capital they have themselves accumulated while working—durable clothes, furniture, an automobile, equity in a house. But for the part of their keep that is perishable goods, especially food and fuel, they are dependent on the currently working generation. In the measure in which they are to consume more of such goods, someone else has to consume less of them. The problem of providing for the old is the problem of making the sacrifice reasonable in the eyes of those working. A well-administered funded scheme testifies that those who are now old have added to the capital of the community in their own working time, and it is the increment of income generated by this capital that they withdraw in their old age.

The degree of social solidarity is determined by history and is not easily manipulated by policy; what policy can do is place the smallest possible burden on the limited amount of solidarity that exists in a modern society. That consideration points to funding at least a part of social security.

CHAPTER **15**

How Birth Control Affects Population

Reduction of births may come by way of abortion, an intervention between conception and birth, or by contraception, which prevents the new life before it starts. Some societies have made abortion their principal method of birth control, and most use it to one degree or another when birth control fails. Let us start by seeing how abortion affects births.

BIRTHS AVERTED BY INDUCED ABORTION

An induced abortion of a pregnancy that is proceeding to term prevents a birth. Do 1,000 induced abortions performed in a population prevent 1,000 births? The answer is no, not even approximately. Here, as elsewhere, the logic of individuals becomes grossly misleading when applied to populations.

An Arithmetical Example

Consider a couple who have just conceived and then decide to have an abortion; the wife might have the abortion in the second month and be sterile for one further month, a total time from conception of three months. To calculate the effect of the abortion we need to consider what happens after. Suppose that the wife is young and fertile again and that the couple resumes intercourse without contraceptive protection. Then the expected number of months before the wife is pregnant again is about five. The three infertile months before and after the abortion, plus the five months to another pregnancy, eight months in all, have brought the couple back to the same condition of just having conceived that it was in when we started our observation. The eight months represent the time unavailable for childbearing due to one abortion. Only if this length of time were sufficient to have a child would one abortion prevent one birth in the population.

In fact, having a child takes much longer. It requires the number of months without protection until conception, say five once again, plus the mean time to term, nine months, plus the postpartum sterile period, which may be as much as another eight months, or twenty-two months in all. Only at the end of this twenty-two months is the woman back in the same condition as at the start of the cycle and susceptible to pregnancy again. To make the discussion concrete, we are supposing a probability of conception in each month of 0.2, that implies, as will be seen, a mean waiting time of 5 months. More precise figures would not greatly affect the conclusions to be drawn.

On this model, childbearing is a matter of time. The eight months accounted for by the abortion are seen as having kept the woman out of exposure for a little more than one-third of the twenty-two months that it would have taken her to have a child. Put the other way, the twenty-two months would have produced one child without the abortion; to prevent childbearing during that period by means of abortions alone would have required $22/8 = 2.75$ abortions.

Hence, the answer to the question of how many births 1,000 abortions in a population prevent is in this example $1,000 \times 8/22 = 364$. Similar arithmetic shows that if the abortion were delayed until the fetus was four or five months old, it would keep the woman out of childbearing longer. However, even abortions taking place just before natural birth are not equivalent to births prevented insofar as the succeeding infertile period is shorter than after a birth.

If on the other hand our model had admitted possible pregnancy terminated by miscarriage, the average time between successive normal births would have been even longer, and the effect of the induced abortion would have been accordingly further reduced. Moreover, the abortion of a conception that was destined to end up as a stillbirth would not have prevented a birth at all, but could even have brought the succeeding pregnancy closer. Far from reducing births, the abortion in this case would on the average have added a fraction of a birth!

The issues here are of general enough application that they have been the subject of a more precise formal model (Sheps and Menken, 1973; Potter, 1970).

The Theoretical Analysis

The model is a renewal process, one that repeatedly reverts to the same situation. Think of two just-married people: they start intercourse, say without contraception; then they have a pregnancy, childbirth, postpartum anovulatory period, and at the end of the cycle they are in the same condition as when they began. They are ready to start over. This is the meaning of "renewal" in this context. Our analysis will be confined to expected values, though a similar argument could tell us about variances or other moments as well. In effect, we will be comparing the renewal process of intercourse, pregnancy, childbearing, intercourse, with the renewal process of intercourse, pregnancy, abortion, intercourse. We will disregard miscarriage and stillbirth and take account only of conceptions leading to live births. Time will be measured in ovulations, and we will suppose these to be one month apart.

First, to find the mean time to conception: suppose that month by month the chance of conceiving is p for a woman in the fertile condition. Then among a number of couples the fraction p will be expected to conceive in the first month, and $1 - p$ will proceed into the second month. Of these, p will then become pregnant, that is to say $(1 - p)p$ of the original women will become pregnant in the second month. Similarly, the fraction $(1 - p)^2 p$ will become pregnant in the third month, and so on.

To check that the probabilities add to unity, which they should do if all cases are covered, we write q for $1 - p$, so that $p = 1 - q$, and the sum for all months is

$$p + (1 - p)p + (1 - p)^2 p + \ldots = 1 - q + q(1 - q) + q^2(1 - q) + \ldots .$$

Removing the parentheses here gives

$$1 - q + q - q^2 + q^2 - q^3 + \ldots ,$$

and all terms but the first cancel. This proves to be p, $(1 - p)p$, $(1 - p)^2 p$, ..., an honest probability distribution.

The expected number of ovulations until pregnancy occurs will be found by multiplying p by 1, $(1 - p)p$ by 2, $(1 - p)^2 p$ by 3, ..., and adding:

$$p + 2(1 - p)p + 3(1 - p)^2 p + \ldots ,$$

if we suppose the process starts with an ovulation.

To sum this expression we write $p = 1 - q$ and have
$$1 - q + 2q(1 - q) + 3q^2(1 - q) + \ldots,$$
or on multiplying out in each term,
$$1 - q + 2q - 2q^2 + 3q^2 - 3q^3 + \ldots,$$
which is the same as the geometric series
$$1 + q + q^2 + \ldots,$$
whose total is $1/(1 - q) = 1/p$. This is the mean number of ovulations (or roughly of months of exposure) if the probability of conception in any month is p.

The feature of a renewal process that makes our task simple is its additivity. Suppose that the number of months of sterility following the onset of pregnancy is also a random variable, with mean value s. Then the expected length of time from the start of intercourse to the end of the sterile or nonsusceptible period is the sum of these two mean values, $(1/p) + s$.

The same proposition applies to abortion, which involves first the random time to pregnancy and then the random time to performance of the abortion. We will find it convenient to incorporate with the time to abortion the length of the postabortion sterile period. Suppose these two add up to a total nonsusceptible period of random length whose expected value is a. Then the total length of the cycle is on the average $(1/p) + a$.

Since the total length of the cycle involving one abortion averages $1/p + a$, and the total length of the cycle involving one birth averages $1/p + s$, the number of the former that would fit into the latter is $(1/p + s)/(1/p + a)$. This is the number of abortion cycles required to fill the time that would be taken by one birth cycle. It is therefore the number of abortions that would prevent one birth, and its reciprocal is the fraction of a birth prevented by one abortion. If $p = 0.2$, $s = 17$, and $a = 3$, we have 8/22 births prevented by one abortion.

The same result may be obtained by thinking of two women with the same constant probability p of conception leading to live birth in any month. The first of the women carries all the conceptions to term, and according to the above argument will have a baby on the average every $1/p + s$ months. The other woman wants no children and uses abortion as her sole method of birth control. She would have an abortion every $1/p + a$ months. Over any long period of time T the first woman would expect to have $T/(1/p + s)$ births; the second woman would expect to have $T/(1/p + a)$ abortions. The second ratio divided by the first, i.e., $(1/p + s)/(1/p + a)$, again tells us how many abortions are equivalent to one birth.

Abortion as a Backup to Contraception

The constants in the above calculation are about right for human populations that do not use contraception. With contraception, the effect of abortion is very much greater, a fact that may not be intuitively obvious. We will see how it follows from the above discussion.

To apply the argument to our new problem, we suppose that the efficiency of contraception is e. If e is 0.95, then instead of the probability of conceiving in a particular month being 0.2, as for unprotected fertile couples, it is reduced to $0.2(1 - 0.95)$ or about 0.01. More generally, in place of p we write $p(1 - e)$ as the probability of conceiving in a particular month. So much for the definition of efficiency of contraception.

Now we go through the whole of the preceding argument again, this time with $p(1 - e)$ instead of p. Nothing else is changed: the mean length of time to pregnancy for fertile couples becomes $1/p(1 - e)$, and the number of abortions that would prevent one birth is now

$$\frac{\dfrac{1}{p(1-e)} + s}{\dfrac{1}{p(1-e)} + a}.$$

Entering $p = 0.2$, $e = 0.95$, $s = 17$ months, and $a = 3$ months gives

$$(1/0.01 + 17)/(1/0.01 + 3) = 1.14$$

abortions to prevent one birth.

This is a very different outcome from the no-contraception case. With unprotected intercourse it takes nearly three abortions to prevent one birth. With 95 percent efficient contraception it takes only about 1 1/7 abortions to prevent one birth. If the efficiency of contraception were higher than 0.95, an abortion would be even more effective.

What conclusion, then, can be drawn from the fact that legal abortions in the United States in 1978 numbered 1,410,000 (*Stat. Abstr.* 1961, p. 66)? We certainly cannot say there would have been 1,410,000 more births if these pregnancies had been allowed to go to term. How many more there would have been depends crucially on how many of the abortions were a backstop to efficient contraception, how many were the only means of birth control used.

Limitations of the Deterministic Model

The argument by which we have found how many abortions in a population are required to avert one birth is deterministic. We compared two women going through repeated cycles, one involving births and the other involving abortions, but without allowing for variation in the length of cycle. We also disregarded variation in fecundity among women. If p is not constant from woman to woman, the resulting expression for births averted has additional terms. The complexities offered by the real world can be met by making the mathematics more elaborate; the art of model-building is to stop the elaboration once the model is realistic enough to draw practical conclusions.

Some kinds of complexity can be defined out of the model. Stillbirths, for example, have been eliminated in what precedes by the device of considering only those conceptions that lead to live births.

BIRTHS AVERTED BY CONTRACEPTION

A similar logic serves to establish the effect of contraception. How many births are averted by the insertion of a loop or by giving a woman a supply of pills? Again let us confine ourselves to contraceptions leading to live births, of which the probability in any month is taken as p. Again we require the proposition proved above that the expected time to conception is $1/p$ months.

Contraception by One Method Continuing Indefinitely

The couple who uses a contraceptive of efficiency e have a probability of conceiving in any month of $p^* = p(1 - e)$. With the same sterile period after conception of s months, the couple will expect a child once in $1/p^* + s = 1/p(1 - e) + s$ months, while an unprotected couple would expect a child each $1/p + s$ months.

This formula tells us that inefficient contraception cannot reduce the birth rate very much. One might think that contraception of 50 percent efficiency would lower the birth rate by half, but its effect is much less. On the present model, with the constants used before, a birth would take place every $1/0.2 + 17 = 22$ months without contraception. With 50 percent efficient contraception a birth would take place every $1/(0.2)(1 - 0.5) + 17 = 27$ months. Contraception of 50 percent efficiency has reduced the birth rate from 1/22 to 1/27, a reduction of only 19 percent.

Frequency of Intercourse

The same model also tells us that childbearing is by no means proportional to frequency of sexual intercourse. To see this, suppose that a woman is fertile one day out of thirty, and that she has intercourse ten times per month on occasions that are random in relation to susceptibility. Then the probability of conception is 10/30 in any particular month and the expected time to conception three months. If the infertile period totals seventeen months, then she would have a child every twenty months; the monthly birth rate of such women would be 1/20. The biology here is crude but sufficient for our illustration.

Suppose now that she reduces her frequency of intercourse to five times per month. If the occasions are still random, then the probability in any month is reduced to 1/6, and the expected exposure time is increased to six months. She will have a baby on the average every $6 + 17 = 23$ months, that is, a monthly birth rate of 1/23. By reducing intercourse 50 percent, from ten to five times per month, people reduce their birth rate from 1/20 to 1/23, or only 13 percent on our assumptions. Restraint with random time of intercourse is not an effective way of holding down births. We revert to contraception.

To assess the consequence of one fitting of a loop or one provision of a stock of pills to a woman who has patronized a birth control clinic, it would be extreme optimism to assume that the loop will stay in place indefinitely or the pills be used forever. Plentiful data now exist on discontinuance rates, and we need to elaborate our model to take these into account (Potter, 1970).

Discontinuance of Contraception

Let the probability of discontinuing the use of the contraceptive for a reason other than pregnancy be d in any month if pregnancy is not considered, and suppose again that among users during a fecund month $p^* = p(1 - e)$ accidentally conceive. Then an expected $d^* = d(1 - p^*)$ drop the contraceptive at the end of the month while still susceptible, and $1 - p^* - d^*$ continue its use into the following month.

Now the probability of pregnancy by an accident during the use of the contraceptive is

$$p^* + (1 - p^* - d^*)p^* + (1 - p^* - d^*)^2 p^* + \ldots = \frac{p^*}{p^* + d^*}.$$

The probability of dropping the contraceptive is exactly the same series, but with d^* rather than p^* at the end of each term. Thus, we have

$$d^* + (1 - p^* - d^*)d^* + (1 - p^* - d^*)^2 d^* + \ldots = \frac{d^*}{p^* + d^*}.$$

If we suppose the process to continue until pregnancy occurs, before or after dropping the contraceptive, then the probability that it occurs after is also $d^*/(p^* + d^*)$. The ratio of the probability of conceiving while wearing the loop, say, is to the probability of conceiving after discontinuance as p^* is to d^*.

To obtain the probabilities month by month for those who are destined to become pregnant while wearing the contraceptive, we divide the unconditional probability of becoming pregnant in each month by $p^*/(p^* + d^*)$. Among these women $p^*/(p^*/(p^* + d^*))$ would become pregnant in the first month, $(1 - p^* - d^*)p^*/(p^*/(p^* + d^*))$ in the second month, etc. Cancelling in these ratios, we find $p^* + d^*$ for the first month, $(1 - p^* - d^*)(p^* + d^*)$ for the second month, etc. Hence, for these women, the mean length of exposure is

$$p^* + d^* + 2(1 - p^* - d^*)(p^* + d^*) + \ldots$$

which works out to

$$\frac{1}{p^* + d^*},$$

using the same argument that summed $p + 2(1 - p)p + \ldots$ to give us $1/p$.

Similarly, the distribution to discontinuance by that fraction $d^*/(d^* + p^*)$ who are destined to discontinue before they become pregnant is the same, and the mean exposure to discontinuance is again $1/(p^* + d^*)$.

Effect of Contraception as Against Natural Fertility

Suppose the $d^*/(p^* + d^*)$ individuals who drop out through discontinuance of the contraceptive use no contraceptive afterward. They will have a further period of exposure while they are unprotected, and this will average $1/p$ months. Hence the time to conception is the time with the contraceptive for everybody, $1/(p^* + d^*)$, and for the fraction $d^*/(p^* + d^*)$ who discontinue is an additional $1/p$. The mean exposure time to conception averaged over all the women in our hypothetical population is

$$t^* = \frac{1}{p^* + d^*} + \frac{d^*}{p^* + d^*}\left(\frac{1}{p}\right) = \frac{1 + (d^*/p)}{p(1 - e) + d^*}.$$

This simple and fundamental formula, due to Potter (1970), enables us to find the effect in births averted of a segment of contraception, for example, fitting a loop to a woman. If we know the three quantities, p, e, and d^* of the expression for mean exposure, then we can calculate the mean months of intercourse until conception occurs. This is to be contrasted with $1/p$, the mean months of intercourse without contraception, and the difference is the effect of the contraception.

For the interval between successive births, we add to the expressions for exposure to intercourse the mean sterile period associated with pregnancy, say s as before, including the time both before and after the birth. The expected interbirth period associated with contraception is then $t^* + s$. Thus, one birth takes place under contraception (including an allowance for dropping the contraceptive) every $t^* + s$ months. If there were no contraception, one birth would take place every $1/p + s$ months, and the expected number of births without contraception during the $t^* + s$ months would be $(t^* + s)/(1/p + s)$. Hence, the births averted by the segment of contraception must number this quantity less the one that did take place:

$$\frac{t^* + s}{\frac{1}{p} + s} - 1 = \frac{t^* - \frac{1}{p}}{\frac{1}{p} + s} = \frac{p - p^*}{(1 + ps)(p^* + d^*)}.$$

The general method for finding births averted by a segment of contraception is thus to calculate the expected birth rate with and without the segment and take the ratio less unity. We can only find the effects of some action by comparing what happens if the action is taken with what would happen if the action were not taken. To say what would happen with or without some proposed action requires a model, and indeed no causal imputation can be made without a model. The more realistic the model, the more precise and certain is the imputation.

To continue with our simple example, suppose that $p = 0.2$, $s = 17$, and (as an approximation for the IUD) $p^* = (0.05)(0.2) = 0.01$, $d^* = 0.03$. Then in the absence of contraception a birth would take place every $1/p + s = 5 + 17 = 22$ months. With the IUD, t^* would be 28.75, and a birth would take place every $t^* + s = 45.75$ months. Hence, the births averted by the segment of the IUD are $45.75/22 - 1 = 1.08$, supposing it to be replaced by no contraception after it falls out.

When Modern Contraception Takes the Place of Premodern

One direction of realism in the model is recognition that many of those who are fitted with a modern means like the loop have already been using contraception of lower efficiency. The number of births averted that can properly be credited to the loop is only the difference resulting

Table 1 Calculation of births averted by contraception

	LOOP SUPERIMPOSED ON	
VARIABLES	NATURAL FERTILITY	90% EFFICIENT CONTRACEPTION
p	0.2	0.02
$p^* = p(1-e)$	0.01	0.01
d^*	0.03	0.03
s	17	17
$\dfrac{p - p^*}{(1 + ps)(p^* + d^*)}$	1.08	0.19

from the superiority of the loop over the method used previously; it would be quite improper to credit the loop with all the births averted through its use, as calculated above, where no other method was taken into account.

By a simple alteration of the meaning of the preceding symbols, we can deal with the case where the modern contraceptive does not replace natural fertility, but supplants some other less efficient method already in use. Suppose that when the modern method is discontinued—the loop falls out, for instance—the couple goes back to the earlier method. All that is needed to make the above argument apply is to redefine p, making it refer now not to natural fertility, but to the probability of conception in any given month under the earlier method of contraception.

If the alternative to which a woman falls back on discontinuance is 90 percent efficient, the p would become $(0.2)(1 - 0.9) = 0.02$, and $1/p + s$ is $50 + 17 = 67$. Then t^* is now $(1 + d^*/p)/(d^* + p^*) = (1 + 0.03/0.02)/(0.04) = 62.5$, and $t^* + s$ is 79.5. Births averted by the segment of contraception in this situation are $(79.5/67) - 1 = 0.19$.

The contribution of a fitting of a loop to a birth-control program is less than one-fifth as great if the alternative is 90 percent efficient contraception than if it is natural fertility.

Delay in Exposure

Often a loop is fitted just after a child is born. It is an administrative convenience that the woman is already present in the hospital, and after having a baby she is likely to be receptive to birth control. For the months of postpartum sterility, the loop cannot affect the chance of childbearing, and on the other hand it is subject to the risk of accidental or deliberate removal. If this risk is d per month in the absence of pregnancy, and the woman has A months to go before she becomes fertile again, then the chance that the contraceptive will begin to work as assumed in the above model is $(1 - d)^A$.

The argument needs to be broken down for (1) the conditional probability if the loop stays in place A months, and (2) the conditional probability if it is discontinued. If the loop stays in place A months, then the subsequent expected exposure time is t^*; and if it does not, the subsequent expected exposure time is $1/p$. Hence, the unconditional expected exposure time is

$$t_A^* = (1 - d)^A t^* + (1 - (1 - d)^A)(1/p),$$

where we start counting at the beginning of the fertile period. Now births averted would be a smaller quantity than before:

$$\text{Births averted given } A = \frac{t_A^* + s}{\frac{1}{p} + s} - 1 = \frac{t_A^* - \frac{1}{p}}{\frac{1}{p} + s}.$$

This is a smaller quantity because t_A^* is a decreasing function of A, so that for positive A the births averted will also be a decreasing function of A. Intuition must be in accord: loops inserted in temporarily sterile women cannot make as much difference to the birth rate as loops in fertile women.

These considerations pose an operations-research type of problem for the family planning administrator. He can more easily arrange for loops to be fitted while women are in hospital, but some of the loops will be lost before they can come into effective use. What part of his effort should go into this immediate postpartum fitting, as against the part that goes into other birth control activities? If the woman leaves the hospital unfitted, when should she be reminded to return for fitting? The lactation period and the temporary sterility associated with it is a random variable, and one would aim to come as close to the end as possible. The optimum solution would compromise between the waste of loops inserted too early and the risk of an unprotected fertile gap.

Again, what amount of effort should be put into providing contraception to women in their twenties, and what to those in their thirties? We know that the dropout rate is higher for younger women, so the expected time they will wear the loop after its insertion is shorter. Yet they are more fertile, and so while the loop is in place it prevents more births. Aside from this, a birth prevented to a younger woman helps to lengthen the generation, which, as we shall see later, in itself lowers the annual rate of increase of the population.

The large amount of data on costs and effectiveness now being gathered ought to provide a basis for rational decision of these and other points.

A Contraception Balance Sheet

The theory sketched here, along with data now becoming available to provide the constants, suggests an overall account of the childbearing activities of a country. Starting with the number of married couples of different ages and of different degrees of susceptibility, we can say how many children would be produced if there were no contraception. From the actual number born before the advent of modern loops and pills, we can estimate the efficiency of older style contraceptive methods. With estimates of the number of loops fitted and pills provided, we can say what additional births are being averted, using the above outlined theory. The balance sheet starts in effect with the amount of intercourse, and accounts for all of it, including the part that results in the bearing of children.

With a target number of births set as acceptable at the end of twenty years, for example, we can calculate what amount of further modern birth-control activity will be necessary, recognizing alternative routes to the target.

OTHER EFFECTS OF BIRTH CONTROL

Childspacing and the Efficiency of Contraception

Those advocating contraception have argued that it would advance the welfare of mothers by allowing them to space out their children, and indeed "childspacing" was a euphemism for contraception in the days when mention of the direct term was injudicious. Today we observe in groups using contraception a tendency to concentrate children within a few years of the mother's reproductive life. The interchild interval seems to go down as the efficiency of contraception goes up, so that if we needed a euphemism for contraception today, child-concentration would be more appropriate than childspacing. The reason is a further aspect of the mathematics of birth control.

To present a simplified case, suppose that a husband and wife want no more than two children, that they command a technology of birth control that is 95 percent efficient, and that they have a reproductive life of 25 years. They would have a probability of conceiving in any month of $(0.2)(1 - 0.95) = 0.01$ with their 95 percent efficient contraceptive, and over the 25 years they would have an expected 2½ pregnancies. The couple could not afford to let up for any part of their fecund life; using contraception for each of the 300 months they would have over two children on the average, and these would appear at random intervals spread through the 25 years.

At the other extreme, a husband and wife who command a sure method of contraception can go ahead and have two or three children early in their married life, or at any juncture they find convenient, with complete confidence that they could then stop. Not needing to allow for accidental pregnancies, they can enjoy the advantages of having their children in a clump. These advantages include especially the economies in the mother's time—she has to stay home whether she is looking after one child or three—and the companionship that the children provide for one another. If the mother is tied up until her youngest is aged ten, then having three children at ten-year intervals takes thirty years; having them at two-year intervals takes fourteen years. In the latter case, childbearing interrupts her career for only half as long as in the former.

A very high efficiency of contraception is necessary for the couple to concentrate its children with confidence; even 99 percent efficiency is not good enough. For with 99 percent efficiency, the chance of bearing in a particular month with $p = 0.2$ is $(0.02)(1 - 0.99) = 0.002$. The couple who marries young, has all three children in a clump, and then has twenty years of fertile life remaining must realize that its chance of avoiding a fourth pregnancy over 240 months is $0.998^{240} = 0.618$. The chance is almost 40 percent that the couple will bear an unwanted child with a contraceptive of 99 percent efficiency.

When contraception of 0.999 efficiency is attained, then the chance of the unwanted child in the same circumstances is reduced to $1 - 0.9998^{240} = 0.047$, that is, 5 percent or one in twenty. At about this point in the technology of contraception, couples can fully accept the advantage of concentrating their children and disregard the risk of unwanted pregnancies. Before this point they may in some degree concentrate their children, but prudence requires deferring one wanted child as an allowance for accidents.

Preference for Boys

With the advent of the perfect contraceptive, most of the problems dealt with above will disappear. The perfect contraceptive would be 100 percent efficient, so no one would have to allow for accidental pregnancy; not only would it always work, but it would be so simple and automatic that no one could forget to apply it, and there would be no need for abortion as a backup. It would be entirely harmless and inoffensive, so no one could feel a disinclination to use it. Such a perfect instrument is still many years of research distant.

Certain problems of the present day will, however, persist into the era of perfect contraception. An enduring contradiction seems to exist between the desire of parents for children and the capacity of the earth's crust to maintain population.

One aspect of the contradiction arises because parents usually want children of both sexes. If parents are satisfied to have two children who would grow to maturity, but insist that the two include one boy and one girl, it turns out that they would need to average more than three children in all. Let us see by what probability mechanism the two children, who on the average would keep the population at a desirable constancy, become three children and, ultimately, an intolerable burden on the ecology, merely because parents continue to reproduce until they have a child of each sex.

If the probability of a boy on a particular birth is b, then the chance that the couple will have first a girl and then a boy is $(1-b)b$. Let us continue with those instances where the couple ends up with a boy. The probability of having two girls in succession and then a boy is $(1-b)^2 b$; of having three girls and then a boy is $(1-b)^3 b$. The expected number of children in this series is

$$2(1-b)b + 3(1-b)^2 b + \ldots.$$

Comparing this with our analysis of the mean months of exposure to conception, in which we required the sum $p + 2(1-p)p + 3(1-p)^2 p + \ldots$, we see that the two are identical, except that now our sum lacks the initial term b. The sum of the p series was $1/p$, and hence we now have the sum $1/b$, but need to subtract b, to obtain $(1/b) - b$.

The argument for the contingency where the couple achieves one child of either sex but ends up with a girl is exactly the same, but we have to replace b by $1 - b$, to obtain $(1/(1-b)) - (1-b)$.

The expected number in total is the sum of the expected number ending with a boy and that ending with a girl, or

$$\frac{1}{b} - b + \frac{1}{1-b} - (1-b) = \frac{1}{b} + \frac{1}{1-b} - 1.$$

If b equals ½, the mean number of children on this last works out to 3; if b departs from ½ the mean is greater than 3. With a departure of $(b - ½)$ the mean number of children can be shown to be approximately $3 + 16(b - ½)^2$, which gives an average number of children of 3.002 for the usual sex ratio at birth of 105 boys per 100 girls.

What in fact are the sex preferences of parents? The first stage of a study in Hull, England, shows that 45.7 percent of recently married couples want one boy and one girl; 15.4 percent want two boys and one girl; 12.6 percent want two boys and two girls. Considering the three-quarters of parents that fall into these three categories, we find that on the average they want 2.55 children. But because of their preferences for certain boy-girl combinations they will on the average actually attain about 3.7 children.

All this would change drastically with the advent of control of sex in the offspring. Parents wanting one boy and one girl would average two children rather than three or more. The mean for the surveyed group above would go down from 3.7 to 2.55. In many less developed countries boy preference is strong, and sex control would correspondingly reduce the number of births.

Moreover, a secondary effect would appear with the ability to determine sex. Preferences for boys being stronger on the average, the next generation would have a predominance of men—anything up to 60 percent is conceivable. The proportion of the population that could get married would decline. Abstracting from any change in the total population, a drop to 40 percent women from the usual 50 percent would in itself cause a fall in the birth rate of one-fifth, supposing the birth rates of women to be the same as before.

A further effect would follow in what one might call the dynamics of the sex ratio. With abundance of boys the tastes of parents would alter. Before even the first generation of children under the regime of free choice of sex grew to marrying age, parents would have an increased appreciation of girls. They might even respond with an excess of girls. Some swaying back and forth between boys and girls would subsequently occur.

The transitional behavior of parents following the invention of sex control is hard to forecast, but we can suggest the hypothesis that the immediate effect would be an excess of boys, and the ultimate effect something close to the present sex ratio. This would mean a considerable temporary reduction in the birth rate over the transitional period and a permanent reduction through the mechanism earlier described, when parents no longer need to average three children in order to be assured of one boy and one girl.

The demographic outcome would be paralleled by a social change. Societies in which boy babies are more highly valued tend to be those in which males monopolize power and prestige. Insofar as this is so, the advent of an easy method of sex control may bring about an unprecedented degree of equality. Fifteen years or so after the start of sex control women will start to be in short supply, both for marriage and for those tasks of production that are customarily performed by women, and the shortage is bound to increase the value of women. The fewer who exist will be offered higher wages for commercial tasks, and be more sought after in marriage. Whether single or married, women would have more independence of their fathers and husbands by virtue of their greater job opportunities, and this effect could well be permanent.

These considerations apply especially to countries where husbands make decisions and wives execute them, which hardly includes the United States. Such countries show high fertility. The advent of sex control would seem likely simultaneously to lower the birth rate and to move the sexes closer to equality of power and prestige.

Family Size and the Population Rate of Increase

The new demography, written with the accent on birth rather than death, and in terms of decisions by individual couples on having and not having children, still requires a link to the old, which stressed populations and their annual rates of increase. We want a way of going from average family size to the rate of increase of the population.

Suppose a community in which married couples average c children, and where the age at which they have these does not change over time. How fast will that community grow from year to year? The answer to this question depends on the proportion of individuals who marry, the average age at which they have children, the distribution of their children by sex, and the probability of babies surviving to have children themselves. Let us consider the female side of the process only, though an analogous argument would apply for males.

If married couples have c children, and a fraction m of women marry, then the average number of children per (married or single) woman is the product of these, cm. If the proportion of births that are girl babies is f, a number close to 0.49 for most populations, then the average number of female progeny to a woman is cmf. If the proportion of these who live to reproductive age is on the average l, the surviving children per woman number $cmfl$. Finally, if the age at childbearing is T, then the ratio per generation $cmfl$ is converted to a ratio of increase per year by taking the Tth root: $\sqrt[T]{cmfl}$.

In order to allow for variation in ages at childbearing, we have to take as the generation a number slightly greater than the observed arithmetic mean age of childbearing. However, the excess is usually a year or less. Similarly, the mean chance of survival has to be an average of survivorships weighted by the ages of childbearing; but with low mortality this is close to the probability of surviving to the mean age of childbearing. Moreover, the annual increase is usually reckoned on a compounding basis, with the period of compounding infinitely small, while we have calculated a simple ratio of increase per year. These refinements alter the results very slightly, and we need not be detained by such details here.

The result, that the ratio of population in one year to that in the preceding year is $^T\!\!\sqrt{cmfl}$, tells us that when mortality was high, variation in proportion surviving could make a good deal of difference. The fact that the proportion of babies surviving to bear children themselves has gone up from about 0.5 just three or four decades back in many less developed countries to 0.9 now is what underlies the contemporary population problem; further increase cannot make much difference.

The proportion f of births that are girls is up to now a biological fact and does not change much. The mean age of childbearing T has gone down with today's earlier marriage; in Sweden of the nineteenth century T was as high as thirty-two years, and now for some countries is as low as twenty-six. If everything else remains the same, the younger average age means a shorter generation and correspondingly more rapid turnover, which has exactly the same effect on growth as an increased number of children per family. In at least one recent year Canada showed a higher ratio of births to women than the United States, but a lower rate of increase because the mothers were older.

A further development of this logic shows that children born to a woman of age forty have only about half the impact on the long-term rate of increase that children born to women of age twenty have. Birth control programs tend to attract older women first, and only later do they attract young women. Insofar as the new confidence in birth control encourages couples to have their children in a clump while they are young, rather than having the same number spread over twenty-five years, the birth control program could actually increase the rate of growth of the population. Fortunately, most couples use birth control to have fewer children as well as to have them younger.

CHAPTER **16**

Equity Between the Sexes: The Pension Problem

The expectation of life at birth for a girl child is fully eight years longer than that for a boy child; at age sixty-five the difference is less, but a woman still has an expected 4½ years more than a man of the same age who retires at the same time. These figures are based on current mortality rates; since the gap is widening, the real difference for women retiring in 1981 is likely to be five years or more.

It has been actuarial practice to take this difference into account, both for insurance and annuity calculations. Women pay substantially lower insurance premiums and substantially higher annuity premiums per dollar of annual income. The general principle has been that price should equal cost.

This principle is being modified by several court decisions that redefine equity. Unlike actuaries and statisticians, the courts have no convenient way of dealing with contingent events. Since not every woman outlives every man, the courts find it discriminatory to charge a woman more; since we do not know how long any individual will live, equity requires that all be charged the same per dollar of monthly income.

Little controversy can arise on the desirability of equity among different classes of policyholder. No one argues in favor of sex discrimination. What is difficult is to know just of what equity consists. To simplify the issues initially, let us forget about interest, as well as individual variation in mortality, taking it that everyone will live the expected number of years for his or her sex.

A man of sixty-five wishes to buy a life annuity of $1,000 per year. Since his expectation of life is 13.9 years (United States White Males Table for 1977), on our assumption of expected values and no interest he will ultimately receive $13,900. A woman seeks an annuity of the same $1,000 per year. On the assumptions and the same data, but for females, she will on the average collect $18,400 during the succeeding 18.4 years.

What is a fair charge to these two annuitants? What does "treating the sexes equally" mean? One school says that it means charging them the same amount, based on a unisex table, say $16,200. The man would pay $16,200 and get back only $13,900; he would lose $2,300. The woman would pay $16,200 and be ahead about the same amount.

Is the example credible? It disregards (1) interest that the company receives on the premium while it holds and invests it; (2) variation among individuals in mortality; (3) office expenses. To take all of these into account would complicate the arithmetic, but the conclusion would come out exactly the same as in the simplified case: on unisex pricing men would be subsidizing women.

Thus it is not enough to say we favor equity between the sexes. The question is which of two approaches constitutes equity: (1) charging men and women alike the average cost; per $1,000 of initial payment women would get the same *monthly benefit* as men; (2) charging men the cost for men and women the cost for women; per $1,000 of initial payment women would get the same *lifetime benefit* as men on the average.

The fact that individuals do not get the same per month is what the courts see as a special problem. Yet we accept such inequality in many fields. A man of sixty pays much more for a $1,000 insurance policy than a man of twenty-five, and no one says that this is unfair to the aged, even though the man of sixty might live another twenty years and the man of twenty-five die tomorrow. We are perfectly satisfied to buy light bulbs with an average life of 1,000 hours, knowing that one bulb might burn out in the first minute, while another will last 5,000 hours. What is needed is better understanding of the way that probabilities enter everyday life and the way in which we cope with them.

Actuaries and statisticians have given contingent events a great deal of thought and devised the best means we have for coping with them. The pivot of their technique is expected values, but they also know how distributions that are unsatisfactory can be altered. You believe that your new car will have an expected life of ten years, but nonetheless you do not want to run the risk of having it break down in the first weeks of use. Very well; the company offers you a guarantee for the first year; this suitably modifies the probability distribution—at a cost that you will pay, of course. You do not want the risk of dying in the first few years of your annuity; very well, you can have a guaranteed ten years certain, so that your heirs, at least, will get back some of your investment.

However, whatever is done to shape the distribution, the average return is the usual criterion of fairness in anything from a church lottery to a government bond that is chosen for redemption according to a set of random numbers.

The above argument in terms of annuities can be adapted to apply to insurance. There are again two opposing principles, each of which can be argued to represent equity: charge everyone the same amount per dollar insured, or charge everyone the expected amount that their heirs will get back. To charge all the same amount is to ask those of lower mortality, the women, to subsidize the men who will get back more. Would those who want unisex premiums also legislate them for insurance? To do so would not by any means offset the inequity, because different individuals buy insurance and annuities.

The question is whether the group that is overpaying is justly required to subsidize the group that is underpaying; in the annuity case, whether men buying annuities ought to subsidize women; in insurance, whether women ought to subsidize men.

At this level of abstraction the volume of business is unaffected, and the company could well be indifferent on the pricing. However, the demand for insurance or annuities *is* affected by the prices charged for them. If, as in the above example, men are required to pay $16,200 for a return of $13,900, that is, to pay $1.17 for each dollar they get back, then some men, or some male institutions if individuals have no choice, will decide that there are better ways to invest their money than in an annuity. Women, on the other hand, since they will be paying only $0.88 for each dollar they get back, will tend to buy annuities as a preferred form of investment.

Insofar as there are any individuals or groups who can change their annuity arrangement, the pricing will act back on the selection of policyholders, shifting it toward the favored group, if the unisex table is used. This means that the mix of the sexes in the body of policyholders will shift against the company, which will have to raise the rates above the unisex table (too low for such a selected group) if it is to come out even.

The result of the distortion of rates through the use of the unisex table is, thus, in the first instance to cause one group to subsidize another; in the second to raise the rates because of selection; in the third, to reduce the amount of business done.

Women have been unfairly discriminated against in many respects, of which employment is the most serious, and the discrimination continues. The proportion of women in the higher reaches of business and of the military, to name two sectors of prestige and power, is much short of the one-half that would represent their fair share. Efforts to recruit women into these fields should be unremitting. The use of unisex tables for annuities is an altogether trivial attempt to make up for such major injustices. The amount of subsidy to women that it would provide is hardly large enough to satisfy anyone who takes the injustices seriously.

In any case, the use of this way of subsidizing women can benefit them only if they are willing to buy annuities. If we insist on this kind of compensation to women, they will buy more annuities than they otherwise would, perhaps more than they need. Why should we make our help to women take this restricted form? Why compel them to buy annuities beyond what they would buy at cost? A unisex table for annuities is like an automobile priced lower for women buyers than for men. If we want to make up for past injustice to women, we ought not to compel them to buy an automobile, or an annuity, to get the compensation.

CHAPTER 17
What Difference if Cancer Were Eradicated?

The demographer sees medicine as a means of prolonging the average duration of life in a population. He takes a stand necessarily different from that of the physician, who is concerned with individuals rather than averages, treats many conditions not likely to prove fatal, and cannot afford much concern with how long the patient will live if he is cured of his present ailment. His task is to treat particular ailments affecting particular patients at the time of consultation.

Yet at some point society—consisting of people who are mostly neither physicians nor demographers—has to make collective decisions about how the conservation of life is to be pursued. Finite resources have to be allocated somehow among three kinds of activities: healing of individual sick persons, public health, and scientific investigation that will provide new medical tools. And within each of these three categories resources have to be allocated among special causes of death; for example, how much research should be devoted to cancer as against heart disease? Mounting costs of health care are bringing into public consciousness issues that once were hidden. This chapter attempts to clarify those issues related to length of life.

Official mortality statistics implicitly treat a population as homogeneous. They overlook the fact that some people are sick and others well, that those who are sick may have many things wrong with them, any one of which could prove fatal. In the official statistics so many people are alive at a given moment, and so many die during a year of observation centered on that moment; the death rate is the year's deaths divided by the mid-year population. The probability that a person will die during a year is deaths divided by the beginning-of-year population exposed. The probability that a person will die of cancer is the cancer deaths divided by the population at the beginning of the year.

Yet people frequently suffer from more than one ailment. When the time comes to record cause of death, it is not easy to pick out the operative cause among the several whose conjuncture was associated with the death. A special analysis of United States data for 1969 (Pitts 1976) shows that for the 94,000 persons dying from cancer of the digestive organs, only 19 percent were reported by the attending physician as having no other trouble; 81 percent had some other ailment that could have proved fatal in the absence of the cancer of the digestive organs. For the 29,000 deaths from breast cancer, only 14 percent showed no other cause; for cancer of the genital organs, only 16 percent showed no other cause.

The tendency of ailments to cluster in some individuals is clear for smokers, who have higher death rates from lung cancer, as would be expected, but more surprisingly also have higher death rates from other kinds of cancer, from heart disease, and indeed from causes scattered through the entire list.

Whatever the hazard, some people are more subject to it than others (Shepard 1976; Vaupel et al. 1980). If we knew enough, we could divide the population into two groups and say that for one group the chance of cancer is negligible, for the other it is substantial. In fact, we cannot allocate individuals to membership in two such classes, but this is not necessary to draw inferences on the effect of a medical improvement. Simply knowing the proportions and levels in the high-risk and the low-risk group is all that is needed. (Even this knowledge we have only in certain restricted cases.) Still less is it necessary for our purpose to know why some individuals are accident-prone, or why a disproportionate number suffer from combined cancer and heart disease. The statistical facts may be forever beyond explanation, but they still need to be taken into account in calculating the effects of a medical improvement.

In a homogeneous population, the expected survival time is simply the reciprocal of the death rate. If the chance of a person's dying in a year is μ, say 1/5, then the expected number of years he has to live is $1/\mu$, or five years. To lower the chance of dying by 1 percent is to raise the expectation of life by 1 percent. Hence, we are accustomed to measuring the benefit of a medical improvement by how much it lowers the death rate.

THE DEATH RATE: WHO CARES?

Yet in fact no one really cares about the death rate as such; what we all care about is years of life added by a medical improvement. As long as the two are in the simple reciprocal relation it is proper to target on the death rate; once we are in a situation where the expectation of life is something different from the reciprocal of the death rate, then it is the expectation on which attention has to be focused.

And the expectation of life becomes something very different from the reciprocal of the death rate as soon as we recognize heterogeneity in the population. Heterogeneity is present everywhere, and to overlook it is to produce wrong answers on the effect of an improvement that lowers the chance of dying. If the improvement mostly benefits the part of the population with high mortality, the usual way of calculating (taking as the expectation the reciprocal of the chance of dying) overstates the benefit; if it mostly affects those of low mortality, the usual method understates the benefit.

Age and sex are the major exceptions to the general statement that vital statistics neglect the heterogeneity of populations. Official statistics painstakingly present breakdowns of deaths from each cause by age and sex. Because these are two breakdowns almost universally recognized for statistical purposes, our argument on cancer will, perforce, be largely confined to them. But before embarking on the use of actual data, it may help to give a partly hypothetical example. This is a modification of one due to Shepard (1976, pp. 36ff), and estimates the saving of life due to discovery of a cure for cancer or other ailment if the whole population is equally vigorous, in contrast with supposing some individuals more vigorous than others.

Suppose that all members of a population have a chance of dying each year equal to 0.02, so that the expectation of life is $1/0.02 = 50$ years. Then comes a medical improvement that lowers the probability of dying by 0.001, bringing it down to 0.019. The expectation of life goes up in proportion and becomes $1/0.019 = 52.6$ years. The overall death rate has gone down by 5 percent and the expectation has gone up by about 5 percent, or 2.6 years. Such is the common analysis.

But now suppose that, unknown to the analyst, the population really consists of two kinds of people in equal numbers. The first kind has a chance of 0.01 of dying each year; the second, a chance of 0.03. And suppose also that the medical improvement affects only the second group, bringing its rate down to 0.028. This group had an original expectation of life of $1/0.03 = 33.3$ years, but now its expectation rises to $1/0.028$ or 35.7 years. Thus, the effect of the medical improvement is that half the population gains $35.7 - 33.3 = 2.4$ years, so the average gain for all is 1.2 years, or less than half that of the preceeding paragraph. This despite deaths directly averted being the same in the two cases.

Thus the estimate of the benefit based on the supposition that the population is homogeneous was 2.6 years, while the benefit recognizing heterogeneity is only 1.2 years. The example is too simple, but it illustrates numerically that an improvement that affects only those who are going to die soon anyhow will have less impact than an improvement that affects everyone.

A measure to ensure safety at ski resorts affects the healthier part of the population, and if it reduced deaths by 1 percent would increase life expectancy in the population as a whole by more than 1 percent. But this kind of improvement is less typical than a new way of treating cancer, prehospital emergency care for victims of heart attack, or kidney dialysis. While data to prove such a statement directly are scarce, the general impression, based on the statistics of multiple causes of death earlier cited, is that they affect a part of the population subject to higher than average death rates for their ages.

What can frustrate any medical system is self-inflicted mortality, which includes that due to smoking, alcohol, lack of exercise, obesity and overconsumption of animal fats. Here again is a source of heterogeneity within populations to which this argument applies.

ELIMINATING CANCER: SMALL EFFECT

We go on to the recognition of the twenty or so five-year age groups in which life tables are ordinarily presented. The usual way of doing this is to work out the life table with all deaths, and then to do the work all over again as if cancer deaths did not occur. The difference is the effect of eliminating cancer, and it turns out to be surprisingly small: the United States male expectation of life with the cancer rates of 1964 is increased by only 2.3 years if cancer mortality is taken as zero. Thus dropping the one-sixth of total deaths due to cancer increases the expectation of life by only about one-thirtieth. This takes account of the heterogeneity due to age for males. Similar results are obtained for females.

But use of age does not end the matter, for within a given age interval there is heterogeneity—some individuals of that age are subject to greater risk than others. If we had the data, a further application of this argument would produce a further diminution in the apparent effect of eliminating cancer. Thus the above result going only as far as age must be regarded as an upper bound of the effect of lowering cancer deaths. It is an upper bound rather than an exact figure because those individuals subject to cancer risk above average for their age are also subject to above-average mortality from a variety of other causes.

This standard method for evaluating the effect of one disease on survivorship supposes that we will retain the full present amount of cancer until the day when someone miraculously comes across an absolute cure. It is more realistic to expect a gradual reduction in the cancer rate. Let us discuss the effect of a reduction of 1 percent in the incidence of cancer at all ages; what would be the effect of this on the expectation of life?

A first answer would be 1 percent of the 2.3 years that we found for the total elimination of cancer, or 0.023 years. This would be 0.023/66.9 or 0.00034 as a fraction of the expectation of life. It would seem to justify the statement that a 1 percent reduction in cancer mortality would increase the expectation of life by 0.034 percent, an approximation to the quantity that will be called $H^{(cancer)}$ in what follows.

Such an approximation will turn out to be reasonably close in many instances, but it involves a gratuitous error. The effect on expectation of life of the first 1 percent reduction in mortality from any cause is not the same as the effect of a second reduction of equal amount, and so on. This nonlinear or nonproportional feature can easily be taken into account.

Suppose a population classified by age in which the chance of dying at a given age is the same for everyone. When people are saved from dying from a given cause, they move up in age and so fall into the higher mortality from the causes that remain. Cancer deaths are one-sixth of all deaths, so when cancer deaths are reduced by 1 percent all deaths would seem to be reduced by one-sixth of 1 percent, and, therefore, the expectation of life ought to be increased by one-sixth of 1 percent. But this is not so if the population is distributed through the several ages. Recognizing the increasing mortality by age but no other heterogeneity, the result of a 1 percent decrease in cancer deaths is to increase life expectancy by only one thirty-third of 1 percent, a more exact approximation to $H^{(cancer)}$. Technically, $H^{(cancer)}$ is calculated as the derivative of expectation of life with respect to a small fractional increase common to all ages (Keyfitz 1977, p. 69) and turns out to be 0.030 percent.

The reason the effect of curing 1 percent of cancer deaths is only 0.030 percent rather than 0.17 percent is that cancer occurs mostly at late ages, and other causes, especially heart disease, are there to take off the person saved from cancer. This (like the 2.30 years mentioned above as being added if cancer were entirely eliminated) is a measure of the difference in timing between cancer and other causes. The benefits of saving people from infectious disease or automobile accidents are much larger in proportion to total deaths because those causes strike people younger than does cancer.

All this takes the expectation of life as the criterion for measuring the effect of a health improvement. In a homogeneous population, where everyone is subject to the same risk, the reduction in the rate and the increase of the expectation of life are the same thing, and no one can object to using either one as the criterion. But in a heterogeneous population, a value judgment in the selection of the criterion is inescapable. A man of thirty could well say that he is not especially interested in increase of expectation at age zero, but only in expectation at age thirty. Or that insofar as a person has heard that he stands in special danger from cancer, he will favor research on cancer rather than on heart disease. The most that one can say for the use of expectation of life at age zero is that it includes mortality at all ages and is not grossly biased toward any one group.

Joel E. Cohen (1975) takes the argument one stage further. He goes on to find the lifetime earnings of the individuals whose lives would be saved by a medical innovation, and thus is able to establish a dollar value for the benefit. For example, he finds $20 billion as the lower bound of the benefit from eliminating kidney and related diseases in the United States. In the present paper, we stop with the expectation of life rather than earnings as the ultimate criterion.

The decision on what direction medical research ought to take, if it is to be directed toward increasing life expectancy, requires three elements discussed above:
1. The criterion, which for us will be the expectation of life at age zero.
2. The effect on this criterion of a 1 percent diminution of mortality from any cause, say $H^{(cancer)}$.
3. The effect, say $\delta^{(cancer)}$, of a given expenditure in reducing mortality from the given cause.

Having these elements for two causes, say cancer and heart disease, with each of which are associated the quantities H and δ, we can say that if the products stand in the relation

$$H^{(cancer)} \times \delta^{(cancer)} > H^{(heart)} \times \delta^{(heart)}$$

then research ought to be devoted to cancer; if the inequality goes the other way, to heart disease.

We have, thus, found a guide to the strategy of medical research. Indeed the above inequality can go beyond medicine; it can tell whether we should spend our money on building more fire stations or, rather, devote the resources to mandatory airbags in automobiles. $H^{(i)}$ is larger the younger the deaths from the ith cause; $\delta^{(i)}$ is greater the less expensive the treatment for the ith cause.

One of the numerous applications of this general principle is among social classes. The quantity $H^{(i)}$ is appreciably larger for those diseases that strike early—especially contagious diseases. In addition, doing something about contagious diseases costs less than doing something about heart disease and cancer, which makes $\delta^{(i)}$ larger for the poor. These relations more than offset the consideration that a given reduction of death rates in the higher mortality part of the population produces a smaller increment in the expectation of life.

But the guide remains merely formal until we know the quantities H and δ. We have seen the difficulties in regard to H, arising from our ignorance of the degree of heterogeneity in the population of a given age and sex, despite an abundance of statistics that tell us many other things. We can only surmise that for most causes a comprehensive H, taking account of sources of variation beyond age, would be smaller than here stated, because of this heterogeneity within age groups.

It is even more difficult to set a number for the result δ of a given expenditure. Millions of dollars can be spent on research without attaining any new scientific knowledge. And even if scientific knowledge is obtained, it may not be of a kind that has direct application to saving life. The question of how much research is needed to gain the knowledge that will reduce deaths from a given cause by 1 percent is not easy, but an explicit estimate would make for better decisions.

The importance of heterogeneity for interpretation of rates is by no means confined to mortality. Divorces in the United States are now approaching the 1¼ million mark, and if one takes all marriages and all divorces to form a marriage table it will show that a very high proportion of marriages end in divorce. But suppose underlying the statistics is the fact that a minority of the population marry and divorce many times, while the majority marry only once and never divorce. In that situation an overall marriage and divorce table is misleading. To say (*Stat. Abstr.* 1981, p. 80) that the mean duration of marriage in the United States was 6.8 years in 1979 is not very informative. As a minimum one ought to separate the data for first marriages from those for later marriages. By making that distinction one would obtain a more realistic probability that a given marriage would end in divorce.

The consequences of heterogeneity in various branches of population study deserve more attention than they have had. Our constant H measures heterogeneity as among ages; data should be sought to apply it within age categories.

BIBLIOGRAPHY

Adelman, I. 1963. An Economic Analysis of Population Growth. *American Economic Review* 53: 314–339.
Arthur, B. 1981. Personal communication.
Artle, R. 1980. The Economics of an Aging Population: Regional and Interregional Implications. Paper presented at the International Congress of Arts and Sciences. Cambridge, Mass.
Balinski, M. L., and Young, H. P. 1982. *Fair Representation: Meeting the Ideal of One Man, One Vote.* New Haven: Yale University Press.
Barker, E. 1959. *The Political Thought of Plato and Aristotle.* New York: Dover.
Barr, N. A. 1979. Myths My Grandpa Taught Me. *The Three Banks Review* 124: 27–55.
Becker, G. S. 1960. An Economic Analysis of Fertility. In National Bureau of Economic Research [editor] *Demographic and Economic Change in Developed Countries.* Princeton, N.J.: Princeton University Press.
Bell, D. 1973. *The Coming of Post-Industrial Society: A Venture in Social Forecasting.* New York: Basic Books.
Bellamy, E. 1951 (1887). *Looking Backward.* New York: Modern Library.
Berelson, B. 1969. National Family Planning Programs: Where We Stand. In *Fertility and Family Planning: A World View.* S. J. Behrman, L. Corsa, and R. Freedman, eds. Ann Arbor, Mich.: University of Michigan Press.
Bixby, L. E. 1977. Statistical Data Requirements in Legislation. Prepared for Committee on National Statistics, Assembly of Behavioral and Social Sciences, National Research Council. Washington, D.C.: National Academy of Sciences.
Bladen, V. W. 1956. *An Introduction to Political Economy,* rev. ed. Toronto: University of Toronto Press.

Blake, J. 1967. Income and Reproductive Motivation. *Population Studies* 21: 185–206.
Bonar, J. 1885. *Malthus and His Work.* London: Macmillan.
Boserup, E. 1965. *The Conditions of Agricultural Growth: The Economics of Agrarian Change under Population Pressure.* Chicago: Aldine.
Botero, G. 1956 (1589). *The Reason of State.* D. P. Waley, ed. New Haven: Yale University Press.
Boulding, K. E. 1955. The Malthusian Model as a General System. *Social and Economic Studies* 4: 195–205.
———. 1964. *The Meaning of the Twentieth Century.* New York: Harper and Row, Inc.
———. 1966. The Economics of the Coming Spaceship Earth. In *Environmental Quality in a Growing Economy.* H. Jarrett, ed. Baltimore: Johns Hopkins Press.
Bourgeois-Pichat, J. 1978. Le Financement des retraites par capitalisation. *Population* 6: 1115–1136.
Brackett, J. W. 1968. The Evolution of Marxist Theories of Population: Marxism Recognizes the Population Problem. *Demography* 5: 158–173.
Brown, H. 1954. *The Challenge of Man's Future.* New York: Viking.
Brown, L. R. 1968. New Directions in World Agriculture. *Studies in Family Planning* 32. New York: The Population Council.
Cannan, E. 1895. The Probability of a Cessation of the Growth of Population in England and Wales. *Economic Journal* 5: 505–515.
Cantillon, R. 1952 (1755). *Essai sur la nature du commerce en général.* Paris: Institut National d'Etudes Démographiques.
Chen Huan-Chang. 1911. *The Economic Principles of Confucius and His School.* 2 Vols. New York: Columbia University Press.
Chenery, H. B. et al. 1974. *Redistribution with Growth.* London: Oxford University Press.
Chesnais, J. C., and Sauvy, A. 1973. Progrès économique et accroissement de la population: Une expérience commentée. *Population* 28: 843.
Choucri, N. 1974. *Population Dynamics and International Violence: Proportions, Insights, and Evidence.* Lexington, Mass.: Lexington Books.
Clark, C. 1940. *Conditions of Economic Progress.* London: Macmillan.
Clark, C. 1964. Overpopulation — Is Birth Control the Answer? In *Population, Evolution, Birth Control.* G. Hardin, ed. San Francisco: Freeman.
Clark, C. 1967. *Population Growth and Land Use.* London: Macmillan and Company.
Clark, R. L., ed. 1980. *Retirement Policy in an Aging Society.* Durham, N.C.: Duke University Press.
Coale, A. J. 1956. The Effects of Changes in Mortality and Fertility on Age Composition. *Milbank Memorial Fund Quarterly* 34: 79–114.
———. 1957. How the Age Distribution of a Human Population Is Determined. *Cold Spring Harbor Symposia on Quantitative Biology* 22: 83–89.
———. 1968. Should the United States Start a Campaign for Fewer Births? *Population Index* 34: 467–479.
———. 1969. Population and Economic Development. In *The Population Dilemma*, P. M. Hauser, ed. 2nd ed. Englewood Cliffs, N.J.: Prentice-Hall.
———. 1970a. Man and His Environment. *Science* 170: 132–136.

———. 1970b. Review of Ehrlich and Ehrlich, *Population, Resources, Environment*. *Science* 170: 428–429.

———. 1978. T. R. Malthus and the Population Trends in His Day and Ours. Ninth Encyclopaedia Britannica Lecture. Edinburgh, Scotland: University of Edinburgh.

———. 1979. The Use of Modern Analytical Demography by T. R. Malthus. *Population Studies* 33:329–332.

Coale, A. J., and Demeny, P. 1966. *Regional Model Life Tables and Stable Populations*. Princeton, N.J.: Princeton University Press.

Coale, A. J., and Hoover, E. M. 1958. *Population Growth and Economic Development in Low-Income Countries: A Case Study of India's Prospects*. Princeton, N.J.: Princeton University Press.

Cohen, J. E. 1975. Livelihood Benefits of Small Improvements in the Life Table. *Health Services Research* (Spring): 82–96.

Coontz, S. H. 1957. *Population Theories and the Economic Interpretation*. London: Routledge and Kegan Paul.

Darwin, C. 1961 (1876). *Autobiography*. Sir F. Darwin, ed. New York: Collier.

———. 1962. (1859). *The Origin of Species*. New York: Collier.

Davis, K. 1955. Malthus and the Theory of Population. In *The Language of Social Research*. P. F. Lazarsfeld and M. Rosenberg, eds. Glencoe, Ill.: Free Press.

———. 1963. The Theory of Change and Response in Modern Demographic History. *Population Index* 29: 345–366.

———. 1967. Population Policy: Will Current Programs Succeed? *Science* 158: 730.

Doll, R., and Hill, A. B. 1952. A Study of the Aetiology of Carcinoma of the Lung. *British Medical Journal* 2: 1271–1286.

Dorn, H. F. 1950. Pitfalls in Population Forecasts and Projections. *Journal of the American Statistical Association* 45: 311–334.

Duesenberry, J. 1960. Comment on Becker, *op. cit.*, pp. 231–234.

Dumont, A. 1890. *Dépopulation et civilisation: Etudes démographiques*. Paris: Lecrosnier et Babé.

Duncan, O. D. 1969. Inequality and Opportunity. *Population Index* 35: 361–366.

Dupâquier, J. 1980. Avez-vous lu Malthus? *Population* 35: 280–290.

Durkheim, E. 1960 (1902). *De la division du travail social*. Paris: Presses Universitaires de France.

Ehrlich, P. R., and Ehrlich, A. H. 1970. *Population, Resources, Environment*. San Francisco: Freeman.

Ekanem, I. 1972. A Further Note on the Relation Between Economic Development and Fertility. *Demography* 9: 383–398.

Enke, S. 1963. *Economics for Development*. Englewood Cliffs, N.J.: Prentice-Hall, Inc.

Euler, L. 1970 (1760). A General Investigation into the Mortality and Multiplication of the Human Species. N. Keyfitz and B. Keyfitz, trans. *Theoretical Population Biology* 1: 307–314.

Feldstein, M. 1974. Social Security, Induced Retirement, and Aggregate Capital Accumulation. *Journal of Political Economy* 82: 905–926.

———. 1976. Savings Behavior: New Influences and Consequences. *Journal of the American Economic Association* 66: 77–86.

Freedman, R., and Takeshita, J. Y. 1969. *Family Planning in Taiwan: An Experiment in Social Change*. Princeton, N.J.: Princeton University Press.

Frejka, T. 1981. World Population Projections: A Concise History. Center for Policy Studies Working Paper no. 66. New York: The Population Council.

Friedlander, S., and Silver, M. 1967. A Quantitative Study of the Determinants of Fertility Behavior. *Demography* 45: 30–70.

Furstenberg, G. M. von, ed. 1979. *Social Security Versus Private Saving*. Cambridge, Mass.: Harper & Row, Ballinger.

Geertz, Clifford. 1971. *Agricultural Involution*. Berkeley: University of California Press.

Glass, D. V. 1963. John Graunt and His *Natural and Political Observations*. *Proceedings of the Royal Society* 159 (Series B): 2–37.

Glick, P. C., Heer, D. M., and Beresford, J. C. 1963. Family Formation and Family Composition: Trends and Prospects. In *Sourcebook on Marriage and the Family*. M. B. Sussman, ed. Boston: Houghton Mifflin Company.

Godwin, W. 1793. *An Enquiry Concerning Political Justice and Its Influence on General Virtue and Happiness*. London: G. G. J. and J. Robinson.

Gonzalez, M. E. 1978. Statistics for Allocation of Funds. *Statistical Reporter* 78: 217–220.

Gonzalez, M. E., and Waksberg, J. 1973. Estimation of the Error of Synthetic Estimates. Prepared for Presentation at the First Meeting of the International Association of Survey Statisticians, Vienna, Austria. Washington, D.C.: U.S. Bureau of the Census, Census Vertical File, Staff Papers.

Goode, W. J. 1963. The Role of the Family in Industrialization. In United Nations, Conference on the Application of Science and Technology for the Benefit of the Less Developed Areas. *Social Problems of Development and Urbanization* 7: 32–38. Washington, D.C.: U.S. Government Printing Office.

Graunt, J. 1964 (1662). Natural and Political Observations ... Made Upon the Bills of Mortality. Republished with an introduction by B. Benjamin, *Journal of the Institute of Actuaries* 90: 1–64.

Halley, E. 1693. An Estimate of the Degree of the Mortality of Mankind. *Philosophical Transactions of the Royal Society of London* 17: 596–610.

Hawley, A. H. 1950. *Human Ecology: A Theory of Community Structure*. New York: Ronald Press.

Heer, D. M. 1966. Economic Development and Fertility. *Demography* 3: 423–444.

Henry, L. 1968. Essai de calcul de l'efficacité de la contraception. *Population* 24: 265–278.

Henry, L., and Gutierrez, H. 1977. Qualité des prévisions démographiques á court terme: Etude de l'extrapolation de la population totale des départements et villes de France, 1821–1975. *Population* 32: 625–647.

Hicks, J. R. 1939. *Value and Capital*. Oxford: Oxford University Press.

Himes, N. E. 1936. *Medical History of Contraception*. Baltimore: Williams & Wilkins.

Ho, Ping-Ti. 1959. *Studies on the Population of China, 1368–1953*. Cambridge, Mass.: Harvard University Press.

Horlick, M. 1979. The Impact of Aging Population on Social Security. In *Social Security in a Changing World*. Washington, D.C.: U.S. Department of Health, Education, and Welfare, Social Security Administration, HEW Publication (SSA) 79–11948.

Bibliography **249**

———. 1980. Private Pension Plans in West Germany and France. Research Report No. 55. Washington, D.C.: U.S. Department of Health and Human Services, Social Security Administration.
Horlick, M., and Skolnik, A. M. 1978. Mandating Private Pensions: A Study of European Experience. Research Report No. 51. Washington, D.C.: U.S. Department of Health, Education, and Welfare, Social Security Administration.
Hoselitz, B. F. (ed.) 1960. *Theories of Economic Growth*. Glencoe, Illinois: Free Press.
Hutchinson, E. P. 1967. *The Population Debate*. Boston: Houghton and Mifflin Company.
Jacobson, P. H. 1959. *American Marriage and Divorce*. New York: Rinehart and Co.
Jaffe, A. J. 1966. Education and Automation. *Demography* 3: 35–46.
Janowitz, B. S. 1971. An Empirical Study of the Effects of Socioeconomic Development on Fertility Rates. *Demography* 8: 383–398.
Keech, W. R. 1979. Elections and U.S. Public Pension Policy: A Working Paper. Paper presented at the Second International Workshop on the Politics of Inflation, Unemployment, and Growth, University of Bonn, West Germany.
Keyfitz, N. 1971. Migration as a Means of Population Control. *Population Studies* 25: 63–72.
———. 1977a. *Applied Mathematical Demography*. New York: John Wiley & Sons.
———. 1977b. What Difference Would It Make If Cancer Were Eradicated? An Examination of the Taeuber Paradox. *Demography* 14: 411–418.
———. 1980. Why Social Security Is In Trouble. *The Public Interest* 58: 102–119.
Keyfitz, N., and Flieger, W. 1968. *World Population: An Analysis of Vital Data*. Chicago: University of Chicago Press.
———. 1971. *Population: Facts and Techniques of Demography*. San Francisco: W. H. Freeman.
Keynes, J. M. 1920. *The Economic Consequences of the Peace*. London: Macmillan.
———. 1936. *The General Theory of Employment, Interest and Money*. London: Macmillan & Co.
———. 1937. Some Consequences of a Declining Population. *Eugenics Review* 29: 13–17.
———. 1972. Economic Possibilities for Our Grandchildren. In *Essays in Persuasion*, Vol. 9 of *The Collected Writings*. London: Macmillan.
Kuznets, S. 1960. Population and Aggregate Output. In National Bureau of Economic Research, *Demographic and Economic Change in Developed Countries*. Princeton, N.J.: Princeton University Press.
Ladejinsky, W. 1970. Ironies of India's Green Revolution. *Foreign Affairs* 48: 758–768.
Landry, A. 1909. Les Idées de Quesnay sur la population. *Revue d'Histoire des Doctrines Economiques* 2: 41–87.
Lee, E. S. 1966. A Theory of Migration. *Demography* 3: 45–57.
Lee, E. S. et al. 1957. *Population Redistribution and Economic Growth, United States: 1870–1950*. 2 Vols. Philadelphia: American Philosophical Society.
Lee, M. P. 1921. *The Economic History of China, With Special Reference to Agriculture*. New York: Columbia University Press.

Lee, R. D. 1978. Appraisal of the Fertility Assumptions Employed in the Social Security Projections. Unpublished Ms.
———. 1980. Aiming at a Moving Target: Period Fertility and Changing Reproductive Goals. *Population Studies* 34:206–226.
Leibenstein, H. 1963. *Economic Backwardness and Economic Growth*. New York: Wiley & Sons.
———. 1974. An Interpretation of the Economic Theory of Fertility: Promising Path or Blind Alley? *Journal of Economic Literature* 12: 467–479.
———. 1975. The Economic Theory of Fertility Decline. *Quarterly Journal of Economics* 89: 1–31.
Léridon, H., and Henry, L. 1968. Influence du calendrier de la contraception. *Population* 24: 1009–1054.
Leslie, P. H. 1945. On the Use of Matrices in Certain Population Mathematics. *Biometrika* 33: 183–212.
Lipton, M. 1977. *Why Poor People Stay Poor: Urban Bias in World Development*. Cambridge, Mass: Harvard University Press.
Lorimer, F. 1959. The Development of Demography. In *The Study of Population*. P. M. Hauser and O. D. Duncan, eds. Chicago: University of Chicago Press.
Lotka, A. J. 1907. Relation Between Birth Rates and Death Rates. *Science, N. S.* 26: 21–22.
———. 1939. *Théorie analytique des associations biologiques. Part II. Analyse démographique avec application particulière à l'espèce humaine*. Actualités Scientifiques et Industrielles, No. 780. Paris: Hermann & Cie.
Mackenroth, G. 1953. *Bevölkerungslehre*. Berlin: Springer.
Mahdi, M. 1957. *Ibn Khaldûn's Philosophy of History*. Chicago: University of Chicago Press.
Malthus, T. R. 1959. *Population: The First Essay*. Foreword by K. Boulding. Ann Arbor: University of Michigan Press.
———. 1960a (1798). *On Population*. G. Himmelfarb, ed. New York: Modern Library.
———. 1960b (1830). A Summary View of the Principle of Population. In Malthus et al. *Three Essays on Population*. New York: Mentor.
Marx, K., and Engels, F. 1959. *Basic Writings on Politics and Philosophy*. L. S. Feuer, ed. New York: Doubleday.
McCleary, G. F. 1953. *The Malthusian Population Theory*. London: Faber and Faber.
McKeown, T. 1976. *The Modern Rise of Population*. London: Edward Arnold.
McNeill, W. H. 1963. *The Rise of the West*. Chicago: University of Chicago Press.
———. 1977. *Plagues and Peoples*. New York: Anchor Press/Doubleday.
Meek, R. L. 1953. *Marx and Engels on Malthus*. London: Lawrence and Wishart.
Mehring, F. 1962. *Karl Marx, The Story of His Life*. Ann Arbor, Mich: University of Michigan Press.
Mill, J. S. 1876. *Principles of Political Economy*. 5th ed. New York: Appleton.
Morgan, J. N. 1977. Myth, Reality, Equity, and the Social Security System. *Economic Outlook USA* 4: 58–60. Ann Arbor, Mich.: University of Michigan, Survey Research Center.
———. 1978. Summary Statement for the Public Assistance Subcommittee Hearings, Senate Finance Committee May 1. Ann Arbor, Mich.: University of Michigan, Institute for Social Research.

Myrdal, G. 1940. *Population, A Problem for Democracy.* Cambridge, Mass.: Harvard University Press.
Nee, V. 1980. Post Maoist Changes in a South China Production Brigade. Unpublished manuscript, Ithaca, New York: Center for International Studies, Cornell University.
Nelson, R. R. 1956. A Theory of the Low Level Equilibrium Trap in Underdeveloped Economies. *American Economic Review* 46: 894–908.
Noonan, J. T., Jr. 1965. *Contraception: A History of Its Treatment by the Catholic Theologians and Canonists.* Cambridge, Mass.: Belknap-Harvard University Press.
Notestein, F. 1945. Population — The Long View. In *Food for the World.* T. W. Schultz, ed. Chicago: University of Chicago Press.
Notestein, F. et al. 1944. *The Future Population of Europe and the Soviet Union: Population Projections 1940–1970.* Geneva: League of Nations.
Nurkse, R. 1953. Population and the Supply of Capital. In *Problems of Capital Formation.* Oxford: Basil Blackwell.
Ogburn, W. F. 1964. Why the Family Is Changing. In *William F. Ogburn on Culture and Social Change.* O. D. Duncan, ed. Chicago: University of Chicago Press.
Ohlin, G. 1967. *Population Control and Economic Development.* Paris: Development Centre of the Organisation for Economic Cooperation and Development.
Okun, B. 1960. Comment on Becker, *op. cit.*: 235–240.
Overbeek, J. 1970. *Comparative Thoughts on Overpopulation Between the Two Wars.* Rotterdam: Drukkerij Princo.
Pan Ku. 1950. *Food and Money in Ancient China.* N. L. Swann, trans. Princeton, N.J.: Princeton University Press.
Peacock, A. T. 1952–54. Theory of Population and Modern Economic Analysis. *Population Studies* 6: 114–122; 7: 227–234.
Petersen, W. 1964. *The Politics of Population.* New York: Doubleday.
———. 1969. *Population,* 2nd ed. New York: Macmillan.
———. 1971. The Malthus-Godwin Debate, Then and Now. *Demography* 8: 13–26.
———. 1979. *Malthus.* Cambridge, Mass.: Harvard University Press.
Petty, W. 1691. *Political Arithmetick.* London: Clavel.
Pitts, A. M. 1976. Some Notes on the Collection of U.S. Multiple Cause of Death Data with Illustrative Multiple Cause Tabulations for 1969. Durham, N.C.: Duke University Center for Demographic Studies.
Place, F. 1822. *Illustrations and Proofs of the Principle of Population.* London: Longman, Hurst, Rees, Orme, and Brown.
Pollard, J. H. 1979. Factors Affecting Mortality and the Length of Life. Proceedings of an IUSSP conference on science in the service of life, Vienna. In *Population Science in the Service of Mankind.* Liège, Belgium: International Union for the Scientific Study of Population.
Population Council, The. 1970. Governmental Policy Statements on Population: An Inventory. In *Reports on Population-Family Planning.* New York: The Population Council.
Potter, R. G. 1960. Some Relationships Between Short Range and Long Range Risks of Unwanted Pregnancy. *Milbank Memorial Fund Quarterly* 38: 255–263.

———. 1967. The Multiple Decrement Life Table As an Approach to the Measurement of Use Effectiveness and Demographic Effectiveness of Contraception. In *Proceedings,* International Union for the Scientific Study of Population, Sydney (Australia) Conference.

———. 1970. Births Averted by Contraception: An Approach Through Renewal Theory. *Theoretical Population Biology* 1: 251–272.

Potter, R. G., Jain, A. K., and McCann, B. 1970. Net Delay of Next Conception by Contraception: A Highly Simplified Case. *Population Studies* 24: 173–192.

President's Commission on Pension Policy. 1980. *An Interim Report.* Washington, D.C.: 736 Jackson Place N.W.

Preston, S. H., Keyfitz, N., and Schoen, R. 1972. *Causes of Death: Life Tables for National Populations.* New York: Seminar Press.

Quesnay, F. 1908. Hommes. *Revue d'Histoire des Doctrines Economiques* 1: 14ff.

Ryder, N. B. 1964. The Process of Demographic Translation. *Demography* 1: 74–82.

Ryder, N. B., and Westoff, C. F. 1967. The Trend of Expected Parity in the United States; 1955, 1960, 1965. *Population Index* 33: 153–168.

Rogers, A. 1975. *Introduction to Multiregional Mathematical Demography.* New York: John Wiley and Sons.

Sauvy, A. 1956. *Théorie générale de la population,* 2 Vols. Paris: Presses Universitaires de France.

———. 1958. *François Quesnay et la Physiocratie.* Paris: Institut National d'Etudes Démographiques.

———. 1963. *Malthus et les deux Marx.* Paris: Denoel.

———. 1968. Population Theories. *International Encyclopedia of the Social Sciences.* 12: 349–358. New York: Macmillan and Free Press

Schultz, T. W. 1964. *Transforming Traditional Agriculture.* New Haven: Yale University Press.

Shepard, D. S. 1976. Prediction and Incentives in Health Care Policy. Doctoral dissertation. Cambridge, Mass.: John Fitzgerald Kennedy School of Government, Harvard University.

Shepard, D., and Zeckhauser, R. 1977. Interventions in Mixed Populations: Concepts and Applications. Discussion Paper Series, 49D. Cambridge, Mass.: John Fitzgerald Kennedy School of Government, Harvard University.

Sheps, M. C. 1967. Uses of Stochastic Models in the Evaluation of Population Policies. San Francisco: *Proceedings of the Fifth Berkeley Symposium on Mathematical Statistics and Probability* IV: 115–136.

Sheps, M. C. and Menken, J. A. 1973. *Mathematical Models of Conception and Birth.* Chicago: University of Chicago Press.

Sheps, M. C., and Perrin, E. B. 1963. Changes in Birth Rate as a Function of Contraceptive Effectiveness. *American Journal of Public Health* 53: 1031–1046.

———. 1966. Further Results from a Human Fertility Model with a Variety of Pregnancy Outcomes. *Human Biology* 38: 180–193.

Shubik, M. 1981. Society, Land, Love, or Money: A Strategic Model of How to Glue the Generations Together. Unpublished Manuscript.

Siegel, J. S. 1975. Coverage of Population in the 1970 Census and Some Implications for Public Programs. Washington, D.C.: U.S. Bureau of the Census, Current Population Reports. Special Studies, Series P-23, No. 56.

Siegel, J. S. 1977. Developmental Estimates of the Coverage of the Population of States in the 1970 Census: Demographic Analysis. Washington, D.C.: U.S. Bureau of the Census, Current Population Reports, Special Studies, Series P-23, No. 65.

Smith, A. 1921 (1776). *The Wealth of Nations,* 2 Vols. London: G. Bell.

Spencer, H. 1867. *The Principles of Biology,* 2 Vols. New York: Appleton.

Spengler, J. J. 1942. *French Predecessors of Malthus: A Study in Eighteenth-Century Wage and Population Theory.* Durham, N.C.: Duke University Press.

———. 1963. Arthasastra Economics. In *Administration and Economic Development in India.* R. J. D. Braibanti and J. J. Spengler, eds. Durham, N.C.: Duke University Press.

———. 1966. Values and Fertility Analysis. *Demography* 3: 109–130.

Stangeland, C. E. 1904. *Pre-Malthusian Doctrines of Population.* New York: Columbia University Press.

Statistics Canada. 1954. Memorandum on the Projection of Population Statistics, 1954. Ottawa: Dominion Bureau of Statistics.

Stockwell, E.G. 1972. Some Observations on the Relations Between Population Growth and Economic Development During the 1960s. *Rural Sociology* 37: 628.

Stoto, M. A. 1979. The Accuracy of Population Projections. Working paper 79–75. Laxenburg, Austria: International Institute for Applied Systems Analysis.

Stouffer, S. A. 1940. Intervening Opportunities: A Theory Relating Mobility and Distance. *American Sociological Review* 5: 845–867.

Süssmilch, J. P. 1788 (1741). *Die göttliche Ordnung in den Veränderungen des menschlichen Geschlechts, aus der Geburt, dem Tode und der Fortpflanzung desselben Erwiesen,* 3 Vols. Berlin: Verlag der Buchhandlung der Realschule.

Sutter, J. 1953. Un Démographe engagé: Arsène Dumont (1849–1902). *Population* 8: 79–92.

Taeuber, C., and Taeuber, I. B. 1958. *The Changing Population of the United States.* New York: John Wiley & Sons.

———. 1971. *People of the United States in the Twentieth Century.* Washington, D.C.: U.S. Government Printing Office.

Taeuber, I. B. 1960. Japan's Demographic Transition Re-examined. *Population Studies* 14: 28–39.

Tietz, C., 1959. Differential Fecundity and Effectiveness of Contraception. *Eugenics Review* 50: 231–234.

———. 1967. Intra-uterine Contraception: Recommended Procedures for Data Analysis. *Studies in Family Planning* 18 (Supp.): 1–6.

Tufte, E. 1978. *Political Control of the Economy.* Princeton, N.J.: Princeton University Press.

United Nations. *Demographic Yearbook,* annual series.

United Nations. 1953. The Determinants and Consequences of Population Trends. Population Studies No. 17. New York: United Nations Press.

———. 1958. *The Future Growth of World Population*. Population Studies No. 28. New York: United Nations Press.

———. 1966. *World Population Prospects as Assessed in 1963*. Population Studies No. 41. New York: United Nations Press.

———. 1973. *World Population Prospects as Assessed in 1968*. Population Studies No. 53. New York: United Nations Press.

———. 1979. *World Population Trends and Policies. 1977 Monitoring Report. Volume 1. Population Trends*. Population Studies, No. 62. New York: U.N.

U.S. Bureau of the Census. 1965. *Projections of the Population of the Communist Countries of Eastern Europe, by Age and Sex, 1965–1985*. J. L. Scott. International Population Reports, Series P-91, no. 14. Washington, D.C.: Government Printing Office.

———. 1975. *Population Estimates and Projections: Projections of the Population of the United States: 1975 to 2050*. Current Population Reports, Series P-25, no. 601. Washington, D.C.: Government Printing Office.

———. 1980. *Statistical Abstract of the United States*. Washington, D.C.: Government Printing Office.

U.S. Department of Health, Education, and Welfare. 1964. *Smoking and Health*. Report of the Advisory Committee to the Surgeon General of the Public Health Service, Public Health Service Publication No. 1103. Washington, D.C.: Government Printing Office.

U.S. Department of Commerce. 1978. Statistical Policy Working Paper 1: Report on Statistics for Allocation of Funds. Prepared by Subcommittee on Statistics for Allocation of Funds, Federal Committee on Statistical Methodology. Washington, D.C.: Office of Federal Statistical Policy and Standards.

Vaupel, J., and Yashin, A. E. 1982. The Deviant Dynamics of Death in Heterogeneous Populations. Working Paper 82–47. Laxenburg, Austria. International Institute for Applied Systems Analysis.

Vialatoux, J. 1959. *Le Peuplement humain*, 2 Vols. Paris: Editions Ouvrieres.

Waite, L. J. and Stolzenberg, R. M. 1976. Intended Childbearing—Labor Force Participation of Young Women: Insights from Nonrecursive Models. *American Sociological Review* 41: 235–252.

Waugh, W. A. O'N. 1971. Career Prospects in Stochastic Models with Time Varying Rates. *Fourth Conference on the Mathematics of Population*. Honolulu: East-West Population Institute.

Westoff, C. F. 1978. Marriage and Fertility in the Developed Countries. *Scientific American* 239 (December): 51–57.

Whelpton, P. K. 1963. Cohort Analysis and Fertility Projections. In *Emerging Techniques in Population Research*. New York: Milbank Memorial Fund.

White, C. L. 1965. Geography and the World's Population. In Ng, L. K. Y., and Mudd, S. (eds.), *The Population Crisis: Implications and Plans for Action*. Bloomington, Indiana: Indiana University Press.

Widjojo Nitisastro. 1970. *Population Trends in Indonesia*. Ithaca, N.Y.: Cornell University Press.

Wright, H. 1923. *Population*. New York: Harcourt, Brace.

Wright, Q. 1965. *A Study of War*. Chicago: University of Chicago Press.

Wrigley, E. A. 1969. *Population and History*. New York: McGraw-Hill.

Wynne-Edwards, V. C. 1962. *Animal Dispersion in Relation to Social Behaviour*. Edinburgh: Oliver and Boyd.

Index

Abortion, 216–221
  arithmetic example in, 216–218
  as backup to contraception, 220
  limitations of deterministic model in, 220–221
  theoretical analysis in, 218–219
Abu Dhabi, 104
Adelman, Irma, 104
Africa
  birth control in, 60
  development in, 105, 137
  fertility in, 59
Age at marriage, and fertility, 40–41, 100–101
Age distribution in populations
  birth and death rates and, 95, 98–99
  census and, 88, 89
  death rates in cancer and, 239
  population growth and, 106–107
  proportion of old people and, 93–97
  of women, and birth rates, 169–172
Age effects, in population growth studies, 114–115
Agriculture
  development and, 144
  population density and, 20, 54–55
  population growth and, 13–16, 127
  slash-and-burn, 54
  world carrying capacity and, 52
Agriculture Department, 150
Air pollution, 16
Alabama, 88
Aluminum, 137
American Indians, 29, 33
Annuities, 233–236
Aquinas, Thomas, 5
Argentina, 93
Aristotle, 4, 5
Arizona, 112
Asia
  birth control in, 60
  development in, 137
  fertility in, 42, 43, 59
Atlanta, 113
Augustine, Saint, 5, 9
Austria, 206
Automation, 55–56
Automobile industry, 55–56, 57
  development and consumption and, 143
  poverty line and, 132, 133, 150–151

Bagehot, Walter, 33
Balinski, M. L., 88
Bangladesh, 45, 114, 143
Barker, E., 4

Index

Barr, Nicholas A., 212
Bauxite, 44, 137
Becker, G. S., 23, 38
Bellamy, Edward, 122
Berelson, B., 60
Bernstein, 19
Besant, Annie, 11
Bias, in censuses, 81–83
Bible, 11
Birth control
   abortion and, 216–221
   Catholic thought on, 5–6
   coupon scheme for, 63
   demographic information and, 91–92
   governments and, 60–61
   moral dilemma in, 62–64
   population and, 216–232
   taxation schemes for, 64
   voluntary, 61–62
   see also Contraception
Birth rates
   age distributions in populations and, 95, 98–99
   age distribution of women and, 169–172
   childbearing intention surveys and, 177
   demographers on, 91
   demographic transition and, 24
   development and, 20
   education and, 31
   numerical study of population and, 8
   projection of constant, 166–169
   ratio of male to female, 100
   Soviet, 19
   women in labor market and, 39–40, 59, 115–116
Bixby, L. E., 83
Bladen, V. W., 22
Blacks, and census, 86, 89
Blake, J., 24
Blaschke, 41
Bodin, Jean, 7
Bolivia, 105
Boring, Edwin, 46
Boserup, E., 20
Botero, G., 7
Boulding, Kenneth, E., 16, 27, 63, 182
Bourgeois-Pichat, J., 208
Bradlaugh, Charles, 11

Brazil, 153
   birth control in, 61
   development in, 105, 125, 126, 141
Breast cancer, 99–100
Brown, Harrison, 16, 21, 99–100
Bureau of the Census, 188
   census estimates from, 80
   choosing convention by, 85–87
   fertility forecasts of, 194
   models used by, 180
   procedures of, 82, 84, 174
Burma, 156

Cairo, 157
California, 65, 88
Canaan, E., 13
Canada, 143, 188, 206
Cancer, 237–243
   death rates and, 239–240
   effect of elimination of, 240–243
   medical research guidelines and, 242–243
Cantillon, R., 8–9, 26, 158
Capital, 159
   development and, 105, 142
   population growth and, 105
   fertility and accumulation of, 24
Capitalism, and population theory, 17–19
Carlile, Richard, 11
Carrying capacity of population
   technical innovation and, 45–46
   world population levels and, 51–53
Casti Connubii (encyclical), 5
Catholic Church, 5–6, 31
Census Bureau, *see* Bureau of the Census
Censuses, 165, 172
   accuracy and completeness of, 79–81
   adjustments in, 89–90
   allocation and use of, 79–90
   apportionment problems in, 88
   choosing convention in, 85–87
   early work in, 8
   English, 29
   illegal immigrants in, 84
   random variation and bias in, 81–83
   residency definitions in, 84–85
   target in, 83–85

Index

techniques used in, 174
Ceylon, 50
Charaka, 11
Chenery, Hollis B., 152
Children
  amount of and held and, 40–41
  economic perspective on, 39
  as extension of parents, 46–47
  income levels and, 104
  in poor families, 32
Chile, 147
  birth rates in, 159
  Cultural Revolution in, 155
  density in, 114
  development in, 126, 142
  famines in, 26, 30
  population control in, 53
  population studies in, 4, 9
Christian thought, 5–6
Cicero, 4
Cigarette smoking
  death rates and, 113
  lung cancer and, 238
Clark, C., 11
Class, and Malthus, 27–28
Coal, 55
Coale, A. J., 20, 22, 30, 178, 179
Coffee consumption, 44
Cohen, Joel, E., 242
Colombia, 44
Colonialism, 50–51, 57
Computers, 56
Condorcet, Marquis de, 9, 11, 28
Congress
  censuses and, 80, 88
  social security legislation in, 203
Consumption
  American patterns in, 149–150
  cultural factors in, 149
  definitions of poverty and, 132–133
  development of poor countries and, 44–45
  ecologists on, 16
  effects on raw materials of, 133–138, 160
  measuring poor and middle class in, 150–152
  middle class patterns in, 148–150, 160
  women in work force and, 117
  world development and, 142–143

Contraception
  abortion as backup to, 220
  balance sheet in, 227
  births averted by, 221–223
  birth rates and, 103
  childspacing and efficiency of, 227–228
  delay in exposure to methods for, 225–227
  discontinuance of, 222–223
  effects of, as against natural fertility, 223–227
  family size and, 231–232
  frequency of intercourse and, 221–222
  historical references to, 11
  income and, 24
  Malthus on, 10–11, 28
  one method continuing indefinitely in, 221
  population growth and, 231–232
  preference for boys and, 228–231
  social change and, 230–231
  use of modern methods in, 224–225
  see also Birth control
Coontz, S. H., 10, 22
Cultural Revolution (China), 155
Culture
  consumption patterns and, 149
  definitions of poverty and, 132
  development and diffusion of, 147–148
  labor force participation and, 117–118
  work preferences and, 152–153

Darwin, Charles, 11, 12
Davis, Kingsley, 24, 180
DDT, 49, 55
Death rates
  age distribution in populations and, 95, 98–99
  cancer and, 239–240
  demographic transition and, 24, 30
  heart disease and forecasts of, 178–179
  male-female differences in, 113–114
  Malthus on, 29
  population control in poor countries and, 59–60

Death rates (continued)
  projection of constant, 166–169
  smoking and, 113
  upward mobility and, 69–71
Demand, and unemployment, 56
Deming, Edwards, 79
Demographic transition, 24, 30, 35, 41–43
Demography
  determination of facts in, 91–110
  early work in, 8
  mortality comparisons in, 111–114
  population appearances and reality in, 111–112
  psychology of research in, 108–110
  use of data in, 107–108
Density of population
  agriculture and, 54–55
  division of labor and, 19–20
  fertility and, 12
  war and, 114
Department of Agriculture, 150
Development
  consumption by developed countries and, 44–45
  diffusion of culture and, 147–148
  elimination of poverty and, 146–161
  fertility and, 24–25, 41–43
  groups and classes in, 147
  knowledge and, 143–145
  middle class and, 125–126
  population growth and, 20–22, 103–106
  raw materials and limits on, 21
  social mobility and, 25
  tariffs and, 159–160
  temporary inequality in, 155
Division of labor
  density of population and, 19–20
  marriage and, 38
Divorce, 38, 116
Dorn, Harold F., 176
Duesenberry, J., 23
Dumont, Arsène, 24–25
Duncan, O. Dudley, 25, 183
Dupâquier, J., 27
Durkheim, E., 19–20

Eastern Europe, 103
Ecologists, 12, 16, 49, 60

Economic development, *see* Development
Economics, and population theory, 35, 37–40, 47
Education
  birth rates and, 31, 42
  class differences and, 28
  middle class and, 147, 158–159
Egypt, 60
Ehrlich, A. H., 16
Ehrlich, P. R., 16
Ekanem, I., 104
Electric energy, 133
El Salvador, 106
Emigration, see Migration
Encyclopedia Britannica, 30
Energy
  consumption and, 143
  development and, 45, 137
  population theory and, 36–37
Engels, F., 18
Engineering, and population theory, 35, 36–37
Enlightenment, 9–11
Environment, and population theory, 16
Ethologists, 12
Euler, Leonhard, 8
Europe
  development and, 41–42, 137
  fertility in, 41–42, 59
Evolution
  biological, 11, 48
  economic, 43–44

Family
  development and, 155
  division of labor and, 38
  microeconomic theory of fertility and, 22–24
  Poor Laws and, 32
  social security and, 214
Famine, 26, 30
Fertility
  Census Bureau forecasts of, 194
  children as extensions of parents and, 46–47
  development in Europe and, 41–43
  economic response to, 39
  economic theory of, 22–24
  evolution theories and, 43–44

Index 259

institutional context of, 40–41
Malthus on, 29
marriage age and, 40–41, 100–101
microeconomic theory of, 22–24
poor families and, 58–59
population density and, 12
proletarianization and, 41–43
women in labor market and, 39–40
Finland, 206
Flieger, W., 178
Forecasting, 163–198
    age distribution of women and birth rates in, 169–172
    aggregating past experience in, 185–186
    as aid to analysis, 175–183
    calculation of error in, 197–198
    childbearing intention surveys of, 177
    components method in, 176–177
    constancy over different projection spans in, 191–193
    counterpredictions in, 180–181
    differences among forecasters in, 186–187
    distribution of error in, 193
    failure and success definitions in, 177–181
    improvement in, 190–191
    lessons from failed, 122
    limits of, 184–198
    Malthus on, 29–30
    mechanics of, 165–174
    migration and, 179
    models in, 179–181
    overall error in, 187–190
    projection of constant birth and death rates in, 166–169
    reliability of predictions in, 173–174
    subnational data in, 194
    turning points in, 181–183
Foreign aid, and investment, 143
Food supply
    energy sources and, 36
    famine and, 26
    Malthus on, 53–54
    pesticides and, 55, 183
    population ceilings and, 53–54, 182
    population growth and, 49–50
    rural-urban migration and, 156, 158

France, 64, 142, 206
    birth and death rates in, 24
    fertility in, 41
Franklin, Benjamin, 26
Frederick the Great, King of Prussia, 7
Freedman, R., 61, 180
Frejka, Tomas, 194
French Revolution, 32, 33
Friedlander, Dov, 104

Gandhi, Mohandas, 10–11
Germany, 30, 160
    birth rates in, 103
    development of, 142
    social security in, 202, 206
Glass, D.V., 8
Glick, Paul C., 180
Gnosticism, 5
Godwin, William, 9, 27
Government
    birth control and, 60–61
    industrial growth and, 14
Graunt, John, 7–8
Great Britain, 58, 64, 136, 160, 230
    birth rates in, 103
    eighteenth century demographic conditions in, 29
    production and population in, 15
Greece, ancient, 4, 26
Green Revolution, 49, 144, 182

Halevy, Elie, 31
Halley, E., 8
Hansen, Alfred, 21, 79
Harris, John, 156
Hauser, Philip, 79
Hawley, Amos H., 179
Heart disease, and death rates, 178–179
Hebrew thought, 5
Heer, David, 104
Henry, Louis, 185
Herodotus, 11
Hicks, J.R., 22
Himes, N.E., 11
Himmelfarb, Gertrude, 33
Honduras, 106
Hong Kong, 58, 130, 160
Hoover, E.M., 20
Horlick, Max, 204
Hoselitz, Bert F., 8

House of Representatives, 88
Housing
　migration and, 157
　population growth and demand for, 21
Hume, David, 9, 108
Hungary, 19
Hutchinson, E.P., 9

Ibn Khaldun, 6
Illegitimate births, 116
Immigrants, illegal, and censuses, 84
Immigration, see Migration
Imperialism, 17, 18, 19
Income
　birth rates and, 103–104
　family size and, 58
　fertility and, 23–24
　population growth and average per head, 128–131
　poverty line in, 150
India, 4, 26, 57
　birth control in, 10–11, 60–61
　development and, 20, 142
　marriage age and fertility in, 100–101
　population growth in, 20, 186
　poverty in, 152
Indians, American, 29, 33
Indonesia, 45, 55
　birth control in, 60, 61
　colonialism and, 50–51
　migration programs in, 120–121
　population growth in, 179
　poverty in, 152
Industrialization, 30
　consumption by developed countries and, 43–44
　population growth and, 21–22
Industrial Revolution, 28, 136
Industry
　environmental factors and, 16
　population control and, 15–16
　production as function of population in, 13–14
　rural-urban migration and, 157, 159–160
　upward mobility and, 73–74
Intrauterine device (IUD), 224–225
Investment
　development and, 143
　population growth and, 21–22, 105

Iran, 142
Ireland, 31
Iron ore, 137
Islam, 11
Italy, 41

Jacobson, P.H., 180
Jakarta, 157
Jamaica, 42, 44, 137
Janowitz, B.S., 104
Japan, 160, 206
　fertility in, 59
　industry in, 57, 58, 160
Java, 40–41, 179
Jevons, William, 15

Kahun Papyrus, 11
Kautilya, 4
Kenya, 60
Keyfitz, N., 178, 179, 206
Keynes, J.M., 15, 21, 32, 122, 183
Kidney disease, 242
King, Gregory, 8
Korea, 58, 130, 160
Kuznets, Simon, 22

Labor
　automation and, 55–56
　cultural shifts and, 117–118
　demand and unemployment in, 56
　development and, 142
　fertility in women and, 38–40, 59, 115–116
　forecasts and, 122
　service occupations in, 116–117
　social security participation by, 206–207
　technical innovations and displacement of, 56–57
Lambeth Conference, 5
Land
　development and, 105, 142
　number of children and amount of, 40–41
　population growth and, 13, 105
　technical innovations and availability of, 45
Language, 148
Laos, 54
Latin America
　birth control in, 60, 61
　development in, 20, 105, 126

population growth in, 20, 93, 94, 105
Lee, Ronald D., 39, 187, 194
Lenin, Nikolai, 19
Leslie, P.H., 176
Less developed countries
   average per head income and population growth in, 128–131
   economic development in, *see* Development *see also* Poor countries; Underdeveloped countries
Liebenstein, H., 22, 23
Life table, 167
Lipton, M., 156, 158
Literacy
   consumption and, 148
   fertility and, 42, 59
London, 7
Lorimer, F., 8
Los Angeles, 113
Lotka, A.J., 179
Lung cancer, and smoking, 238
Luther, Martin, 10

McCleary, G.F., 11
Machiavelli, Niccoló, 6–7
Mackenroth, G., 7
Macroeconomic models, 22
Mahdi, M., 6
Malaysia, 60
Malthus, Daniel, 9
Malthus, Thomas Robert, 7, 9–10, 11, 16, 17–19, 35, 59, 105, 142
   class distinctions in, 27–28
   comparison of editions of, 33
   contraception and, 10–11, 28
   demographic conditions of eighteenth century and, 28–29
   education and birth rates and, 31
   evolution of thought of, 26–33
   food supply and, 50, 53–54, 55, 182
   as forecaster, 29–30
   late marriage and fertility in, 30–31
   on poverty, 31–32
   predecessors of, 9–10, 26
   preventive check theory of, 10
   use of data by, 29
Manicheism, 5
Mao Tse-Tung, 142, 154, 155
Marriage
   division of labor and, 38
   fertility and age for, 40–41, 100–101
Marshall, Alfred, 156
Martinique, 93
Marx, Karl, 17–19, 43, 142
Medical research, 242–243
Meek, R.L., 17
Mehring, R., 18–19
Men
   birth rate ratio between women and, 100
   death rate comparisons between women and, 113–114
   equity in pensions and, 233–236
   marriage and division of labor and, 38
Menken, Jane, 218
Mercantilism, 7, 9
Mexico, 158, 180
   mobility and death rates in, 70
   population growth in, 93, 96, 105
Mexico City, 157
Microeconomic models, 22
Middle class
   consumption and, 142–143, 148–150, 160
   development patterns and, 125–126
   education and, 147, 158–159
   location of poverty line and, 131–133
   measuring, 150–152
   production and, 152–153
   relief of poverty and, 153–155
   resources and, 135, 137–138, 160
   rural-urban migration and, 156–159
   window restricting passage into, 138–142
Migration, 30
   birth rates and, 7
   development and, 156–159
   equilibrium point in, 156
   food supply and, 156, 158
   forecasting population figures and, 179
   housing problems and, 157
   Malthus on, 32–33
   population control and, 15–16, 120–121
   transport and, 157–158
Mill, John Stuart, 13, 19, 105

Minerals, consumption of, 44
Mining, 55
Mississippi, 150
Mobility, *see* Upward mobility
Models, 109
    demographic information and, 99–101
    population changes and, 34
    population characteristics in, 179–181
    population theory and, 47, 48
    stable population, 118–121
Moheau, 11
Montesquieu, Baron de La Brede et, 26, 28
Morgan, J.N., 83
Mortality
    comparison studies of, 111–114
    population density and, 12
    see also Death rates
Moscow, 157
Multinational corporations, 152–153
Myrdal, G., 15, 22

Nationalism, 51
Natural gas, 55
Natural resources, *see* Resources
Nee, V., 147
Netherlands, 51, 55, 114, 202
New Hampshire, 112, 150
Noonan, J.T., Jr., 5
Notestein, Frank, 24, 180, 188
Nurske, R., 21

Ohlin, G., 20
Oil, 55, 133
Okun, B., 23
Organization of Petroleum Exporting Countries (OPEC), 142
Overbeek, J., 15

Pakistan, 61, 152
Paraguay, 105
Pensions, 202
    equity between sexes in, 233–236
Pesticides, 183
Petersen, W., 10, 18, 29, 30, 31, 32
Petty, Sir William, 7, 8
Phnom Penh, 157
Pitts, A.M., 238
Pius XII, Pope, 5
Place, Francis, 11

Plato, 4, 52, 114
Poland, 30, 206
Polanyi, Karl, 43
Pollution, 16
Poor
    impact on natural resources and, 135
    location of poverty line and, 131–133
    measuring, 150–152
    window restricting passage into middle class for, 138–142
Poor countries
    economic development of, *see* Development
    technical innovations and, 58
    see also Less developed countries; Underdeveloped countries
Poor Laws, 32
Population
    birth control and, 216–232
    causes and consequences of change in, 34–48
    models in forecasting, 179–181
    production as function of, 13–14
    world carrying capacity and, 51–53
Population control
    Chinese, 53
    demographic information and, 91–92
    governments and, 60–61
    migration and, 120–121
    nature of ceiling in, 53–55
    values and, 49–64
    voluntary birth control in, 61–62
    world carrying capacity and, 52–53
    see also Birth control; Contraception
Population growth
    age distribution and, 106–107
    age effects in, 114–115
    average per head income and, 128–131
    development and, 20–22, 103–106
    division of labor and, 19–20
    effects of differential, 126–127
    family size with contraception and, 231–232
    food supply and, 49–50, 182
    housing demand and, 21
    in late eighteenth century, 28–29
    peaking of rate of increase of, 126–127

proportion of old people and, 93–97
self-determination of nations and, 51
stable model in, 118–121
stationarity in, 121–122
upward mobility and, 65, 66–69, 70, 76
zero, 22, 121
Popularity theory
in antiquity, 4–5
biological perspectives in, 11–12
Christian thought on, 5–6
economics in, 35, 37–40
energy transfer system in, 36–37
Enlightenment and, 9–11
environment and, 16
evolution theory and, 11
historical survey of, 3–25
Malthus and, 26–33
natural resources and, 13–16
numerical study of population in, 7–9
socialist writers on, 17–19
uses of, 25
Portugal, 41
Potter, R.G., 180, 218, 223
Poverty
birth rates and, 58–59
development and elimination of, 146–161
Malthus on, 31–32
middle class and relief of, 153–155
technology and, 143–145
Price, 29
Production
cultural preferences for work and, 152–153
development and, 144, 145
ecologists and, 16
as function of population, 13–14
marriage and division of labor and, 38
middle class and, 152–153
national politics and, 58
population growth and, 127
socialist writers on, 17–19
Proletarianization, and fertility, 41–43
Property, Malthus on, 32
Protestant thought, 5
Proudhon, Pierre Joseph, 10
Puerto Rico, 93, 150

Quesnay, François, 9

Race, and censuses, 86
Random variation in censuses, 81–83
Raw materials
consumption and, 43–44
development and, 43–44, 130
world development and, 21, 142–143
Razi, al-, 11
Reagan, Ronald, 202
Rempel, H., 156
Research
medical, 242–243
psychology of, 108–110
Resources
birth control policies and, 61
effect of affluence on, 133–138
middle class and, 135, 137–138, 160
population levels and, 12–16, 160
Rhythm method of birth control, 5
Ricardo, David, 17
Roman Catholic Church, 5–6, 31
Roman Empire, 4–5, 6
Rostow, Walt W., 43
Royal Society, 8
Rural population, 30
development and, 20–21
education and urbanization and, 147
migration from, 156–159
Russia, see Soviet Union
Ryder, Norman B., 177, 182

Sahel, 26
Samuelson, Paul A., 210, 213
Saudi Arabia, 142
Sauvy, A., 4, 14, 18
Saving, 159
Saxony, 41
Schultz, T.W., 21, 39
Self-determination of nations, 51
Servants, 149
Service occupations, 116–117
Sex
censuses and, 88, 89
death rates in cancer and, 239
Shepard, D.S., 238, 239
Sheps, M.C., 180, 218
Siegal, J.S., 88, 89
Silver, M., 104
Singapore, 58, 60, 130

Smith, Adam, 9–10, 17, 22, 26, 140, 154, 155, 158
Smog, 113
Smoking
　death rates and, 113
　lung cancer and, 238
Social change
　contraception and, 230–231
　evolutionism and, 43
Socialism, and population theory, 10, 17–19
Social mobility, *see* Upward mobility
Social reform movement, 19
Social sciences, and population theory, 47–48
Social security, 201–215
　demographic analysis in, 204–206
　differences in bookkeeping systems in, 209–210
　labor force participation in, 206–207
　legislative history of, 203–204
　limits on independence of cohorts in, 210–213
　social cohesion and, 213–215
Social Security Administration
　measuring poor by, 150, 151
　poverty definition of, 131
Sociology, and population theory, 35, 43, 47
South Korea, 58
Soviet Union, 155
　development in, 125, 126, 137, 140, 142
　population theory in, 19, 21
Spain, 41
Spencer, Herbert, 12, 43
Spengler, Joseph, J., 4, 8, 182
Sri Lanka, 159
Stalin, Joseph, 19
Starvation, 12
Statistical Abstract, 150, 151, 192, 205, 243
Stolzenberg, Rafe D., 39
Stoto, Michael A., 187
Stangeland, C.E., 7
Strip mining, 55
Sukarno, 61
Sumatra, 54, 179
Süssmilch, J.P., 7, 30
Sutter, J., 25

Sweden, 121
　birth rates in, 178
　consumption in, 143
　mobility and death rates in, 70
　population growth studies in, 93–95, 98
　social security in, 202, 207, 208
Switzerland, 30
Synthetics, 45–46, 55, 57

Taconite, 137
Taeuber, Conrad, 79, 179
Taeuber, I.B., 24, 179
Taiwan, 58
　birth control in, 61–62
　development of, 130
　mortality comparisons with, 111–112
Takeshita, J.Y., 61
Tariffs, 159–160
Taxation
　birth control and, 64
　social security and, 202, 203
Technology
　development and, 142, 143–145
　labor displacement and, 56–57
　population carrying capacity and, 45–46
　raw materials and, 134–135, 138
Telephones, and poverty line, 133
Thant, U., 62
Third World
　fertility in, 42
　self-determination in, 51
Tietze, C., 180
Tilly, Charles, 41–43
Todaro, Michael, 156
Transportation, and migration, 157–158
Treasury Department, 79, 87
Tufte, Edward, 203
Turkey, 60

Uganda, 152
Underdeveloped countries
　birth control policies of, 60–61
　see also Less developed countries; Poor countries
Unemployment, and demand, 56
Union of Soviet Socialist Republics (U.S.S.R.), *see* Soviet Union

United Arab Republic, 60
United Kingdom, 206; *see also* Great Britain
United Nations, 4, 19, 126, 180, 188, 189, 191
United Nations Development Decades, 137
United States
  mortality comparisons with, 111–112
  upward mobility and death rates in, 70
Upward mobility, 65–76
  basic equation in, 66–69
  chain-letter analogy to population and, 74–75
  death rates and, 69–71
  demographic models in, 101–103
  economic development and, 25
  hierarchical organization and, 65–66
  industrial expansion and, 73–74
  rate of change equation in, 71–73
Urbanization
  education and, 147
  energy supply and, 36–37
  fertility and, 42
  population growth and, 29
Uruguay, 93

Vaupel, James, 238
Venezuela, 44, 98
  birth rates in, 178
  development in, 130
  population growth in, 105
Vialatoux, J., 4, 10

Vital statistics, 8, 29

Waite, Linda, 39
Wallace, Alfred, 9, 11
War, and population density, 114
Weber, Max, 28
West Germany, 103, 202, 206
Westoff, C.F., 177
Whelpton, P.K., 176–177, 179
Widjojo, N., 179
Women
  birth control and, 64
  birth rate ratio between men and, 100
  birth rates and age distribution of, 169–172
  breast cancer and, 99–100
  childbearing intention survey of, 177
  consumption aspirations of, 117
  death rate comparisons between men and, 113–114
  equity in pensions for, 233–236
  fertility and employment of, 38–40
  labor force and, 59, 115–116
  marriage and division of labor and, 38
Working class, and population theory, 17–19
Wright, H., 15, 16
Wynne-Edwards, V.C., 12

Young, H.P., 88

Zaïre, 143
Zero population growth, 22, 121